ON BORROWED LAND

A Refugee's True Story of
Escaping a Homeland
and Finding a Heartland

BOUNTHAVY SOUKTHIDETH

OVERVIEW PRESS

For my little brother, Thurng, who showed me that I had to live every moment of life like it's my last. And to my mom and dad, who gave me the opportunity to do so.

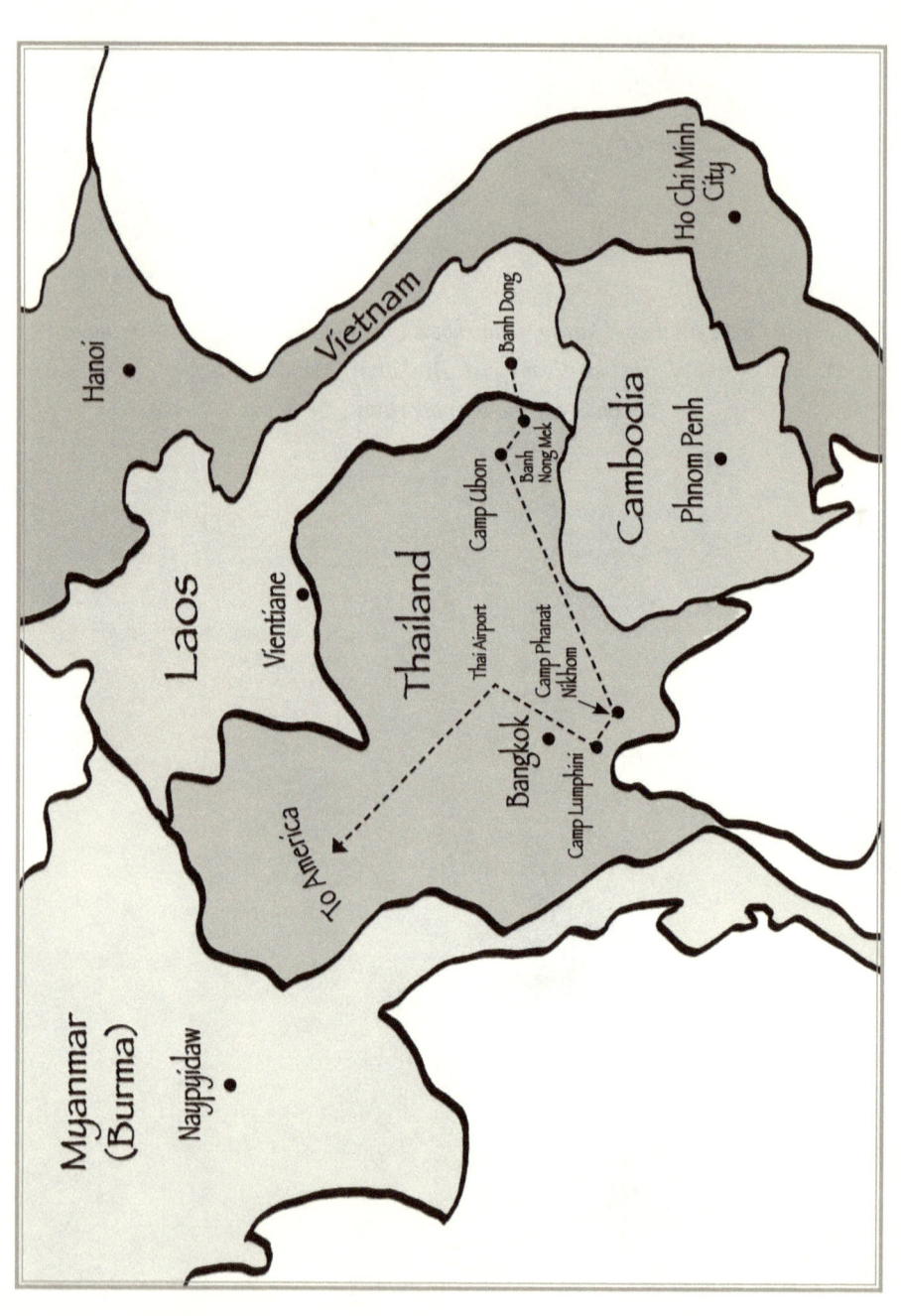

CHARACTERS

Immediate Family
E-Paw (father)
E-Mae (mother)
Vung (eldest brother)
Narng (eldest sister)
Somnurk (older brother)
Nok (older sister)
Boun (Author)
Thurng (youngest brother)

Paternal Family
Grandpa Oosu
Grandma Dom
Aunt Pen (eldest sister,
    Jour Peng's mother)
E-Paw
Uncle Wan (youngest brother)
Aunt Dee (his wife)
PuMaa (eldest son)
Champa (eldest daughter)
Lasamy (second daughter)
Lasee (youngest daughter)

Maternal Family
Grandpa La
Grandma Dao
Aunt Putt
Uncle Saun
Aunt Paa
Yai (eldest daughter)
Som (second daughter)
Gun (eldest son)
Vee (second son)
Bee (third daughter)
Buc Dur (youngest son)
E-Mae

Special Characters
Kubar Somdee (beloved Therevada
    Buddha Monk)
Jour Peng (aka Cousin Peng)
Uncle Lun
Brother Dang (Son)
Sister Thong (His wife)
Paw Seel (E-Paw's lifelong friend)
Mae Seel (his wife)
Paw Yai Tut
Mae Yai Tut (his wife)
Ku Mai (E-Paw's Thai friend)
Mae Mai (his wife)
Paw Yai Lerm
Mae Yai Lerm (his wife)

CONTENTS

Author's Note ix

Chapter 1: *The Village of Banh Dong, Laos* 1

Chapter 2: *The Unexpected Goodbye* 16

Chapter 3: *The Flight Through Darkness* 24

Chapter 4: *Climbing the Mountain* 37

Chapter 5: *Reunited* 46

Chapter 6: *Banh Nong Mek* 54

Chapter 7: *Leaving the Nest* 67

Chapter 8: *Moving Again* 77

Chapter 9: *The Sirindhorn Reservoir* 88

Chapter 10: *A Year in Paradise* 110

Chapter 11: *Visitors* 125

Chapter 12: *Arriving at Ubon Refugee Camp* 143

Chapter 13: *Life in the Camp* 153

Chapter 14: *A Brief Return to Paradise* 164

Chapter 15: *American Dreams and Thai School* 174

Chapter 16: *A New Home in the Camp* 191

Chapter 17: *E-Paw Jailed—Confined in a Confinement* 209

Chapter 18: *Camp Phanat Nikhom and Camp Lumphini* 221

Chapter 19: *On Our Way to America* 236

Chapter 20: *Arriving in America* 254

Epilogue 259

Acknowledgments 264

About the Author 267

AUTHOR'S NOTE

On Borrowed Land isn't just my story (I alone couldn't have forged anything on my own except the will to dream), and if you unintentionally ran away from your village looking for a new home, and were handed one grace after another, this is your story, too. At the heart of my story is the human kindness that existed within the miracle hands that reached out to us during the days of our darkness.

In writing this book, I recounted several memories from my childhood—many of those vivid images still linger indelibly in my mind today. For what my own mind couldn't reconstruct from its own memories, my mom, my eldest brother (Vung), sisters (Narng and Nok), and cousins were there to help me fill in the gaps to capture the human essence of my family history. Beyond my siblings' memories of latent tales and images, I also had my father's precious diaries, where he kept on flimsy notes the story of our journey to America (the land that Laotian refugees proclaimed to be "The Land of Heaven"). And far more than intangible memories were his photographs of himself as a soldier and our family as refugees. Along with his ancient relic that he worshiped, our story was written on clothes, notepaper, and tiny sheets of copper plate . . . all of which existed in a moment when we laughed and cried together under our own glorious sunshine.

I

THE VILLAGE OF BANH DONG, LAOS

December 1975

One night when I was almost five, my fourteen-year-old sister Narng held me and my seven-year-old sister Nok close, as we stared at two men with rifles sitting on the bench underneath our hut. Through a small hole in the wooden plank of our floor we could see their eyes gleaming under the moonlight.

"Don't speak," Narng whispered to us. "They're watching us and waiting for E-Paw." That was when Narng said that men in army uniforms were counting us.

It all started right after the monsoon water had receded, and the dry season heat was approaching. E-Paw, my father, went missing. Our village of Banh Dong had two seasons that were vivid to me: wet or dry. Both were hot and humid, but I hated the heat during the dry season for baking my back in the sun.

One afternoon, I pulled myself to the railing of our balcony, hoping for E-Paw's return. I stared down at the dirt road that cut through our village and our hut, then stretched my eyes over the jungle, but he was nowhere to be found. On the horizon before me, the blue vivid sky was bursting under the sultry sun with random thuds of gunfire and explosions emanating from the mountains and jungle beyond the verdant rice fields and the bending bamboo forest.

It was there the world began shifting its foundation, making me the person I am today. Life was evolving in my ever-absorbing mind, where I learned that our fate is handed to us by chance, and the *peace* that existed was no more than a fragile bond.

When it was broken, it would change us forever.

We lived in Grandpa La's large teakwood hut sitting on rough lumber stilts—a "two huts sandwiched under one tin roof" contraption. A pair of thick ropes were attached to the crafted wooden removable ladder, leading to the above floor and the main kitchen on the far end with its own tin roof and a large clay pot of water on the open deck with a coconut bowl affixed to a wooden handle.

In the tight-knit rectangle-shaped village of nearly 100 families, we lived with Aunt Paa and our six cousins. They occupied the right side of the hut, and my family inhabited the opposite end where two windows opened to a balcony facing the dirt road. Banana and coconut trees lined the small pond, and tin huts like ours sat nestling next to one another before the jungle, where the Village of Banh Dong got its literal name: The Village of Jungle. The main entrance to the village ran perpendicular to the beaten path from our hut, leading to the sandy ground of the temple.

Like most mornings, I was lying on my blanket over the reed mat on the hard wooden planks of our floor, but the temple woke me up with the beat of the gong, reminding me that the village was by the temple and of the temple. The reverberating soft "thongs" etched themselves into my head, along with squawking and squabbling chickens and crowing roosters wandering beneath us. Under our tin roof, I could hear Grandma Dao's voice encouraging the entourage of busy hands: "As long as someone from our hut makes an offering, whether in the morning or at the temple before noon, we won't have sinned."

My mother, E-Mae, and my sister Narng were rising to the rhythm of Grandma Dao's words. On the opposite end of the hut, over by the wooden balusters and the gate at the top of the main stairs from the ground, Aunt Paa and her five children were also getting up to embrace the daily routine. Our cousins were older, and Aunt Paa's eldest son, Cousin Gun, had already been sent to the war front at Mount Somlee, where E-Paw was said to have gathered with his platoon of Royal Lao soldiers before he became a member of the village watchmen.

From the jungle end of our hut, I'd watched E-Mae and my elder sisters working diligently, preparing the morning alms for the monks. Most of the food would be our meal for the rest of the day. Cousin Yai, the eldest, was tossing the sticky rice inside the bamboo steamer basket, flipping then rolling the large clump of steamy rice into a round bamboo tray. Quiet, long-haired Cousin Bee, at ten, was fanning the fire with her usual friendly reserved eyes focused on her chore. Chatty Cousin Som was adding anchovy sauce and stirring her fish, crab, and snail bamboo soup. Narng was helping with the cleanup, while E-Mae and Aunt Paa were peeling and shredding unripened papaya picked from the yard for our hot spicy papaya salad, which was one of our staples.

I heard them as they urged one another to "Hurry, get *Khao Niew* (sticky rice) and *Khao Thom* out from the rice steamer." It was 6:00 a.m., so I was hit with the aroma of *Khao Thom* (the sweet ripened banana in coconut milk wrapped in banana leaves), a treat that I could eat every day for the rest of my life.

It was not even breakfast time, but my stomach was already growling. I knew that soon the monks would be circling around the village before they reached our hut. They would first stop at our neighbors, Aunt Putt (E-Mae's eldest sister) and her brother, Uncle Saun, whose hut sat next to the temple ground, then to the friendly sisters Mae Kem and Mae Bout, with their adopted teenage daughter, Sister Koon. Before sweeping by our hut, they'd come to Uncle Kao's (E-Paw's friend), Brother Liam's, and Uncle Paay's. Our chatty, puffy-haired Uncle Paay was not really our biological uncle, but we called everyone uncle and aunt—it was a lineage tradition of respecting our elders.

There was a small opening in the wooden planks of the hut by our pillows that I loved peeking through each time the monks strolled by. I'd stare down to see E-Mae, Narng, and our cousins kneeling with their offering before the monks on the clayish ground. In their bright, meticulously wrapped robes, they paraded by in a single file like an orange stream flowing along with alms bowls at their waists held by their shoulder straps. I looked for my brother Vung and cousin Peng, who were in the line with the marching monks. They were both teenagers and had been ordained as *Jours* (young monks) five months earlier at the temple in a spiritual ushering to the heaven of our Grandma Dom, E-Paw's mother, who had recently passed away.

I got up. I needed to eat. I took my hungry belly to E-Mae.

Before I made it to the wooden deck with the steaming rice and food inside the kitchen, Cousin Yai warned me, "Stay away from the monks' offerings, don't you know it's a sin to touch the monks' food with your dirty hands? You got snots sticking to your cheeks," when my little hands reached in to grab a ball of sticky rice. I heeded her words. She was taller and a lot older than me, but I knew there was kindness in her.

"Listen to your elders; give them respect." E-Mae gave me a ball of rice, then added, "You want to ripen like a sweet banana and not rot when you get bigger."

So, I ran back to the wooden plank of my bed and stayed inside with Nok and Thurng, my infant brother.

Nok said, "Cousin Yai is not nice. But Narng said she's teaching us to be patient."

I was used to this repetitive routine. Even if it made me get up early, I found it humbling.

One evening we were having dinner in the kitchen by the balcony. E-Mae had Thurng on her lap, and Narng, Nok, and I were next to one another enjoying a quiet dinner of mudfish and bamboo soup, herbaceous herbs and aromatic rice paddy weeds we'd picked along the rice field, and a basket of sticky rice. Vung remained at the temple, and, still, there were no sign of E-Paw.

"E-Mae, why didn't E-Paw take his motorcycle and his medical syringes?" Nok asked.

"Don't talk so much. Your father has work," E-Mae said.

"When is he coming home?"

"Sh . . . don't ask anymore. Your father is busy, and he'll come soon. Don't call for him," E-Mae hushed Nok.

We accepted E-Mae's answers that night. But I was still looking forward to E-Paw's warm smiles and the happy glow of his shining brown eyes.

Without E-Paw, E-Mae kept our hands from boredom, and she taught us to forage food for a meal. I'd get up with zest in my own eager feet on the floor to her words, "Hurry, hurry, we can't be lazy, quickly get up. Wash your face. You're going to sin. Put on your shoes, we have to leave before we don't have anything to eat."

When she was not at the temple listening to the monks chanting, E-Mae loved reciting Theravada Buddha's Pali scripts and telling fortunes. She did this with a captivated audience full of excitement that made her a bigger social butterfly than E-Paw. She was also religious like Grandpa La and Grandma Dao, but it was food that drove her—it was her sole maternal purpose during those days to get us food. She needed to put as much food as she could on our reed mats for the entire family under that roof.

E-Mae's obsession with finding food became my favorite pastime. I loved straggling along with her during her daily food foraging and prepping meals, which often became an entire day's production. We didn't have electricity or running water, but E-Mae said that it was a lot more fun to use our legs and hands. On most of our food-gathering trips, she tied Thurng to her hips, and she strung a woven bamboo basket on her back. She held my hand, while in the other hand she carried a shovel and fishing net, and Nok trailed behind us.

I waved to Narng. "Narng, I go with E-Mae." Normally I went with her, riding on Buc Ang, our water buffalo. She'd let out a soft smile and gentle words and give us her usual "you kids be careful and be good," while pulling the noose on our water buffaloes, leading them to our *nah* (farm) where there was tree shade and green grass with soothing mud for them to lay on.

Nok said, "Narng is like E-Mae, she cries without tears, and she's still crying to herself for the loss of our brother Somnurk."

I cried for our nine-year-old brother, too. I still remembered his brave brown marble eyes and dark round face, *the two of us little frogs*, floating in the little lotus pond before our *nah* hut when the previous relentless monsoon water came. It was when E-Paw ran out of medications and couldn't save our brother from what he'd believed was malaria. I cried for him when he died, then I cried for my favorite gray military blanket E-Paw wrapped him in before carrying him away in that little bamboo crate.

Keeping up with E-Mae's steps, we'd walked for almost two kilometers toward Banh Jik to reach the Paleeng River, where she scooped little mud fish, tadpoles, and a handful of grass shrimp with her fish net, dug in the sand for the little sand frogs and crickets, fumbled in the muddy water for snails, and even chased the little rice field crabs along the way to scavenging mushrooms.

That day, on our way back to the hut from picking mushrooms, we saw men in green military uniforms passing by our hut with rifles dangling off their shoulders. They made foreign sounds in groups of no more than twenty. The soldiers with round cone-shaped hats moved along our paths with rifles and daunting grim looks on their faces, speaking words that we didn't understand. Broken syllables like "Ma Tik . . . Ma Tok" were all that my little head could gather from what was said in their passing conversation. E-Mae said that they were *Gael and Kaar* (Vietnamese and mountain people). She held us at a distance.

"Don't go near them. Fear them."

E-Mae wanted to warn us about the strange men in their army boots, carrying their guns in our village. That was the first time I saw the men who were said to be the communists.

In Banh Dong, the Lao Dang leader was a man we knew. It was Jan Lee, our neighbor three huts down toward the village temple. He was a tall man who carried a pistol at his hips with a sharp face and dark pointy lips. Jan Lee was said to have been given the title of Banh Dong Lao Communist Chief for his natural ability to set fear into others by brutal force. Within two months after E-Paw disappeared, Jan Lee and his men gathered the women whose husbands he believed to be associated with the random cracks of gunfire emanating from the gray peaks in the distant jungle. One day, Jan Lee's men came for E-Mae, staring up at us from the bottom rung of our wooden steps.

"*Pai* (Go)," the men ordered E-Mae to hasten herself with a hard gesture of their hands.

Unable to detach from E-Mae, who had Thurng in her arms,

we ran after Narng and E-Mae down the stairs, kicking on our dusty dirty sandals. We ran past Grandpa La stirring his tea pot by his work bench.

"Don't go!" His grave voice stopped our little feet dead in their tracks.

Narng grabbed our shoulders, pulling us upstairs toward the large clay pot of drinking water. Then we went to our side of the hut; we sat and waited for E-Mae, wondering what Jan Lee wanted with our mother.

When E-Mae came home that day, she told us that Jan Lee stood before a circle of frightened mothers. He was barking orders with his hand resting over his pistol belt; his face was dark red, gleaming under the sun.

"Your husbands can come back peacefully if they stop the random attacks on the village. Do you understand?! If you want to see your children, you will listen. Those who don't listen, we will toss them in the river with a rope tied to their neck, attached to a large rock."

By the next morning, E-Mae took her handwritten note from Jan Lee, then held Thurng in her nursing arms. Before leaving, she turned to Narng's gloomy face and said, "You take care of E-Nok and Buc Boun. I won't be gone long." Then she stepped into the back of a pickup truck that was dropping a handful of women off near the gray pale peaks by the Nong Mek Border, where E-Paw and his Patigan comrades were said to be hiding.

That evening, I began sobbing for E-Mae's maternal touch, after realizing she and Thurng hadn't come back. Nok added to the chaotic calamity in our mosquito tent with her own shrieking cries. Her outburst instantly aggravated Cousin Yai, who came stamping her feet across the dark planks of our floor and pulled our tent open. Then she'd grabbed Nok by the arm, dragging her outside. Nok fought to stay with all her child's futile might to an angry yank of a grown woman. Cousin Yai then picked up Nok, carried her down the wooden ladder, and left her crying on the ground in the dark.

"I want my E-Mae . . . E-Mae . . . " Nok rubbed her eyes while pulling from the grip of the dark tall woman.

"I want you quiet!" yelled the honeymooning woman. But before she returned to her new husband waiting for her in their own mosquito tent, she shoved the ladder attached to a thick rope outward, suspending it by the attached ropes at just above the top rung like the villagers did when they wanted to prevent people and even stray animals coming to the above living space of the hut.

"E-Mae . . . E-Mae!" Nok continued to elevate her wailing cries, stirring up the neighborhood.

That night, Narng kept a watch over her through our little hole in the wooden plank. She saw Nok's dark figure crawling and fighting to get back on the dangling ladder leading to the upstairs. By the time Nok was silenced by the dark of the night, my tears had already dried on my cheeks as I lay asleep in the soothing arms of Narng, my soft-spoken, fair-skinned sister. The days became weeks, and the weeks became months, and soon my cries for E-Paw and E-Mae faded away with the sound of crickets at night.

Ever since that night, Narng held us tight, cuddling us in her arms with her comforting words: "*E-Laa, Buc-Laa* (Dear girl, Dear Boy), don't cry, E-Paw and E-Mae will come for us . . ."

It was by Grandpa La's workbench that my cousin Buc Dur and I bonded like two fatherless brothers under the watchful eyes of our grandfather, who we also called *Paw Yai* (big father). Buc Dur was a stout boy with a round face and dark-pointy lips. Under that tin awning of Grandpa La's workbench and his hammock, Buc Dur and I chased the snots out of one another, then through alleys of huts and dirt road. When we got mud smudged on our face and dirt caked into a dark ring around our neck, Grandpa La would usher us to the little shower shanty in the backyard. The bamboo-thatched shack with grass roof housed a large clay pot for washing water. The communal pot filled with water—and it stayed filled. It was everyone's responsibility to replenish it with the water drawn from the well at the temple ground. Like most of the families in that village, it was collective—everyone had to lend a hand.

"If you're old enough to tend a fire, you can help," Grandpa La drummed into us while sitting by his own glowing flame.

Next to the outhouse, there was a tall leaning coconut tree; a tamarind tree we'd climb, picking every dangling sour and sweet brown fruit; and a guava tree that stood as high as our kitchen balcony. The guava reminded me of a mild green pear; when it's young, the fruit has a hard white inside with little chewable seeds. Unripened it's still refreshing with a crunchy bite to the sour and tropical fruit, and when I'd eat it with salt and ground roasted pepper mix, it left my mouth salivating for more. When our guava grew soft to the touch, its insides ripened into a light pink flesh, making it a sweet juicy snack. I'd cram and crunch the fruit inside my little mouth like a bartlett pear with its sweet tropical aroma and hint of fruitiness that enticed my little hands to stretch out to its limbs from the balcony, leaving Narng yelling at me, *"Buc Shour* (Silly Boy), you're going to fall off the balcony and die!"

Grandpa La and his family were originally from Thailand. They were Thai Isan living in a village called Honghee. The small village was in the northern part of the Ubonrachatani province of northeastern Thailand.

According to E-Mae, who was twenty years old when her family moved to avoid the crime and robberies, "There in that village, there were some poor people. They were so poor they would steal our banged-up and dirty soup bowl. At night we'd light torches, keeping a lookout for the rice storage shack. They'd sneak our grains of rice out through a poke-hole underneath the wooden cabin. So, your Paw Yai picked up the family, and moved us to Laos, to where your Aunt Putt and Uncle Saun happened to be living."

If he wasn't found with a machete in his hand, clearing the evasive bamboo trees at the rice field, Grandpa La was at the hut by his work area next to the vegetable garden. The disciplined and religious man was also a goldsmith. It was said that he tucked away the gold and money he had accumulated in the satchel that he carried under his armpit. It was also said that the man liked his money and liked to be in control. Each year the entire family would spend half the year working hard on growing the sweet rice encompassing many acres. But when the crop was harvested, Grandpa La kept most of the money. E-Mae speculated that this was why Aunt Paa's husband left her with six children, crushing her heart and breaking her will to live (she jumped off the hut).

Out of all my vivid memories of my tall, large-eared, sharp-faced grandpa, I found him to be soft-spoken with a low sensitivity to foolishness. He didn't say much except when we crossed paths and ruffled his state of peace, then he'd lose it. He was soft and shrewd, never yelling at us kids, only in those quick surprising moments I would witness a hint of human emotion from his grave face. I learned this vicariously through my cousin Buc Dur. Buc Dur was a few years older than me and had a mouth on him with little filter. Even after being swatted by Grandpa La like a mosquito and running with snot and tears dripping down his face, he was daring enough to say, *"Ma See Mae Murng!"* Translated, it means "the dog screwed your mother!"

But in his work area, there was a harmony between the well-disciplined grandfather and the mischievous grandson who existed there. By the time Buc Dur's tears dried up, Grandpa La would be sitting next to him, apologizing with his calm words, "I'm sorry, *Buc Laa*, I thought it was a mosquito on the back of your neck." It was his way of reconciling with a fatherless child, of saying "please don't provoke me again, I love you, and I really don't want to crack your head."

When the monsoon water came pouring on us during the wet season, we didn't return to our *nah* to seed the rice in the paddies or patch up the dikes that held pools of water that the swaying rice stalks loved soaking up. We kids put our best efforts into helping Grandpa La and our cousins with their own *nah*. But without E-Paw and Vung, there wouldn't be anyone tilling the soil with the water buffaloes, or even hauling the heavy bags of rice grains from the mill by the village school.

When we were out at the farm, I'd stretch my eyes over the rice paddies, and I'd think of E-Paw. I was still waiting for him to show up like the swell of water filling dry clay cracks and dikes, refreshing every earthly bowl of dirt in the ground, then rushing down toward the Paleeng River, by Grandpa Oosu's fruit orchard. There was a calling within those paddy weeds that grew with soft petals of purple, white, yellow, and green that spread through the fields. Frogs, tadpoles, and giant boatman bugs (reminding me of an oversized cockroach) could be seen with stalks of grass half submerged in the muddy water. Standing there smelling the fragrance of rice paddy weeds and lotus in the pond in front of our *nah* hut, and watching birds sail across the sky in their own jubilations over buffaloes roaming the fields made me as happy as a child running through a lush green field during the dawn of life.

Some days, we would return home to be under Grandpa La's tin roof, listening to heavy raindrops. In the beginning of the season, the rain would be sporadic, short and sharp, yet relieving the hot and humid air. Then the relentless rain gradually became a consistent bombardment of raindrops crashing down on us like pebbles tossed over our tin roof. By mid-monsoon season, Buc Dur and I were already used to it, and we'd made several dives headfirst into pools of water near our *nah*. Then we'd go home, and the elder cousins would tell stories of monsters, spirits of people who had been recently cremated over a pile of burning wood right there at our temple ground, especially with the bellowing smoke still fresh in the air.

Standing tall before us kids, my older cousins would point their sharp fingers at us, and I could see the whites of their eyes when they'd say, "Did you see the late *mister Khao*, white like a ghost sitting there staring down at people on the Bo tree by the entrance of the temple?"

This form of scaring, intended to be humorous entertainment left me in the dark with my own frightful imagination by the kerosene lamps. The stories were a lot more vivid to me when we had to go to the outhouse to relieve ourselves, where I hated when the flickering flames of our lantern light blew out with the flashing sky, leaving me in the dark with a thud of lightening. So, I'd stay away from the elders and their scary tales and huddle inside our mosquito tent covered under our gray blankets with my sisters.

Still, the *nah* was my favorite place to be. If we were out in our *nah*, it was a time of plenty, and we could relieve ourselves from the sweltering heat in the pool of water in front of our hut. From our *nah* hut balcony, I had a good view of other grass tops scattered along the dirt road that cut through our farm. It was the main road that led east toward the Mekong River and Pakse, closer to Vietnam, and the opposite direction was the border of Chong Mek, Thailand. There were few cars and trucks passing through the roads of our villages, but I still have a vivid picture of this road from the balcony of our dilapidated *nah* hut.

Toward the west stood the looming peak *Hin Soung* or "High Rock," which separates Laos from the northeastern part of Thailand. The gray pale mountain is still etched in my brain like an indelible painting over the swaying bamboo forest and dark jungle in the distance, over the verdant rice paddy and the village of Banh Dong.

Uncle Wan, E-Paw's younger brother, was a little like E-Paw and Grandpa Oosu—small-framed, narrow-nosed, soft-spoken, and light-skinned. When he would come to get me, he'd sit there on his bicycle in front of our hut with a warm smile on his face, chiming the bell on the handlebar—*gling, gling.*

"*Buc Laa,* do you want to come to the *nah* with me?" he would say excitedly.

"*Err. Er* (Yes. Yes) . . . " I'd run to him.

He'd pick me up and say, "Hang on, I won't let you fall," as we would ride along the bumpy dirt road until we got to his *nah* hut. It was just up the same side of the main road leading to Chong Mek Thailand.

Along the unpaved and bumpy road, Uncle Wan's hut was just beyond Aunt Paa and our cousins, and where Grandpa La and Grandma Dao stayed when they came to our *nah.* Back then, he and Aunt Dee had four children: one boy (PuMaa) and three girls (Champa, Lasamy, and Lasee). In Uncle Wan's *nah,* I didn't feel like an orphan; I was treated like the member of my cousin's family. When I heard him call me "Buc Laa," I'd picture him as my E-Paw. Then he mussed my hair and threw me up in the air and said, "Ooops! Look out, you're going to fall to the ground!"

When I returned to Grandpa La's, we'd learned through the adults' quiet conversations that good neighbors and E-Paw's old comrades were disappearing, some overnight. E-Mae's adopted brother, Uncle Taa, in the Village of Banh Hai—a village two miles west beyond the village temple—was also said to have disappeared overnight with his family. Our next-door neighbors Mae Kem, Mae Bout, Sister Koon, and Uncle Paay, who kept to themselves, were hunkering down because their own family had also disappeared. And the neighborhood dogs were no longer howling—they too had gone missing.

The following day, our eldest brother, Vung, still wrapped in his celibate robe, came to Grandpa La's hut. He stared at us kids then whispered softly to Narng, "I'm leaving now, don't say anything to anyone, take care of yourself and E-Nok and Buc Boun. Someone will come for you."

Then he disappeared.

2

THE UNEXPECTED GOODBYE

November 1976

Five days before E-Paw came for us, I was lying on my bare belly on the floor of Uncle Wan's farm hut. The hut stood on rough lumber stilts high enough for a water buffalo to pass through with ease. I was looking through a hole in the worn plank of floor board, staring at the ground below and the blades of green rice stalks swaying side to side just a few paces from the hut. Narng was next to me as we heard the repeated "Toom!" Then, "Tup, Tup, Tup, Boom!" emanated from the direction of Hin Soung Mountain. By the time I was four, I was used to hearing gunfights and explosions that randomly echoed from the jungle and the looming mountains in the distance.

That evening, Grandpa Oosu and I were sitting on the wooden bench next to Uncle Wan's *nah* hut. I could smell the tobacco lingering on his breath. Uncle Wan stood next to us with his hands on his hips; a puzzled look on his face replaced his casual warm smile. We stared at the open sky, which blended into a bluish orange over us and the swaying verdant field of rice below. Then Uncle Wan stared into the green paddies, then at the coconut, banana, and tamarind trees that towered over his shoulders in the yard.

As the dusk slowly crept upon us, there underneath the unsettled sky, a man emerged from the rice paddy, his grayish-green clothes soiled and army boots scuffed with mud. His skin was dark red. He moved toward us like a phantom casting a shadow along the green field. Grandpa Oosu held me close, and I returned a taunt grip on his rough hand.

Almost in an instant jolt of excitement for whatever bonds each of us together, I realized that the man was E-Paw. In that very moment of surprise, I freed my hand from the safety of Grandpa Oosu, and I ran to him. He picked me up before I'd sprung my little feet and knees upward, and then he threw his arms around me while he mussed my hair. If he had faded out of my memory in his absence, then his warm smile and playfulness had brought him back to life. I couldn't believe that E-Paw had returned once again.

E-Paw had been coming in and out of our lives like a magician when E-Mae and Thurng were still living with us at the village, appearing in our bedroom closet one day and vanishing the next. Now he stood in front of us with his eyes sunken and disarrayed. For five days while Narng stood vigilant next to a tamarind tree, keeping watch over the verdant rice field for E-Paw, he had been crawling in the mud. And Uncle Wan had snuck food wrapped in banana leaves to him as he walked past where E-Paw had been lying. E-Paw was hiding from the Lao Dang, waiting silently for the right moment to sneak us out from the village.

In that moment, I was overly excited to see my E-Paw, who was then holding me, rubbing my hair, and calling me *Buc Shour*. I'd missed his soft pinches on my calves or pulling my ears. It was this sense of humor in E-Paw that filled me with a sense of peace in my childhood memories—it made the kid in me wish to live forever. Besides calling me "Silly Boy," E-Paw also called me *Buc Na Ma* (Dog-face Boy). To me, it was sweet to hear E-Paw's teasing terms of endearment, but strangely that day E-Paw had lost quite a bit of his humor, and he was rather serious. His displays of affection were cut short, and soon after he had set me down, he turned to Uncle Wan and Grandpa Oosu.

They began a hushed conversation next to a wooden stilt holding up the hut. It would be the last time the three men were found huddling together. Seeing them standing there talking was like watching marionettes with their strings gradually pulled back and forth. I heard a few mumbles and instinctively kept my distance and watched the dark furrowed brows and frowns on their faces. This would be E-Paw's final goodbye to his father and only brother.

They had spent so much time together clearing and plowing fields, building the dikes of the rice paddies to hold back the water, fishing and hunting down by the Paleeng River, and they had each accomplished achievements in honor of the family. E-Paw became a village doctor and Uncle Wan the village teacher.

Grandpa Oosu stood close to his two boys, desperately trying to keep them together. "Let me come with you and we'll all escape together!" he sobbed.

"It's too dangerous," E-Paw said, holding back his tears.

"If they catch up with us, they'll kill us all," Uncle Wan agreed with E-Paw.

"*Bor, Bor, Pai num gun . . .* (No, no, we go together . . ." Grandpa Oosu plead for the last time.

I wished we could be there with them forever, but the evildoing was upon us, and its intention was to take over our livelihood. E-Paw didn't have any options but to run—he was with the wrong political party. As a former soldier to the Royal Laos army, the town's watchmen, and with ties to the anti-communist Patigan, E-Paw had to run. He had been moving nomadically along Hin Soung Mountain and the jungle with the Patigan and fighting in guerilla-warfare tactics and hiding in caves. This had been E-Paw's third attempt to save us. He fell short on his first two attempts with his comrades, only to encounter gunfights with the Lao Dang near the base of Hin Soung Mountain, and eventually gunfights led them to retreat to the border of Chong Mek, Thailand.

There in that very moment, it was as if the whirling wind of E-Paw's life came to a standstill; he stood staring at another pivotal point of no turning back. The narrative of his entire life was now at hand. He was balancing the scale of life and death, weighing the potential casualty to the family. To take my sisters and me meant he was sacrificing the lives of Uncle Wan's family. To be caught by the Lao Dang with everyone could be the demise of the entire pack.

"Go . . . go take care of yourself and be careful," Uncle Wan urged E-Paw with his vigilant eyes on the looming horizon.

I stood there for a while as Grandpa Oosu touched me on my head, and Uncle Wan looked at me while he patted me on my back. It would be the last time I looked upon their faces. In their brown eyes, the despair had already mixed with fear as they gazed upon each other.

"*Err* . . . " Then the three men exchanged their final looks and touches with one another, now falling into a heavy silence.

"I'm leaving. Take care of yourself and the family," E-Paw said.

As E-Paw touched both Uncle Wan and Grandpa Oosu on their arms and shoulders, his words died with a sullen silence on his face. Then finally the three men looked at each other with despair.

Aunt Dee and our little cousins were still on the above balcony, alert like a pack of meerkats. She had been busy preparing food earlier that day. Cousin Pu-Maa's job was to fetch Nok from the village of Banh Dong to join Narng at the edge of the *nah* near the Paleeng River. In the meantime, Cousin Champa, who was then a teenager, had the role of "watcher" from the balcony. In her silence, she stretched her view over the green fields with her dark marble eyes and round dark-red face high above the rice stalks, her jet-black hair pinned high in a ball behind her shoulders.

Then with almost a swoop from E-Paw's arms, he pulled me closer to him, and I felt my spirit rise with his reassuring touch. I was on top of the world again as he placed me on his back and he carried me out from underneath the hut. I wrapped my arms around his shoulders and straddled my bare legs around his gray army jacket. I was still unsure of where E-Paw was taking me, but I was overjoyed just to be reunited with him.

"Goodbye, be careful, and good luck," they whispered to us.

Why were we saying goodbye to each other? I thought. They had always been there for me and my family.

As E-Paw moved us away from the family we left behind, the cool breeze picked up and we watched the sun sinking together, the orange sky slowly fading into the gray mountains ahead of us. I tried to turn around to see Uncle Wan and Grandpa Oosu for the very last time. But I couldn't, and my legs were being brushed by the stalks of rice.

E-Paw quickly trudged through the rice fields and finally stopped before exiting to the main road that ran through our village farm. Before crossing, E-Paw set me down on the ground and kneeled next to me, so he could poke his head out through the blades of rice stalks to see if there was anyone in sight. He stared to his left, where the main road led to our *Banh* (village), and to his right, where the road led to the stretch of mountains on the border of Thailand, the birthplace of E-Mae.

"Now remember to be very quiet and don't make any sounds, okay," he said to me in his soft voice.

"*Err,*" I gave him a guttural grunt through my nostrils.

"Don't talk, *Buc Laa* (Dear boy)," he said, scanning the edge of the jungle. Then he bent to the ground, staring at tracks next to human footprints.

I'd seen those animal tracks before and they belonged to our water buffaloes, Buc Ang, a bull, and E-Don, our young calf. I began to wonder why he was so curious about such common tracks. I wanted to ask E-Paw why we were heading into the dark jungle and not going home to Grandpa La, but E-Paw was consumed, and his mind was focused elsewhere. Something was disturbing him, and I didn't dare to ask him. I felt as though E-Paw had not been himself that day. The father I knew was so full of life and his antics had always kept us amused, but as he placed me on his back again and we entered the woods, there was another side of him that I hadn't seen before.

It was the first time I recalled venturing into the woods during sunset. Now we were past the edge of Grandpa Oosu's fruit farm. Here the mangoes, tamarinds, and even starfruits dangled high above my head in abundance beyond what could have ever filled our bellies. The dense vegetation tangled E-Paw's feet and branches poked at me even while I was riding on his back. With the light gradually diminishing, I began seeing the ominous images of bug-aboos from stories the adults had told, intending to add fear to our childish imaginations. They were tales of man-eating pythons and tigers, of poisonous snakes striking with sharp fangs, and of leeches that would latch onto your body to suck your blood as you trudged through the hot jungle, never mind commingling them with the dreaded images of the squatting Hanuman, a depiction of the Hindu god tattooed on E-Paw's arm. I was spooked by its imagery when I first saw it on his body. I had neither the strength or courage of E-Paw's god, even with E-Paw's assurance that I'll be fine, if I kept quiet.

I was still on his back as E-Paw moved us closer to the dark forest, the sounds of flowing water grew louder with the diminishing light behind us. Continuing along the edge of the wood, E-Paw appeared to be picking up speed with the brisk wind. Then, abruptly, we came upon a clearing at the bank of the Paleeng River.

From E-Paw's back I was still staring at our familiar ground. I thought back to my recent visits to this part of the river with Uncle Wan, Narng, Nok, and our cousins. I was reminded of the playful sounds of laughter that lingered from the time when we had all come down to cool off at the fresh pool of water. I swam in the stream of the swirling water that gathered at the bend until my eyes turned red and the snot dripped out of my nose. Narng lathered my hair with the simmering leaves of the sudsy bush that were found along the water's edge by breaking up the plants and mushing them into her hands until they formed a handful of foam. I'd always loved how the pool of water filled up this pristine setting, as it appeared to gently replenish the life of fishes, frogs, and the wild and sweet colorful tropical fruits. After a fun-filled day of water, stuffing my face with *maak vaa* (a small cherry-like fruit that left my lips and hands purple), figs, and mulberries, we would dig along the sandy banks with twigs and sometimes our bare hands for crabs and the little sand frogs. The sand frogs were my favorite; sometimes they were found floating in the water with us. Since they were the size of our thumbs, E-Mae had to stretch a bowl full of these bouncing critters to make us a tasty meal. On our way home through Grandpa Oosu's fruit farms, we climbed the *taa-gholp* for a snack. The *frogs' eyes* fruit, a shiny little red fruit, came with an aromatic fragrant of sweet flower. It was always a delicious treat, as their sweet juice popped in my mouth.

Then a sudden shake brought me back to reality as E-Paw shifted me up higher on his back, keeping me from sliding off. The rush of water flowing down the river became loud, as he hopped on the first big gray rock on the edge of the water.

"We're going to cross here, you hold on tight, and no matter what happens, you must keep quiet," he said, his soft voice fading out with the sounds of rushing water.

"*Err.*" I let the air out of my nose as I tightened both my arms around his neck. My pulse raced from his words and the looming darkness. I hung tautly to his neck and shoulders, and his hands tightened their grip on my dangling legs.

The Paleeng River was a playing ground for us, and for E-Paw it was a place where he would hunt and fish. We were familiar with this part of the river—we had crossed on several occasions—but in the darkness, my untrained eyes saw only invented childish fears of shadows and ominous images.

There were many streams near our farm hut, but small pools of water turned to cracks of clay during the dry season. The Paleeng River had shallow areas and deep areas where water would gather and flow throughout the year. In some locations of the river, the pool of water would be so deep that a water buffalo would submerge itself, hiding from the hot days. Since E-Paw used to come to this part of the river to cast his fishing net, he knew this area well, and he did not want to chance slipping into the deeper pools of water. He stood at the bank for a while and then decided to hop nimbly from one protruding rock to another, working desperately to get us safely to the other side.

3

THE FLIGHT THROUGH DARKNESS

I was still clinging tightly to E-Paw's warm body as he skipped along the rocks to the other side of the Paleeng river, where the sandy slope rose upward toward the thickets and dark towering trees. Here the river curved with gentle waterfalls cascading down the hill and tall trees with vines that coiled around its huge trunks. Glancing side to side over E-Paw's shoulders, I watched the water running through the rocky channel. Then I stared down to my side, my brown sandals dangling off my feet by E-Paw's thighs. The rushing water overpowered E-Paw's heavy breath, but I felt him bouncing us along the gray boulder. While gripping tighter on my legs, he hopped off the last rock, to where he sank knee deep into the flowing water and forded across for the final stretch. When we reached the sandy hill, E-Paw stopped, and we both gazed at the hill in front of us. Then without any hesitation, E-Paw lunged forward, pulling our weight upward on the tree limbs and draping vines that stood in our path, as I felt the loose branches whip my face, legs, and arms. My only defense against the swinging limbs was to bury my face into E-Paw's gray uniform and wait for a clearing.

When we arrived at the top of the slope, E-Paw was still shaking the sand from his boots. He found an opening and made his way through teak trees that towered over our heads. Behind us, the hazy sky was slowly disappearing as E-Paw took us further into the interlocking bough of trees. He rushed us quickly to the dark surrounding of thick brushes.

"Don't speak and keep quiet," E-Paw reminded me again after a long silence.

"*Err, Err.*" I nodded pressing my face against his back.

The next time I looked up I saw the orange robe of Jour Peng with Buc Ang's noose in his hands. He stared at us with a brown satchel on his shoulder, while Buc Ang stood there like an oversized pet with his gray horns tilting toward us. At the sight of Jour Peng, E-Paw nodded at him as if they shared one common thought, then stared at the direction he wanted to take us.

"*Err.*" Jour Peng agreed and nudged the noose on Buc Ang.

E-Paw quickly pointed us deeper into the woods with Jour Peng and Buc Ang behind us, until we came to a small clearing where there was a giant tree so tall that the sunset cast its shadows deep into the green field below. It was then that I saw Narng and Nok standing there stiff like the trees behind them, both wearing brown sandals and dressed in sarongs that were wet from the waist down, as if they were hanging them to dry from their hips. Narng carried a brown bag on one shoulder while hanging onto Nok, who also had a bamboo rice basket almost the size of her waist with a cotton string dangling from her own shoulder. Narng's fair skin accentuated her glow, with her hair neatly tucked in a ponytail resting on three different buttoned-up shirts she had layered on top of one another. Nok was still clinging tightly to Narng's hand with a frightful look on her heart-shaped face, her dark trimmed hair draped over her forehead. Cousin PuMaa (Uncle Wan's eldest son) had pretended that he was taking Nok to Uncle Wan's *nah*. Instead, he had sneaked Nok from the village for a rendezvous with Narng by the edge of the Paleeng River next to Grandpa Oosu's fruit farm. The bamboo rice basket Nok carried had been hand-woven by Grandpa Oosu, and it was filled with sticky rice, grilled chicken and some hard-boiled eggs that Aunt Dee put together for us earlier that day.

Not a peep came out from any of them, as E-Paw lowered me, and I slid off his back to the ground. Then Narng's voice came out like the soft crackling sounds of a little kitten. "E-Paw," Narng finally said, acknowledging his presence.

"*Pai!* (Go)!" E-Paw said, as he moved toward Narng and Nok, then exhaled the pocket of air that appeared to have been gathering in his lungs.

Narng and Jour Peng nodded in sync.

"Did you see anyone?" E-Paw asked.

"*Err*," Narng whispered the soft "*yes*" through her nose. "We crossed paths with Paw Seel (E-Paw's best friend) and E-Laa (his youngest daughter) along the rice field. They were walking their water buffalo back to the village of Banh Bok. He asked us where we were going, and we told him that we were going to Grandpa Oosu's *nah*."

"Did you see anyone else?" E-Paw looked at Narng with a frown, pulling his dark brows tighter, pondering the thought of his whereabouts with the interlocking bough of trees growing even darker.

"*Bor (No)*." Narng looked at E-Paw's concerned eyes.

"We have to go quickly." E-Paw picked the thumb-sized leaves from a green bush, then handed a leaf to each of us, except for Jour Peng. I'd seen this before—E-Paw believed in animism.

We followed his cue, as he put the leaf into his mouth. We moved with him as he mumbled the familiar prayers to Buddha and Mother Nature. But this time E-Paw also called upon spirits of the jungle, rivers, and the dark mountain.

"*Saa Tu Hai Kanoi* (I beg of you), please protect me and my family from the danger as we pass through the earth, the jungle, the river, and over the mountain," E-Paw said, pinching a bit of dirt from the ground and dabbing it on everyone's head, except for Jour Peng who was already in his own meditation.

"Please protect us and may our paths be cleared, and I pray to you to shelter us from harm. In return, we shall respect you for life and live peacefully among all people, and when we've safely crossed the mountain, we shall offer you a great feast of wine, chicken, and sweet rice, *Saa Tu* (Amen)." E-Paw whispered his prayer with his hands still clasped together, while he pushed our way through another small opening.

We kept our pace to E-Paw's without any trouble until my sandals got stuck against the coiled roots at the wide base of a tree trunk, as I tried to keep up with Narng. Seeing that I was up against a challenge, Narng helped me and said, "Don't speak, *Buc Laa*!"

I followed Narng along a path that Buc Ang had squeezed through. Now in the dim light, E-Paw's figure was still working hard to push a path through the bushes that lead us farther into the woods. E-Paw moved vehemently ahead through the trail, studying footprints and broken branches and making way for us through the tangled vines and wild weeds that reminded me of choking rice stalks during harvesting season. But this path that E-Paw was taking us on was leading us in the opposite direction of the mountain, which was leading us westward. We were moving eastward toward Paw Seel's village of Banh Bok. E-Paw had made this maneuver fearing that we could accidentally stumble into the village of Banh Jik, where we would surely fall into the hands of the Lao Dang. It was a strategy that E-Paw and Uncle Wan had been devising for days to fool the Lao Dang into thinking that we took the most obvious route into the mountain.

E-Paw urged us to push our way through the thickets, as the limbs that sheltered us became our obstacle. We were to stay under the covering of trees and bushes until the sun completely disappeared from the horizon and our eyes had acclimated to the moonlight.

"If you see anyone or anything moving, hide yourselves behind the trees or the shrubs, and take your sister and brother with you," E-Paw said to Narng.

I didn't dare say a word, as I watched everyone holding their belongings and trailing behind E-Paw. Narng picked me up, and from her shoulders I saw everyone desperately pushing through without a cry from the prodding pickers and the jabbing branches. There wasn't even a hissing from Buc Ang blowing his nose as he walked heavily behind the line. Jour Peng's rope was still flapping to the slight warm breeze. Nok was in the middle, pushing her way through and trying to study overgrown roots and vines that sometimes tangled her ankles and sandals.

Then suddenly E-Paw stopped dead in his tracks. He pulled out a lighter from his puffy coat pocket to view something that puzzled him. He quickly shut off his lighter, and the inquisitive look on his face disappeared into the dark figure of his statue. With a glimpse, E-Paw had discovered footprints. He was quite sure these fresh marks weren't the ordinary footprints of a peasant wandering through the woods. E-Paw seemed perplexed as he hurried back to us several paces behind him; his brown eyes now darkened with their vigilant nature.

"I saw soldier boot prints in the mud farther ahead on this trail. They may belong to the Lao Dang," E-Paw whispered quietly to Jour Peng and Narng. "We can't follow this path. We have to take a detour into the jungle and the swamp out to the rice paddies, and we can loop back next to the other jungle next to the meadow on the other side of this marsh. That way we can cover more ground and stay out in the open under the moonlight until we reach the jungle before the base of the mountain."

Jour Peng and Narng nodded to E-Paw in silence. They veered into another opening and squeezed themselves through the trees right behind E-Paw. This time E-Paw was taking us away from the accessible path, pushing his way through with minimal light. The darkness that became our friend soon became E-Paw's fear as he was losing his sense of direction under the heavy covering. Our little backward detour took us through Aunt Choum's farm, which was almost directly across the Paleeng River from Grandpa Oosu's vacant fruit farm. Aunt Choum was Grandpa La's younger sister. But before long we found ourselves lost under the towering forest where we lost sight of Hin Soung Mountain.

Fighting through the dimness, we found ourselves surrounded by elephant grass, thick weeds, and the soft swamp ground. The water was up to Nok's knees, while she fought to keep the rice basket from being soaked. Narng reached over grabbing Nok's hand, pulling her up from the water.

"I lost one of my sandals," Nok said, still struggling with the dark water.

"Lost where?" Narng reached down and grabbed the rice basket from Nok.

"We can't find it; I think it's stuck in the mud," Narng whispered to E-Paw.

Narng scrambled to find it. She looked for anything that floated to the surface of the water that resembled Nok's sandal. But she found nothing but disappointment.

"We have to keep moving quickly." E-Paw feared the soldiers closing in on our trail.

Narng heeded E-Paw's words and grabbed Nok's hand. Nok picked up her only sandal and she held it tightly, then pushed herself through the dark water to keep up with E-Paw's pace.

Shortly after we worked our way out of the swamp, we were still surrounded by the dark covering of trees.

"Can you climb that tree and see if you can find the mountain?" E-Paw asked Jour Peng, pointing at a tree with an overgrown trunk and limbs that seemed to stretch in every direction under the stars.

"*Err*," Jour Peng nodded his shaved head. He then lifted the strap of his pouch from his shoulder and hung it on a small protruding branch of the tree next to him. He quickly and silently pulled off the upper half of his orange robe and tied the sweep of the cloth to his waist and kicked off his sandals. Then he grabbed the lowest limb of an adjacent tree and hoisted his sinewy body upward limb by limb until he stood as high to my naked eyes as the skyline. With both hands hanging on the limbs, he gazed into the moonlight filtering through the dark bough of the jungle. I watched him disappearing and reappearing through the dark leaves and branches. And before I realized it, he was on the ground putting on his sandals and grabbing his belongings from E-Paw's hand.

"The Hin Soung Mountain is that way," Jour Peng said as he pointed over E-Paw's shoulders.

"Okay, *Pai* (Go)," E-Paw said, moving quickly toward that direction. He found another opening that stretched itself into another dark jungle ahead of us. The meadow of green grass, bushes, and trees scattered far into the distance to our left and right. We could see a burning torch coming from Banh Jik's small hut (where E-Paw was trying to avoid) to our west just before the mountain where E-Paw said we were supposed to cross.

I wanted to go to sleep under the stars, but my inquisitiveness kept me awake. Tired of carrying me, Narng saddled me on top of Buc Ang. He moved his hooves heavily through grassy fields, picking up muddy soil while I balanced myself with his shifting motions. With my legs far from reaching his large ribcage, I pressed my hands into the course hair of his back.

From behind Jour Peng I gazed up into the dark jungle and saw E-Paw's dark-silvery image several feet ahead of us. Jour Peng, still wrapped in his orange robe, was directly behind him, and Nok kept her stride alongside Narng.

Nok stumbled along patches of grass barefoot and holding her only sandal. I watched her avoiding ditches in the field as if they were going to swallow her whole. Years later, she would tell me that at that moment she was fighting to stay awake, since she was afraid that she would sleepwalk onto her own path into the jungle. I didn't hear much from her except for when she warned Narng about the strange man that was in the woods.

"I saw a man smoking and squatting over there. I think he's going to the bathroom," Nok said to Narng.

"Shh . . . Don't talk. We have to be quiet and not say a word," Narng demanded as she tried to catch up with Jour Peng and E-Paw.

Nok didn't say anything else as she lunged forward over another clump of grass. Once we were out in the open, I was still seeing dark images in the jungle, but E-Paw was now using it as a quick cover. To see our path better, he took us along the grassy fields as we blended in with the edges of the jungle. Narng kept her vigilant eyes on me, but then the worst happened: Buc Ang hit a bump in the field and shook me like an earthquake. I tried to lean forward into his back, wrap my arms around his oversized belly, and plant my face right over his spine like I had done many times on our rice field. But Buc Ang became too big for me and I slowly slipped away from him like a flimsy rag. I tried reaching out to grab anything on his massive body to hang onto, but I grasped nothing but air in the palm of my hands, not even a single coarse hair on him.

"Narng!" I cried, reaching for her hand.

Narng dropped Buc Ang's noose and reached desperately for me, but her arms were too short to reach over his back. Then suddenly, my world went sideways as I sailed through the air hitting the brush of grass and felt a hard thump that shocked my entire body. I couldn't move as I lay there on my back sucking in all the air that I could muster. Then a burst of air came out of me in the darkness, as I finally let out a shrieking cry from the depth of my lungs and burning throat. I felt like I was dying with tears now filling my eyes. I saw that everyone had gathered around E-Paw, as he held me in his arms. On my back I felt Narng's gentle hand probing for wounds. Nok and Jour Peng looked at me without any words.

"Shh . . . shh . . . nothing happened, nothing happened, you're okay, shh, shh." E-Paw held me closer to his chest, absorbing the weeping sounds coming out of me. "Shh, don't worry, everything will be alright, I got you." E-Paw was still cradling me in his arms.

Now I was sucking in the mucus that ran down my throat and the wind began to cool off the burning in my chest. I stopped crying and E-Paw wiped the sliminess off my face.

"Shh, it's okay," E-Paw repeated, rubbing me with his gentle hands.

The shimmering world fell silent once again as E-Paw hoisted me to his shoulder facing his back as he moved onward without hesitation. Looking behind him, I could see Jour Peng's face still glowing as if he was a mirror image of the moon itself. Narng and Nok had exhausted looks on their faces as they were fighting to keep up with E-Paw. But like nomadic people in search of a place to rest, they continued walking under the moonlight and speckled stars that were flickering off and on inside my head. But before I lost consciousness, I saw Nok fumbling over a clump of grass away in her own direction for the last time, and I fell asleep as all the lights went out on me.

I woke up in the arms of Jour Peng. Leaning on his shoulder, I opened my eyes to more dark images all around us. High above our heads the stars were sparkling through the openings underneath the trees. The warm breeze now dissipated into the chilly air, and the dew gathered on the leaves dabbing my skin with moisture. Along the ground, shadows of the trees stretched on the rocks and grasses as the luminescent light of the moon filtered through.

Ahead in the near distance, E-Paw's figure came to view. He moved like a mother cat prowling in the night anticipating trouble for her kittens. He struck his lighter and pointed down to the small pile of leaves by a huge trunk that stood across our path. The orange flame in the palm of his hand illuminated the disturbed look on his face. Something seemed to have daunted E-Paw, but then his face quickly disappeared with the glow on his hand as he tucked his lighter into his pocket. Still edgy, he was ready to act at the end of each trail and each opening. It appeared as if he was searching for a ghost that existed only in his mind. Like when he discovered the footprints in the mud and made us detour from our path.

Then he immediately stopped his forward progress, as he warned Jour Peng with his soft words, "It might be a *Maak Tag* (grenade booby trap)." We all stopped dead in our tracks, fearing the hard truth, the secret truth of why E-Paw kept using his lighter in the darkness. He searched for any signs of broken branches and even unusual yet obvious paths we could've taken.

At the time, I had very little understanding of it, but back in the village of Banh Dong, it was common to hear about the deadly devices leading to incidents that instilled so much fear for travelers, especially along the path by the base of the mountain and the Lao-Thai border. The nightmarish tales of fleeing refugees amputated as their limbs had been torn apart by stepping on the deathly explosives was enough to detour anyone from taking a path known to have booby traps. The horrible and tragic death of a person bleeding and squirming helplessly to their demise filled me with fear. Although I had never seen a limbless person with my own eyes, hearing the constant thud of gunfight and explosions coming from the distance was enough to make me a believer of what the village's tales shared in the adults' hushed corner.

I tried not to let my imagination get the best of me, and I flushed out the thought from my mind. I closed my eyes and then I heard exhaustion coming from Buc Ang, blowing air out of his nostrils, and the sound of Nok whining.

"I'm tired. My feet and legs are hurting," Nok said to Narng, who was now pulling Nok and Buc Ang along the trail.

"We need rest," Narng said to E-Paw as he shortened the distance between us.

"What's the matter?" E-Paw asked, staring down at Nok's heart-shaped face.

"Can we rest a bit before we head on farther?" Narng asked.

"Okay, but it's still dangerous to be here. We should cross the mountain before we take our rest," E-Paw said, patting Nok's shoulders with his hand, calming her from further whining.

E-Paw stood there for a while, his mind still plagued with his concerns. He stared at the dark woods with his keen sense of awareness, as if he was feeling the soft breeze in hope that it might carry a sound of caution. It seemed that with each move he was calculating our chance of getting caught, but at times E-Paw appeared to be playing against himself. He pondered our chances alone, climbed the trees, and scouted the tracks, and most of the time he pointed and waved to us like we were deaf. Now, the agile man seemed to be stopped in his tracks with chiding thoughts of making the right choice in his direction.

"Alright, if I recall there used to be an old vacant hut by the base of the mountain down the ravine. We can sleep there for a while," E-Paw said. "Don't talk, stay quiet, and if you see or hear anything or anyone, hide," E-Paw warned us before jetting off to search for the vacant hut. Then like a silhouette, E-Paw disappeared into the dark trees.

We huddled under the dark covering, as Jour Peng remained alert to any movement or sounds. In Narng's eyes there was still unrest, while Nok and I sank into our exhaustion. Nok and I leaned closer to Narng, for a place to rest our head and for protection. Pressing on each other, we fought to keep our heavy eyelids open, while we waited for E-Paw's return. And in Jour Peng's hands, Buc Ang stood on his hooves staring at us with his huge gray horns and dark shinny eyes, swiping his tail back and forth like a faithful dog. If he could have spoken that night, he too might have requested a pool of mud or patch of grass to lie on.

Without a sound, E-Paw's shape appeared looming from the darkness, then in the moonlight his silvery figure came rushing over to us through an opening on our path. E-Paw's return came with a sense of relief, as we stood up eagerly to hear what he had to say about our shelter for the night.

"There's a vacant hut over there," E-Paw said, pointing in the direction that we would take.

Narng grabbed my hand and hoisted her bundle over her shoulder. Then she took Buc Ang's noose from Jour Peng, and Nok followed without a word. Jour Peng came back for me, and I climbed on his back again. We broke through another opening after E-Paw, and there it was, the vacant hut that E-Paw had spoken of. It stood on dark wooden stilts with a thick field of grass covering the ground underneath it. The dark framed window that had been left wide open was over our heads, and the wooden planks were covered with silvery green algae. On its roof dried grass and bamboo thatch held the hut's covering together, and it reminded me so much of our *nah* hut. Although this hut was a lonely hut, the person who was living here had no obvious neighbor or none that any of us kids ever recalled within sight that night. Thinking back to the story that Grandpa La used to tell of a magical, ancient time they called *"Bo Laan,"* I imagined that this might be the home of a *Pa Lur See*, a mysterious wizard who often lived alone in the wilderness.

This time, I was too tired to stare up into the trees and see their dark limbs casting shadows from the moonlight. I wasn't haunted by the thought of something sitting up there that might just yank me away from my family. Then I felt E-Paw touching the back of my head, as he guided Buc Ang's noose to a dark wooden stilt underneath the hut where the overgrown grass touched the bottom of his exposed belly.

"There shouldn't be anyone up there, but watch your steps, the wood might be rotted." E-Paw pointed to the rungs of the wooden ladder.

"Err." Jour Peng nodded as he was the first to ascend.

Narng and the rest of us eagerly followed him and settled in by the corner next to the open window. She unraveled her bundle and pulled out a cloth and threw it on the wooden planks. Neither Narng, Nok, or even Jour Peng had much to say as they lay down. My head also came to rest on the hard wooden floor next to Nok and Narng, the weight of my little body on my spine, and again the dimly lit world suddenly became completely dark as I drifted away from E-Paw and the dark roof that now covered us from the dew of the night.

4

CLIMBING THE MOUNTAIN

E-Paw shook my shoulders from a dead sleep early the next morning. I laid there almost lifelessly, feeling disconnected from my neck, waist, and legs. It was as if I had landed on a rock instead of a patch of elephant grass on the previous night. I wanted to lay there a little longer, at least until the rooster crowed at the crack of dawn.

Half asleep, I heard E-Paw's urgent voice echo in the dark, "*Pai, Pai* (Go, Go)." He urged us to move. Along with everyone, I stood up quickly rubbing the sleepers stuck in my eyes. My body numb with the dizzy spells that came surging through my head.

"*Pai, Pai,*" E-Paw's repeated words echoed in my head like a dream. "Get up, get up!"

He helped us to gather ourselves and our belongings. Then E-Paw quickly led us down the steps and untied Buc Ang from the post directly below where we'd slept. Jour Peng got out of the hut first, followed by Nok, and then Narng, who carried me down the creaky steps into the open. Buc Ang didn't make a sound as he lay there silently. E-Paw pulled him up and he lunged with his front hooves from his rest on the thick grass; underneath him he'd made a huge impression in the shape with his huge belly.

We walked into the woods, and I looked back and saw the gray hut slowly disappearing behind the dark tall trees with vines choking on its limbs. I noticed the light mist rising from the wet leaves above where the soft rays of sunlight shone through the canopy.

To keep up with E-Paw, who was guiding Buc Ang along the rocky base of the mountain, Narng pulled my hand to hasten our steps. From behind, I could see Buc Ang's hooves crushing broken tree limbs and slipping on the jagged rocks. Then without any notice, a pocket of air shot out of his nostril. The gray smooth rocks made him a clumsy animal. But like a faithful dog, he pushed himself upward toward the small plateau we were trying to reach with all the mass of a bull water buffalo.

Through an open trail, a ray of sunshine cut above the tree line, and I felt its warmth on my face. Although E-Paw was with us now, I was still longing for home. I thought of my family in the *nah* again; I was running along the field and my sisters and brother would help me to hitch a ride on Buc Ang.

Then suddenly I was drawn to the chattering of jungle life that came alive with the sounds of squawking birds and animals shrieking from the branches and below in the thickets. Birds of yellow, red, and brown sailed above my head through the air in the haven of dark green leaves.

Thinking about birds, my belly growled as my mind filled with the thought of food. The hunger drove me to remember the tasty morsels of hot grilled sparrows with sticky rice and spicy papaya salad. My head felt light as I stared into the shiny bushes and the rocky ground surrounding us. I couldn't wait any longer. It was there that I learned that the hunger pang yields to no one. My stomach growled even louder with its dire needs. Then I finally succumbed to the rumbling monster in me.

"Narng, I'm hungry," I said.

"Me too." Nok looked up at us with a sunken face.

"Okay." E-Paw heard us and turned his attention to Narng. "What do we have to eat?"

"We have the grilled chicken that Aunt Dee gave us with the rice that we soaked in a little bit of water last night in the swamp," Narng answered.

"Alright, let's sit down over here and eat a little of what we have and try to save the rest for later," E-Paw said.

We stopped to gather by a large boulder to eat breakfast. Each of us took a few drops of water from E-Paw's canteen as Narng laid out the basket of rice and the grilled chicken. Finally, after waiting anxiously, E-Paw placed the first ball of rice and chicken in my mouth. The savory chicken and rice melted deliciously in my mouth and slowly began to ease my growling tummy and my entire body. I wanted to reach in with my own hands, but this was a true piece meal, as E-Paw slowly fed me the little ball of rice with a pinch of chicken he pulled off the bones with his fingers.

"E-Paw, I'm still hungry," I said when our meal came to an end.

"We should save a bit of our food for later in the day, since our journey is still quite a long way, and we may arrive at nightfall," E-Paw reminded us again.

After we each took a quick swig of water from E-Paw's canteen that he had attached to the loop of his belt, we gathered ourselves again and marched upward toward the rocky terrain. We were now walking on the side of the looming mountain that I could only imagine a few days ago. As we climbed up to its peak, I thought about all those stories that spread throughout our village. I thought of what the world would look like when we got to the summit. I remembered from the village tales that there were supposedly evil monsters and ghosts that roamed its jungle. I wondered if we would run into any of them, how we would defend ourselves if they surprised us with their sharp fangs and claws. Then, on the other hand, if we reached the top, maybe I could see Uncle Wan and the rest of the family farming along the rice paddy. All sorts of images whirled through my mind as we suddenly came to a halt. This time it was because E-Paw could no longer pull Buc Ang up the path, which was too much of an incline for him.

"We have to find another path. Buc Ang isn't going to make it—he'll slip and injure himself," E-Paw said.

We stood looking at the slope of the mountain in front of us as it rose steeply right before our eyes. The rocky terrain became a challenge even for us to pull each other up. Here there were no shrubs to hang onto, and the trees were taller, with limbs stretching high above our heads.

"I'm going to find another way to bring Buc Ang up," E-Paw whispered to Narng and Jour Peng, while pulling Buc Ang's noose along the side of the hill. Then he and Buc Ang made their way parallel to the hill as we pushed our way through behind him, avoiding coiled roots and rocky crevices.

"Get on my back and hang on tight." Narng picked me up when our path became more than a challenge for me. Years later, she would tell me that she was more afraid of my shrieking cry giving away our location if the Lao Dang had been on our trail.

From afar the mountain's incline appeared to ascend sharply into the horizon, but E-Paw finally discovered a path that Buc Ang was able to manage with his hooves. It was a gradual rocky slope that appeared to be formed by rain that flowed down the mountain. After E-Paw gave us the go-ahead, we followed him and pulled each other up the hill, leveraging ourselves with the tree limbs and vines that dangled in our way. Narng decided that it was too dangerous to carry me up the hill. She put me down on the ground and pulled me along with her hand. I felt the rock and tree roots underneath my feet, and I pushed my legs forward with each step to meet everyone's strides. A little farther ahead of us, E-Paw was working Buc Ang up the hill. Buc Ang's hooves kept slipping off the rock. But E-Paw whipped him with a stick to get him to keep on trying. Buc Ang grunted and blew the snots out of his large slimy nostrils and looked back at us. He was giving up and the hill was too steep for him—he didn't want to go any farther. He looked at us one more time, and his curved gray horns swung side to side. Then with another tap from E-Paw's stick, he planted his rear hooves on the protruding rocks and thrusted himself up the hill.

E-Paw stopped Buc Ang and waited for us when they reached the top of the mountain. The small plateau was abrupt, and our descent was gentler on Buc Ang than our incline to its peak. I searched down below and far into the horizon, and I saw the plain field and that reminded me of our *nah*. But it was not our *nah*—it was missing the grass tops of huts along the road, the pond in front our *nah* hut, and the streams of water that ran through our farmland.

We descended to the base of the mountain after E-Paw and Buc Ang. We gazed upon the land below the blue sky as we balanced our way down the hill, clinging on to tree limbs and each other. In the distance, a stretch of land came into view and a hut with its grassy tops baking in the morning sun. Along the green fields, dikes ran like a labyrinth throughout the rice field. Along the slope, my mind wandered to thoughts of E-Mae. I missed E-Mae so much since she had been gone. There were nights I cried for her soothing touch and her calming whispers. And what about little Thurng? I wondered if he still remembered me. If he'd crawl or run to us when he saw us. The more I thought of them, the more my thoughts sailed with the birds in elation. I imagined all of them in the hut below and how soon we'd all be reunited.

Suddenly, an abrupt halt by E-Paw at the bottom of the hill interrupted my imagination. He wasn't entirely relieved to see the other side of the mountain, but he wanted to give us a brief rest. After taking a few more sips of water and exchanging some soft mumbling "*Err, Err*" from our nostrils and gasping needed breaths, we continued along the grassy field and thick weeds until we came to an open farmland. We moved with E-Paw who was deliberately taking caution through the tall grass ahead of us. Since we were now out in the open field of weeds as high as Narng's hip, E-Paw put me on Buc Ang's back. Nok pushed on behind us, still hanging on to Narng's hand. Together we stared into the blue horizon with the bright sun heating up our face. Then we heard dogs barking from afar, and I tightened my grip on Buc Ang's back. But I dare not say a word. I'm both scared and fond of dogs; our dogs were friendly and vigilant like most dogs left to meander in the village, but I knew that some were fierce and territorial. E-Paw was once fined because his dog attacked a child in the village. Still, I long to see their wagging tails and playful barks, as the memory of them flooded back to me running along with them on our *nah* fields.

My thoughts were interrupted again as we stumbled into someone's *nah*. To our surprise there was a family of farmers moving about with their daily duties. From several feet away, the father stood with an inquisitive look on his face. Then the tan-skinned man and his wife, who was dressed in a sarong, stepped out of the field to greet us. The woman reminded me of E-Mae but with long dark hair, and the man had a similar stature to E-Paw, with uncombed hair and skin darkened from too much sun. They welcomed us with warm smiles, especially at the sight of Jour Peng.

"Where did you come from?" the father asked in a familiar language to ours.

As we moved closer to the man, his wife gave us a huge smile and tucked her sarong with both hands against her thigh, keeping it from sweeping the ground. She was wearing brown sandals, and her dark matted hair was tucked in a bun just above her shoulders.

Her three children stood next to her, and they appeared excited to receive us as their guest. From their stature, they appeared to be older than Nok and I.

"We're passing through," E-Paw said to the man.

The man stopped interrogating E-Paw and shifted his attention to welcoming us to his home. He quickly waved to his family to step out of the rice field a few paces from the hut.

"*Sa bai dee* (hello), *Jour*, greetings and come in, it's almost noon." He put his hands together and gave Jour Peng a *wai* (prayer).

"You must be hungry." The wife stared at Nok and I.

"Come on in." They both continued almost bowing to Jour Peng with their friendly welcome, as they escorted him into their hut so that they could pay him respect.

The man's children also sprang to their feet without any hesitation each time a request was made. They worked together almost in sync with one another. They were excited, as if we were the only people who had crossed the mountain and set foot on their fields.

The older sister scooped the little catfish from a small pool of water next to the hut with a handheld net and flopped them into a dark bowl. Then she quickly grabbed the slimy fish and pinched their necks and cracked their heads with the round edge of her machete. After cleaning and gutting the fish in quick strokes, she threw each one into a brown wooden bowl. Meantime, the elder son, a boy with sinewy muscles, was working the fire, keeping the orange flame glowing and steaming the sticky rice using the aluminum pot and bamboo steamer.

"Hurry, bring water—it's getting close to noon, and soon it'll pass the time when the *Jour* will not be able to eat his daily meal before noon," the father urged his family, while pointing his fingers to the younger son to bring us water.

The little boy didn't say a word as he quickly lugged over more water in his white bucket and added it to a large clay pot before us.

Narng picked up the coconut bowl and washed our feet with the refreshing bucket of water.

"My feet hurt," Nok said, staring at her bare feet and regretting the loss of her sandal in the muddy pond. The night before Narng had wrapped her naked foot with a piece of cloth from her sarong.

"You'll be okay, and you can ride Buc Ang with Buc Boun." Narng rewrapped the cloth around Nok's foot, then tightened it with a knot.

Soon after E-Paw tied Buc Ang to one of the stilts of the hut he came over and joined us in washing the dirt from our hands and faces. E-Paw looked at me with his reddened eyes and warm smile and gave my hair another muss with his gentle hand—he often did that when I was a good son, and he was proud of me for not being afraid.

After our warm lunch, I was ready to crash and go to sleep on the reed mat beneath my collapsed legs. But E-Paw and Jour Peng extended our respect for the strangers that hosted us in their humble hut. Jour Peng proceeded to bless the hut and the family. In my exhaustion, I sat there listening to his chanting and staring at the candlelight dancing on the candlestick in his hand. The family gathered before him; the father, mother, and E-Paw were up in the front with the children behind them. Meantime, us kids were in the back, waiting for a cue from E-Paw. The whirling and humming coming from Jour Peng made me wish for my pillow and blanket. I remembered that we'd left them on the hard plank wood of our hut with Grandpa La. But with all the energy I had left in my legs, I fought to stay awake.

Jour Peng finished his blessing by a pouring a cup of water into another cup during his prayers and extinguishing the burning candle in his hand. The family bowed three times on the mat with their hands by their heads then pressed to the ground.

"*Saa Tu!* (Amen!)," said the father, as he took the cup of water and the candle from Jour Peng and smiled with delight and honor.

We followed E-Paw and made our way down the steps, and then he quickly loosened Buc Ang's noose from the wooden stilt. Buc Ang stared at us and gave out neither a huff nor hiss, appearing to be relieved from the heat of the sun. Narng hurried with E-Paw and grabbed her belongings, and Nok took her rice basket that was now filled with a new batch of rice. Then Nok and I climbed up Buc Ang's back with the help of Narng.

We sat there looking at the humble family. The man's wife and children stood behind him as he expressed his warm goodbye.

"Thank you so much." E-Paw leveled his eyes with the man and gave the couple a gentle bow with his head tilted slightly forward.

"No problem, no problem." The man tapped E-Paw's shoulders repeatedly.

"*Soak dee* (good luck)," the woman said, reminding me of E-Mae and keeping her eyes on Nok and I, as if we were her own.

5

REUNITED

We moved onward with E-Paw leading us along a small dirt road, then we detoured into another verdant field of thick grass on the edge of tangling vines and field weeds. Buc Ang trudged along with Nok and I on his back. I wrapped my hands tightly on Nok's waist, as we stared into the blue sky with the sun's heat on our backs. Narng and Jour Peng were walking along next to us on opposite sides of Buc Ang.

Ahead of us stretched out more farmland, and E-Paw said that it was the yuca potato farm. This farm was guarded by two ferocious dogs that E-Paw accidentally ran into on his previous trips to the mountain.

"Stay calm and don't say anything," E-Paw cautioned, preparing us for an encounter with those canines. "They won't bite you if you don't run or panic."

I stared into the potato field anxiously waiting for those snarly faces and piercing fangs to lunge out at us as we walked past the farm. But the ferocious dogs E-Paw spoke of were nowhere in sight and I was relieved. Ahead of us, E-Paw moved hastily, making a new path on the tall grass with his boots, leading us from the open fields toward tall trees running along a ravine. We had crossed the mountain into Thai territory, and each time we came to a clearing, E-Paw reminded us to keep our eyes out for movements in the distance.

"Thai soldiers may be patrolling the border," he told us.

Continuing with our journey that day, I stared into the interlocking bough of trees and saw with my naked eyes the peace and harmony coming to life. As I watched for the birds, sometimes rats or lizards scurried for their life across the dirt road. Above our heads, wild fruits and berries hung with gleaming colors of red, purple, and yellow. On the ground, we were surrounded by the wild berry shrubs; some were bright red, and others were white like shiny little pearls. They were call "*Puk Mek*," E-Paw told us. And as we came into a field of the *Puk Mek*, E-Paw broke a few branches and handed one to each of us. From that moment on, I discovered a newfound appreciation for the taste of the shiny reddish green leaf of the plant. Once I put the pea-sized soft sweet white fruit and shiny reddish white shoots in my mouth, the hint of slightly sour herbaceously tart scent filled my nose. Eating *Puk Mek* leaves will always bring me back to that very moment, to my first time being surrounded by those brilliant aromatic bushes.

E-Paw also told us that the Thai villagers here named their village after this plant. They called it *Banh Nong Mek*, translated as a *Village Pond of Puk Mek*. And after passing through fields surrounded by what seemed to be gullies of water formed by ravines along our path, I could see why the villagers decided to name their village Nong Mek, or Chong Mek, as the Thais officially called it.

At dusk that day, when I no longer felt the stinging of the sun on my back, we stopped by another pool of water for a quick refreshment. This time E-Paw brought us to what seemed to be a dead end, as we stared at a body of dark water. The water appeared to be deeper than the swamp water that we had trudged through the night before. The murky water was full of water weed and lotus flowers suffocating each other.

From above Buc Ang's back I saw another huddle below, as E-Paw's words came out like a whisper. "I'm going to take Buc Ang around and soon Vung will come with a canoe to take you to the other side. But be alert—if you see anything strange, get out of the way and hide." E-Paw stared at us and quickly disappeared into the thickets with Buc Ang trailing behind him.

We waited for any signs of Vung as the sunlight gradually cast its bright orange haze over the skyline behind us. I yearned for E-Paw's return, but instead, I saw two men rolling their wooden canoe toward us. From about 100 feet out from the shore, we could see that one of the men worked the dark wooden paddle at the stern, while the other man worked his paddle at the bow of the canoe. Their faces were tan and darkened by the sinking sun. I moved closer to Narng, Nok, and Jour Peng. Together we stared at the long dark wooden canoe gliding through the water weeds and faces that appeared to be smiling back at us.

As the canoe crashed into the sandy shore, the thin man jumped off the stern and hurried over to us. He was followed by an older and taller man with a darker tan complexion.

"It's Vung!" Narng said happily.

We were all surprised at the sight of Vung, who was now standing there with almost the same features as E-Paw. He was smiling and no longer wearing the orange robe, with his fine dark hair parted in the middle to the sides.

"E-Paw told me and Uncle Lun to come and get you," Vung said with a smile on his face.

"Get in the middle and settle in," Uncle Lun said with a gentle smile on his tan face.

Vung quickly grabbed Narng's belongings then jumped back into the wobbly boat.

"Buc Boun and E-Nok, be sure to hang on, and don't move," Vung said, while trying to steady the canoe.

After Jour Peng followed the Thai man to the farther end of the boat, Nok and I took our seat in the middle. Narng grabbed my shirt tightly from behind as Vung began to push the flimsy vessel into the water. Finally, he jumped in the boat behind Narng with wet feet. Then he took the wooden paddle still in his hand and pushed us out farther into the water. The men propelled us as they paddled from opposite sides of the vessel effortlessly. The canoe slid slowly over the murky water, and my grip grew tighter on the wooden seat. Then my head began to feel light and my stomach became queasy, as I watched the world around me go by in slow motion. But soon the little inlets opened to a sea of water that stretched wide toward the looming mountain beyond the inlet in front of us.

"This is the Sirindhorn Reservoir. Once it was a valley full of trees and birds; now the dam fills this reservoir with water and fish," said the dark tan Thai man, alternating his paddle from side to side.

As I looked at what seemed to be the end of the world, fields of dead treetops protruded from the dark water. In a rush of fear, I held my gaze from looking directly into unimaginable darkness below me, as more tree limbs were now jutting out around us. I looked to the horizon, and to my left I could see the silver skyline touching the water in the far distance—it was the first time that I'd ever gazed upon a body of water and could not see the land beyond it. But my own curiosity kept me fixated on more ghostly trees with dark limbs piercing through the murky water before me. At the bow of the canoe, Vung kept us from crashing into the lifeless limbs.

Vung and the Thai man hurried the canoes along the water with their paddles, racing against the sunset. They maneuvered us toward our right to the inlet, where huts and canoes were strung along the road at the end of the water. On my left the sun's last beams of the day hit the pointy tips of a golden shrine and tomb-stones scattered in the distance not too far from the water's edge.

I stared at the shore, examining the grass and water weeds before us and the huts scattered along the water's edge. The huts were supported by wooden stilts and planks. Some of the huts were covered with tin tops, while others looked like giant mushrooms tipis fashioned out of dried grass and bamboo thatches. Behind some of the huts roamed cattle, chickens, and other livestock in the fenced-in yard. Along the fence stood coconut, papaya, and banana trees. Nearby, more wooden posts were buried in the ground with chicken wire for a vegetable garden.

The dark wooden canoe slid into the small wooden dock. Vung picked up a pile of rope by his feet, jumped off the bow, and secured the boat to the post. Narng got up after him, and one by one we jumped out of the canoe. Once on the pier I glanced up, and I saw a man and a woman with a small child hanging onto her hand waiting for us. Nok and I recognized them immediately—it was E-Paw, E-Mae, and Thurng. Without any hesitation, Nok and I raced toward them. We threw ourselves on E-Mae and held her by her hands and thigh. E-Mae gave us the biggest smile I had ever seen and took us in her arms.

"Are you okay?" she asked, staring at us.

"*Err . . . Err.*" Nok and I broke free from the fears that kept us in silence.

Thurng was excited to see us, too. He stared curiously at us with his dark marble eyes and then he smiled with a child's glee. Startled by all the commotion, he jumped up and down excitedly. Standing on his own, he no longer needed anyone to help him walk, and I thought back to seeing him at Grandpa La's hut on his tippy toes. As a matter fact, his legs looked like jumping beans and they appeared as if they were ready to run. Then E-Paw reached over to me, mussing up my hair and pulling at my ears.

"*Buc shour*," he said with a smile.

"Come on, I have the food ready for you," E-Mae interrupted our reunion.

Marching behind E-Mae, we crossed a dirt road and entered the dome-hut fashioned almost like ours in Banh Dong with tin roofing, wooden planks, and a stairway running up the middle. Standing by the entrance a medium build Thai man and his wife cheerfully greeted us with their warm smiles.

"*Sa bai dee* (hello, hello) Come . . . come . . . come on in," Paw Yai Tut and Mae Yai Tut repeated with their hands together to give a *Wai* prayer to Jour Peng while slightly bowing their heads.

Standing behind Narng, we gave our most friendly and respectable smiles and gestured to the men and women staring at us with warm smiles on their faces.

"Come on in little one," they said almost in a chorus, with Paw Yai Tut's hand on my shoulder.

"First wash your hands with the water before you go up." E-Mae pointed to a large clay jar by the first rung of the wooden stairs.

"This is *Paw Yai* Tut and his wife, *Mae Yai* Tut, and this is their hut." E-Paw introduced us to the friendly Thai couple.

Narng gave them her most venerated smile, while Nok and I followed everyone back into the house.

Then Paw Yai Tut asked Jour Peng, "*Jour*, where are you going to rest for the night? If you would like I can walk you over to the village temple so you can be with the other monks."

"*Err.*" Jour Peng smiled at the humble Thai man. "I'll sleep at the monk's quarter at the temple tonight." He turned to E-Paw still with the warm smile on his face as if he was looking for reassurance.

"*Err . . .* we'll visit you soon," E-Paw said, nodding his head with a gentle bow toward Jour Peng and watching him trail off with Paw Yai Tut.

"Let's eat!" E-Mae quickly got our attention.

We followed E-Mae and settled ourselves before the trays of food and the bamboo rice baskets laid out on the reed mat. We took our seats but waited for the elders to eat first, then we followed suit and dove in. I stuffed my face until a lingering dizziness filled my head and soon the levity took over my body.

After I washed up, I lay down listening to the clanging of aluminum and clay dishes, the chattering from the dinner gathering slowly fading in and out. Now in my tummy I felt a satisfied rumbling of another basket full of sticky rice and one of E-Mae's fish porridges with shredded bamboo, *Goy Pa* (fish salad), small mudfish and catfish grilled on bamboo sticks, spicy and sour papaya salad, vegetables spread on dishes from bitter to tart to sour, and even the *Puk Mek.* For the first time since we left the village of Banh Dong, I was safe. Safe from the vicious people that E-Paw was running from, safe from the rocks, bushes, and prickly vines, and safe from the ghostly images that haunted me within the jungles.

That night after our meal, there wasn't anything more delightful to me than seeing our family reunited under one roof. It seemed as if E-Paw and E-Mae had been running in and out of our lives for so long that I had never thought there would ever be a time when the two of them would be here together before us. But then there was a restlessness that raced through E-Paw's mind while he laid on his end of the mat with the hook of his elbow over his eyes—it was how E-Paw was often found sleeping. Snoring and talking in his sleep, E-Paw would often speak of his troubles. In his sleep, E-Paw moaned about the pain in his injured back and echoed his words during our travel through the mountain again—"*Pai, Pai!*"—urging us to move faster through trees, shrubs, and strangling vines. I listened, but with a child's understanding, grasping only his words, not fully comprehending the fears in his mind. Then I drifted away to the sounds of waves crashing onto the shore, listening to E-Mae catching up with Narng.

"I told *E-Paw Yai* and *E-Mae Yai* that we were leaving. They were the only ones who knew. They wanted me to give you this medicinal pouch and E-Mae Yai's cinnamon stick cutter," Narng said to E-Mae, while unwinding the rolled-up top of her sarong and then furnishing a cotton pouch and the dark tarnished cutter Grandma Dao used when she chewed *Maark* (tobacco concoction).

"What about Mae Paa and your cousins, Yai, Vee, Som, Bee, and Buc Dur?" E-Mae asked. Her head was slightly sunken with her dark wavy hair resting on her shoulders. She looked at us with proud brown eyes, happy to be with us, then she became silent as she turned away lost in her own thoughts.

Before I sank into the darkness, E-Mae's soft smile turned to a worrisome blank look. Then I felt the cool wind blowing through the hut, this time with a different air. It was not the smell of stale water gathered in the billabong or the fragrance of water weeds held by the dikes of the rice fields, but the smell of water weeds and primrose picked up by the misty breeze coming from the water. Staring in the dark, it could no longer hold my curiosity or my heavy eyelids. I began to drift in my own dreams; lingering there in the darkness I saw uncle Wan's face and our family back home waving goodbye as we continued our journey away from home.

6

BANH NONG MEK

The next day, I woke up at Paw Yai Tut's hut by the water, and I learned that Jour Peng also found a home at the ornate temple with a shimmering gold roof on the other side of the inlet. Now staring at us were new faces expressing warm gentle smiles. Customary to our family tradition, they were still using the same naming convention when referring to strangers or non-blood-lines such as ours when it came to adopting someone as a brother, grandpa, and uncle. The way we called each other with respective titles was soon explained to us by E-Mae, who told us that the visitors were Thai Isan, her people.

E-Paw's friend Ku Mai and his wife were also there. They'd passed by to see us. Ku Mai and E-Paw had been friends since they were teenagers. During peaceful times he and his wife also came to visit us in the village of Banh Dong.

"Ah, you made it, little children!" Ku Mai said excitedly through his shiny glasses and fine dark hair parted neatly from the left to the right side of his head. He had on a long-sleeved plaid shirt and dark pants as we recalled in his visit to Banh Dong.

"Good that you made it! You must be tired," his wife added, smiling cheerfully. "Your parents have been staying with us for a long time; now they want to be closer to the water. Brother La, did you catch any more fish for me to take to the Ubon Market?" she inquired with the ambitious look of a businesswoman who had a bamboo basket of money and goods in the hook of her arm.

E-Paw smiled and shook his head and said, "I'll be sure to catch some more for you." And he welcomed the couple in for a drink before they headed back to their hut across the main road from the temple.

That day we gave our warm smiles but kept our respect for them at a distance. And we watched how happy E-Mae was to be surrounded by her friends.

"What are you doing, Mae Mai?" E-Mae asked Ku Mai's wife with enough cheer to make her smile. E-Mae also loved a good crowd like E-Paw; they were always putting in the effort to acquaint themselves with strangers, then welcoming them to their home and calling them brother, uncle, and *Paw Yai* and *Mae Yai*.

Whenever E-Mae spoke of her youth in Thailand, great jubilation filled her eyes and she expressed such pride in her country. "I was born in the village of Honghee, an hour ride southwest from Banh Nong Mek. My home was so close to the temple that it was the first hut monks would come to during their daily ritual of morning offerings throughout the village. We lived there until I was twenty before we moved to Laos," E-Mae recounted. "People would stop and gather at the hut to watch Grandpa La shaping gold and silver, handcrafting them into ornate patterns for necklaces, earrings, and even the silver belts." She was proud to be Thai Isan.

In those days, this simple notion of acceptance by her former country didn't do much for us. We'd soon discover the truth. In the lush verdant fields of E-Mae's familiar land that she used to call her birthplace, we learned that we were clearly illegal aliens.

After staying with Paw Yai Tut by the Sirindhorn Reservoir for a week, we went to live with Paw Yai Lerm, who lived less than a mile on the other side of the woods. He and his wife and their six children lived on the main road—the same road that ran straight to the village of Banh Dong just over the Chong Mek border.

One day E-Paw took us to the local store in Banh Pong, and we soon learned that most of the people in the village were like us, and they even spoke a language we could understand with some slight differences (they had a Thai accent). The men acknowledged the on-goers with "*Kup*," and the women, "*Ka*," politely expressing their "Yes, Sir" and "Yes, Ma'am", or a respectful "Okay." They lived along the main road in raised huts supported by rough lumber and tin roofs. Most of them were simple and kind peasants, and their children had dark hair and marble eyes and offered us kind gestures. They also practiced the same Theravada religion at the village temple where Jour Peng now resided. Along the main road they were often found baking in the hot sun with dark tan faces, tilling soil, getting mud on their hands, and rotating the soil using water buffalos. They were also hunters and gatherers, sometimes bartering goods with one another found right there in the most pristine setting.

We quickly connected with Paw Yai Lerm and his family. He was older than E-Paw and he chewed spit tobacco that we called *Maark*. It was a mixture of red pasty *pboon* limestone, a green betel leaf they called *bai puu*, and thin sliced areca nuts. This mixture didn't just give him a wonderful tobacco spitting sensation, but it also stained his mouth red and teeth dark. That was how we met him and his wife, Mae Yai Lerm, both chewing and spitting this red pasty concoction that was common with some Isan and even in the village of Banh Dong.

E-Paw had been helping Paw Yai Lerm with his farm, and then the two men became fond of one another. Paw Yai Lerm wanted us to live with them and quickly gave E-Paw permission to put up a hut on his land. Paw Yai Lerm and some of E-Paw's Laos friends with familiar and unfamiliar faces came to help. We watched the men drag out the thick, rough lumber from the wood behind the hut, then dig deep holes for the hut's stilt foundation. They used bamboo posts to make the rafter of the hut and strung bamboo strands to the long wooden posts, making a roofline.

E-Mae made grilled fish and bamboo soup, and she asked us kids to pick the sour tamarind leaves from the yard for the base of her fish soup that had a spicy broth full of lime and ground pepper, and even her own anchovy sauce. Narng and Nok helped with steaming the sticky rice, while Thurng and I ran excitedly with Paw Yai Lerm's children around the yard and even pushed each other back and forth on their wooden swing set.

After the men helped E-Paw build the skeleton of the hut, they feasted, drank E-Paw's homemade rice wine, and cheerfully grabbed their belongings and made their way home.

"Thank you!" E-Paw and E-Mae gave their deep appreciation to the men as they made their way out to the main road.

Some went left and others went right with their voices echoing, "Not at all, not at all, *soak dee* (good luck)!"

A couple days later, E-Paw and Vung finished putting up the shell to our new hut with the lumber they gathered from the nearby woods. If it wasn't on Paw Yai Lerm's property, E-Paw hesitated at the thought of cutting down the trees for lumber, since it was illegal. They dug more holes in the ground where they felt were needed to bury more large posts for a small awning that would shade us from the sun. They also attached the additional planks and laid the floors with split bamboo they gathered from the edge of Paw Yai Lerm's farm. When they had assembled the semi-skeleton shape of the shanty, they threw flats of dried grass over it with what had been woven with bamboo strips that they had fastened on the roof of the hut.

Us kids helped with good intent but were told to keep away. Paw Yai Lerm had six children, two boys and four girls. They were no older than us, and we called them by their nicknames in the order of eldest to youngest: E-Dow, E-Noy, Buc Latt, E-Nit, E-Noy, and Buc Joy (still a baby). They had dark straight hair cut short like ours, the boys short military style and the two older kids had hair cut into a bowl shape just above their shoulders. We took to each other like most playful children. There was a wooden swing set that we would play on, and after we were done with the swing and climbing and hanging on the little ladder, we'd yell, "Let's play under the mulberry trees!" There were several mulberry trees throughout their yard. Paw Yai Lerm's wife was a silk maker. She was growing her own silkworms and feeding them with the mulberry leaves. Naturally, she was known to us as Mae Yai (Grandmother).

We kids didn't care much for the mulberries—we stepped on them and had "Yuck!" written on our faces. When we were done chasing the snots out of each other under the shade, we would chase lizards. Sometimes we were truly bored, then we would say, "Let's flip rocks and catch tarantulas." The adults always had one eye on us; they knew we were up to no good when we were quiet, and they would call out from the hut, "*Buc Laa, E-Laa* (little darlings), don't play with those insects that are poisonous. They'll bite you to death!" If we heeded their warning and went on to another game, they would retreat back into the hut like a turtle into its shell.

No more than a month after we'd settled in our new hut on Paw Yai Lerm's land, more men came to visit E-Paw. Some of the faces were familiar, others became more familiar with frequent visits. I later learned that they were E-Paw's comrades who I'd eventually associated with those random crackles of explosions and gunfire. Then there were E-Paw's Thai friends, whom he'd met during a peaceful time traveling to this part of Thailand to study medicine. E-Paw had other visitors who came for a drink, a laugh, or to share news of what was happening back in Laos, and then they left like the occasional wind. When the men visited, Nok and I knew to go outside to play while E-Mae and Narng prepared food and E-Paw passed out his drinks. Some conversations were loud, and others a near hush because they were for "adults only."

There was one conversation that left E-Paw sitting in his dimly lit corner, lost and sunken in the whirling puffs of his tobacco. He was visited by Brother Liam, the small, dark, round-faced man who was known for slipping back to Banh Dong to retrieve his belongings. Brother Liam was also known to have assisted comrades and escapees crossing the border through the Hin Soung Mountain trails. On his way back to Banh Nong Mek, he ran into Uncle Wan and Grandpa Oosu at the *nah*. He delivered the news to them of our safety. Then he told E-Paw what had happened to Uncle Wan the day after we'd escaped from the village.

He said, "The Lao Dang came to his hut the day after you left. They threatened to take his life, pointed a pistol at his temple. They pressed him to tell them which direction you'd traveled. He said he didn't know. Then, they yelled at him some more, and they fired a single shot over his head. They forced him to tell them by threatening to hurt his family, so he pointed in the opposite direction."

One day I finally got to meet our respected Monk, Kubar Somdee, who we also called *Arjan (*teacher*)*. E-Paw and his visitors had mentioned his name through the course of their conversations, but I'd never actually seen him in the flesh. It was on that day that I observed Kubar Somdee to be more than a holy monk. He had a gentle smile on his round face as he walked gracefully toward us. He was wrapped in a traditional saffron robe, carrying a brown cotton satchel hanging down to his side. He appeared unaffected by the heat of the sun and his celibate cloth remained almost wrinkle free in the humid air, as he called out "Brother La!" from where he was standing there on the dirt trail leading to our hut.

In our little grass hut his humming voice asked, "Brother La, what are you doing? And how are you little children?" Kubar Somdee's voice and warm smile came with a glow that grabbed our attention, especially with his magic and treats he'd pulled out from his brown satchel.

Since that day we first met him, we jumped in joy, grabbed, and felt a liveliness with one another whenever we saw his holy face. For us kids, it was more than the holiness that followed Kubar Somdee— on most occasions it meant sweets of candy and honey. But for E-Paw and the other good-humored men Kubar Somdee came with the magical relic they called *Ga-Taar* (the animist and spiritual protection acquired by deep spiritual belief and self-discipline).

After E-Paw rolled out a reed mat for Kubar Somdee with great respect and comradery, he set two pillows for him in the middle of the hut. On the kitchen end of the hut, E-Mae quickly worked on a meal that she offered Kubar Somdee before noon.

Kubar Somdee settled on his seat with a warm smile, and he said, "You kids come here, I have something for you."

Without any hesitation, Nok and I followed Narng as we sank to our knees with respect for Kubar Somdee. We watched him pulling out what appeared to be two-inch squared sheets of tarnished copperplates in his palm.

"Thurng, don't get too close to *Arjan*," E-Mae grabbed Thurng as he was tugging at Kubar Somdee's robe, since he learned that there were sweets in Kubar Somdee's bag.

"It's okay, don't worry, sister Saan." He found humor in the persistent child butting against his shoulder. Then he continued to write with his sharp pen-like metal instrument. "This is going to make you brave, and it'll keep evil spirits away from you," he added as he inscribed the ancient Pali language into the malleable sheets of copper and rolled them around cotton strands long enough to be fastened around each of our necks.

"Hmm . . . here's one for each of you." He cleared his throat and then placed the blessed *Maak Lord* in the palm of our hands.

"*Doi, doi* . . ." We bowed our heads repeating *your holiness* as we received the sacred relic with a great sense of reverence.

Then Uncle Lun and his son, Brother Dang, appeared through the doorway from the top rung of the wooden ladder. The tan dark Thai man and his tall son quickly put their hands together, gave Kubar Somdee a *Wai* and asked, "*Sa bai dee*, and where have you been?"

After receiving our *Maak Lord*, the small rolled-up sacred copper scroll, that day, we joyfully followed Narng outside the hut where we saw that more men and women had come to visit us and to see Kubar Somdee for a blessing. Some were there in search of spiritual enlightenment, a magic relic that he might have bestowed upon them. In what appeared to be happy pleasantries, they sat on the wooden bench, naturally made from a fallen *Du* (redwood) tree, roughly carved with a machete into a workable bench that was left next to the firepit, where laughter echoed over Paw Yai Lerm's rice field and into the woods behind the hut.

Narng said that some of our visitors who followed Kubar Somdee were comrades, the Lao Kao Rebels, and Laotians hiding between the border, and were secretly living amongst the Thai peasants just like us.

Some said that it was kindness and compassion that drove E-Paw and Kubar Somdee to hold deeper bonds for one another. I soon learned that their brotherhood was bonded by the lively spirit and magical relic, and dreams of becoming doctors and healers. Through the thin walls I could hear the men joke that E-Paw and Kubar Somdee were like two brothers.

"Brother La, how can you and Kubar Somdee be so much like brothers?" a man said from inside the hut.

"Well, it's like you're coming from the far left and Kubar Somdee the far right," laughed another man.

There were some truths about these observation of Kubar Somdee and E-Paw, as I would eventually learn that the two men were somewhat overprotective of one another. As if losing each other would be like one hand without the other. Since they ran with the Patigan, their enemies might have been abroad, so E-Paw and Kubar Somdee had to look out for each other in a fragile time.

A few days later, Kubar Somdee waved goodbye as he headed back to a temple he called Mukdahan, in a town three and a half hours ride north on the Thai side of the Mekong River. In his farewell, he blessed us before leaving with his hand on our shoulders, and he told us, "You children be good and listen to your parents."

E-Mae said that Kubar Somdee lived near an ancient fallen monument called *Thaat Phanom.*

"*Doi, Ka Noy*" I bowed with my hand in a *wai* (prayer), in sync with my sisters and brothers.

I wished that Kubar Somdee could've stayed another week.

"He's on the go, visiting friends in the refugee camp and moving with the Patigan, and some nights he doesn't sleep in people's huts, he rests in the *Sim*, where monks sleep at the temple. Monks aren't supposed to be away from the temple for a long time—it's against their discipline," E-Paw told us.

Our days were spent foraging and fishing. Nok and I excitedly trailed E-Mae into the woods to pick leafy greens from trees, bushes, and vines, high and low, mainly by the edge of our hut. It reminded me of how I used to stumble along the wood with Grandma Dao, picking mushrooms and gathering wild berries and jungle vegetables near Banh Jik. This part of Isan had edible plants, such as the bunches of flat stringy green *katin* dangling over our heads, which grew to the average size of my six-inch foot. If the string was soft and crunchy enough for me to chew, we'd eat the entire string whole. If the string grew to longer lengths, and the covering of its pods matured and proved to be a challenge for us to chew through, we'd unpeel it just like a lengthy pea pod. The *katin* was one of my favorite Isan plants to savor with our hot spicy papaya salad, grilled fish, and sticky rice.

There in Paw Yai Lerm's *nah* an entire spread of edible greens grew along the rice field. These plants complimented our chicken or fish Larb, or bamboo and mushroom soup, and E-Mae's fish porridges and her curry noodles. Their distinct taste ranged from mild bitter to nutty and crunchy to sour to gingery or to a very plain taste that was good for dipping hot sauce but made a perfect complement to our hot and sour tamarind leaf soup. Sometimes the textures of these plants could be a little hairy like the edamame bean or a wild vegetable we loved to pick in the rice paddy of Paw Yai Lerm, the *Puk Ga-Doon*, that was a little tart yet nutty enough for any larb or soup loaded with galangal, lemongrass, and kaffir lime leaves.

During the day E-Mae would make her finest dessert, the gelatin-like treat made from sugar, flour, and food coloring that sometimes came from the green leafy long narrow bunch of spiky fan leaves of the pandan plant that she had been growing in the garden. My favorite was her green jelly, which she would extract from the green stems of the leaves and had a savory sweet grassy aroma.

Usually after E-Paw returned home in the morning from checking his fishing net, E-Mae would go out and about in the village and sell some of her specialties for a few Thai *Bahts* and *Satangs,* sometimes her precious *coins* were not enough to even buy a small bag of rice. E-Mae also traded her sweet treats or E-Paw's catches for salt, sugar, fish sauce, or even a few pieces of candy for us. While E-Mae was gone, Narng would babysit Thurng and me. Nok would accompany E-Mae during most her trips to help carry the goods.

I watched E-Mae balancing two baskets on her shoulders with a bamboo stick, and I wished that she had taken me, so I could be part of the festivity on the other side of the village near the temple ground.

"It's too hot. You can help Narng out by watching Thurng and let your dad take a nap. Don't worry I'll take you with me next time," E-Mae said.

"It's not too hot, and I wanted to go with you," I plead fruitlessly.

"When I come back, you can come with me to Ku Mai's land, and we can pick *Dork-Ga-jeal.*" She sweetened me with her promise and quickly disappeared with Nok into the woods behind our hut.

At home, I waited excitedly for E-Mae to take me across the road to gather those stalks of a plant we called Dork-Ga-jeal. The pale green floral shoot of purple and white flowers grew like the ginger plant, and had large thick leaves with soft white stalks. What I remember most of this plant was its soft, crisp and fresh crunchy taste, almost like a cross between a stalk of celery and cucumber, and it accompanied many of our hot and spicy dishes.

That morning, while I waited for E-Mae to come back home with Nok, so she could take me to gather wild vegetables, E-Paw said, "Boun, come with me and we can gather wild mushrooms and jungle fruits."

"*Err . . . Err.*" I nodded those words nasally right away to E-Paw, who immediately broke my boredom with an adventure running in my veins.

"Narng, can you watch your little brother, *Buc* Thurng (the nickname Narng gave him for his set of overly large ears hanging on his skinny body)?" E-Paw said, smiling at Narng with Thurng on her slim hip.

"*Err, Err.*" Narng nodded and she went back to amusing Thurng as if he were her own baby.

With the blue sky above our heads and the sultry heat stinging my neck, I followed E-Paw, kicking up the dust on the main road as we made our way toward the gray pale peaks in the distance. It was the same mountain we had crossed during our escape from Banh Dong.

That day, our hunting expedition took us into the lower valley across the main road from our hut, where thick vines dangled down from the towering trees. Under the cover, the air was cooler and offered me great relief from the baking sun.

When we got thirsty, we drank from E-Paw's canister. When we were low in water, E-Paw did the unthinkable.

"Boun, you step back." E-Paw stared up at the vine that strung itself from the tree above our heads. He took the machete in his hand and with one swoop sliced the hanging vine in half.

"Look!" I said excitedly pointing my finger at the water dripping out of the vine like an elephant's trunk.

"Open your mouth and I'll give you some water," E-Paw said, holding the severed vine over my face.

"E-Paw where did the water come from?" I asked after feeling refreshed with a drink of water from such an unusual source— hanging from what seemed to be the heavens.

"*Buc Shour*, you see, the trees, they drink the water from the ground underneath us." E-Paw pointed to a vine-strangling tree trunk with his machete.

E-Paw made me happy that day, letting me tag along on his hunting trip. Not only that I could brag about such adventure to Narng and Nok, but also because I was excited to do more now to help E-Paw. And from that day on, my little legs became strong enough to break free of the strangling vines grappling my sandals, and I learned how to avoid the thorns of the *Maak Ben* bush, which was thick enough to puncture through a rubber sandal deep into a man's flesh. The excitement kept me waiting for a new surprise, and I was no longer afraid of the thicket that once imbued eerie images in my mind on that dark night we ran away from home. I was now E-Paw's partner, his extra sets of eyes and ears and hands during his food foraging for the family.

7

LEAVING THE NEST

Two months after our little grass shanty had been built, Narng met Mae Tuu and her daughter at the village temple ground. Mae Tuu was a short, tan, perky Thai woman, whose *nah* happened to be on the opposite end of the temple from our hut. Since Narng and Mae Tuu's daughter had several similar features and were both fifteen, their friendship coalesced rather quickly.

E-Paw was happy with Narng's newfound friends, and even better, she could work for the much-needed rice for the entire family. But contrary to his pseudo-happiness, he was plagued with the notion of living on borrowed land as illegal immigrants. The thought left him brooding in the dark corner of our hut, puffing his rolls of tobacco.

"I'm worried for her. She's still young, and men are already staring at her with wanting eyes," E-Paw said as his face lit up with another draw of his smoke.

"There isn't much for them to do here. She's becoming a woman, and if she goes to work for Mae Tuu, at least she can get rice in exchange for work," E-Mae said softly as if she were keeping a secret in her dark corner.

On the day Narng left, I was sunken, but she offered me her soft gentle words: "I'll be back soon. You stay out of trouble and listen to E-Paw, E-Mae, and Nok when I'm gone." Narng gazed down at me and patted my shoulders with her soft hands, then made her way down the rungs of our wooden steps. She was only fifteen and had been a mother to me for what seemed like a lifetime.

"*Err . . . Err.*" I watched her walk away from us along the main road toward Ku Mai's hut and then disappear in the woods before the temple.

Vung also left the family and went to work for Aunt Tai's *nah* in Banh Honghee. It was an hour bus ride into Ubonratchatani to the *nah* where E-Mae was born. It was then I learned that we had relatives in Thailand; they were Thai Isan. The day he left, he led us along the beaten path toward Ku Mai's hut to the pickup area by the temple, where trucks with large cabs awaited their passengers. There was a blank look on his face, he stared straight, then down to the ground, and glanced at us as if he were trying to give the impression of a man but was actually a teenager looking for his confidence.

"Watch yourself and keep your eyes on each other," E-Paw's voice echoed from behind us. It was implied that his words weren't only for Vung, but the rest of us kids. It became his slogan.

We continued kicking more sand between our sandals before Ku Mai's hut at the pickup area, where we noticed more pickup trucks lined the main road. We watched people hurrying along with their belongings, as the drivers were securing their load and passengers climbed up to the back of the cab. Vung quickly jumped up and joined them by taking a seat on one the benches under the oversized plastic canopy cover. Minutes later, we waved *La gon* (goodbye) to each other. Then the truck with Vung and other smiling faces faded away with the widening distance.

Before we came home that day, we walked over the sandy ground of the temple, and we stopped to see Jour Peng. E-Paw led us through the main entrance toward the altar with golden Therevada Buddha statues that sat bigger and taller than the monks, and next to them Jour Peng was sitting in meditation. He noticed our presence and smiled. He waved us to come closer to the altar, and we bent our bodies halfway to the ground, bowing toward the monks. We sat before them, E-Paw offered some money, fruit, and a small bundle of flowers in a small ornate silver bow, and they gave us a prayer in return.

"*Sa bai dee, boor?* (hello, are you well)?" Jour Peng asked with wide smile exposing his nice set of white teeth grinning under his glistening eyes.

"Everything good?" E-Paw asked while slightly tilting his head with a sense of pride for Jour Peng, then lowering himself to a deeper bow, giving great reverence to the head monk and the others in their bright orange robes.

"I'm okay." Jour Peng was still smiling at E-Paw, then he stared at us.

We returned his smile, we looked at him with a sense of reverence, but we kept our silence.

"The *Paw-Ork and Mae-Ork* (women and men) will be serving us food soon."

"*Dee, dee* (good, good)." E-Paw gave a customary revering gesture to Jour Peng with his warmest smile and gratitude. He knew that he didn't want to draw too much attention to us.

In our own circle, we gave each other a smile, and E-Paw led us out through the entrance. We saw Jour Peng every so often, during the morning alms and gathering of festivities at the temple. Sometimes we would go with E-Mae, taking our offering to the temple. E-Mae would carry her bamboo woven basket, and we kids would carry our sticky rice basket dangling from our shoulder and a bowl of fruit in the palms of our little hands. Often our offerings were ripe bananas and fruit we'd picked from the yard.

"Since we are his only relatives in the village, we have to support Jour Peng as much as we can—that way people won't frown upon him as much for taking refuge in the temple," E-Mae said.

Heading back to our hut that day, we saw Buc Ang. He was tied to the wooden post under Ku Mai's hut, and he was munching on the grass beneath his large round belly.

"Look, it's Buc Ang!" Nok said, staring at him like a child who just found her lost pet.

"*Err, err,* Nok, do you think he remembers us?" I asked. I still remembered crying for him. He was my gentle oversized animal who had carried me along the bumpy fields of grass and snapping tangling limbs along our trails on the night that changed us forever.

"*Err.*" Nok nodded. "You see he kept looking at us?"

"Buc Ang lives with Ku Mai and his wife now," E-Paw said, moving us along the dirt trail.

Nok didn't say much after that about Buc Ang. Both she and Narng knew what had transpired and kept the truth inside her little soul. On that day, she looked at him and said her final "goodbye" to Buc Ang and walked away with me following E-Paw, who was carrying Thurng on his back. Buc Ang was almost like a domesticated pet to us kids. But to adults, a thousand-pound animal like him meant tilling rice fields, and worst—some farmers would slaughter an animal like him for meat.

Years later Narng would tell me the truth to what exactly happened to Buc Ang. It was Ku Mai who coerced E-Paw into selling Buc Ang to him. After we crossed the mountain, he came over to visit E-Paw and saw that Buc Ang was a large and healthy animal, and he wanted him. His desire drove E-Paw to sell Buc Ang. Narng recalled the very conversation when E-Paw and Ku Mai were staring down at one another.

"You don't have a place here for this water buffalo," Ku Mai said to E-Paw with his friendly words morphing into something grave.

E-Paw was out of his element; he feared trouble if he didn't comply with Ku Mai's request. He had hope that he would put Buc Ang to work on Paw Yai Lerm's *nah*.

"The authorities will come and take him from you eventually." Now the friend that E-Paw once welcomed to his home as a humble guest came to him with the intent of a foe.

"I don't want to sell him." E-Paw spoke softly in friendship in the hope that such kindness would be returned to him.

"You don't have a choice," Ku Mai said so sternly that the friendship between them died from his face.

"Okay, I can't just give him to you." E-Paw was at the mercy of a friend who he'd known since he was a teenager, and who was on established ground with his desire for Buc Ang.

"I can't give you much for it, but I'll give you something for him," Ku Mai said, as he handed E-Paw far less than the fair price for Buc Ang. Then he grabbed Buc Ang's noose and guided him toward the main road.

That night during our quiet dinner gathering, E-Paw said to us, "Buc Ang is going to a better home, he'll have more grass to graze, and he'll be useful in Ku Mai's field since we no longer have a *nah*. Besides, Buddha taught us that eventually we must let go of everything in life: the good, the bad, and all things we love. Our teeth will eventually fall out, hair grow gray, skin wrinkle, they too, will fall off our body. It's not an easy thing to do, detaching from the tangibles in life, but when we can let them go, we'll find more peace in our heart."

Months went by, then the monsoon rain came, and the green fields swelled up with water in the *nah* fields and the life within it. I was beginning to forget the fact that Vung, Narng, and even Buc Ang were gone during that rainy season. Now it was up to E-Paw to catch fish, frogs, and hunt birds, rats, and whatever meat he could find to keep us going for another day. One day E-Paw and I got lucky; one of our contraptions had snagged a wood rat. The rat was still alive when we got there. The loop was snugged on its hind legs, and it was swinging back and forth like a caught fish on a fishing pole.

"E-Paw, look we got one!" I yelled out with excitement.

E-Paw and I ran to it, and E-Paw took out a large rice bag and scooped the rat from beneath to avoid it escaping. An excitement filled me at the sight of E-Paw's contraption, as I was beginning to hone my skills into a cleverer hunter like E-Paw. I was still baffled at some of E-Paw's knots and the little wood piece made into a lever that held the trigger for the trap as a spring.

"You see the little trail along the bushes? This is a rat's trail. We have to keep it as natural as we can and just tie our string to any of the swinging branches over it." E-Paw showed me how the contraption worked.

"E-Paw we got one for E-Mae!" I said excitedly.

Even though the hopeless dangling field rat was no bigger than a chipmunk, there was a hunger in my little belly. It was a hunger that would drive me to kill, a hunger that ran through my body like water running in the stream and salt in my veins. It didn't matter to E-Mae whether it was a field rat or a possum, she would roast it over the fire to burn off its fur and then turn it into a savory dish loaded with herbs and wrapped up in banana leaves and steamed until it was completely cooked.

That evening that was exactly what E-Mae cooked up for dinner. She kept my hunger at bay and suggested that E-Paw and I travel farther into the woods for tomorrow's hunt. Sometimes we'd end up picking wild mangoes, brussels sprouts, *Maak Vaa,* or *Maak yarng* (the yellow fruit with white oozing sap and sweet-sour flesh on the inside). Then we'd chase lizards or quietly lean on the trunks of a tree, waiting for a bird to land in the nearby branches as they heard the high-pitched birdcalls that E-Paw made by sucking the air through the palms of his hands with his lips. His "cheep cheep, twooth twooth" echoed through the winds of those interlocking boughs of trees, and the birds circled high over our heads.

Day after day, I'd look forward to being in the woods with E-Paw hunting, picking wild fruits of the trees, and taking shelter from the heat. Even when we didn't catch anything that day, we'd sit next to one another leaning on a huge tree trunk, waiting for a bird to perch on the tree high above our heads.

During the day we would set the traps and at night E-Paw would take a lonely trip to the Sirindhorn Reservoir with his fishing net.

"E-Paw, can I come with you when you go set your net?" I asked one night.

"No, it's too dangerous—you can't swim."

"*Err,* E-Paw, I can," I contested.

E-Paw gave me a huge smile, mussed my hair, and gently tugged my ears as he headed out with his fishing gear and a kerosene lantern.

Sometimes E-Paw was gone until the dark of night. "That's when some fish float up to the surface of the water," E-Paw told me.

Some nights we could see E-Paw's lantern glowing through the woods. He would set his fishing net and bait his hook at night, and then the next morning he would get up and go out to see if any got caught in his net. Each day, E-Paw would spend so much time in the water that he'd come home with wrinkled feet that often peeled. But he would often make it up with a good bucket of mud fish, silver featherback, and snakehead fish that were more than we could eat and enough for Ku Mai's wife to take to the local market to turn into money.

When Ku Mai's wife couldn't come down to the fishing docks, E-Mae would take the fish to Ku Mai's wife. Along the way, E-Mae would sell the fish, steamed dumplings, and jelly desserts to the locals. Often it wasn't even enough to buy salt, sugar, or fish sauce, which were the base for most of our meals. But E-Paw would make up for it with his fish and side jobs playing the medical doctor.

Since there wasn't a hospital in the village, some of the villagers who knew E-Paw well would come to him when they were sick. E-Paw was still boiling his syringes and injecting people with vitamins and vaccines just like he did back in Banh Dong. He offered his services only to his Lao and Thai friends who saw him as a sign of comfort in a time of need. Without a Thai medical license, he was afraid of getting arrested. Out of the many things we were supposed to keep hushed, E-Paw was worried about this one the most. His concerns were warranted, because just like any little village, word could spread quickly.

E-Mae enjoyed helping people too; with her machete and shovel she would hike toward the woods to find roots and barks. But most of her pungent and bitter remedies, like the roots of the *An-Ar* and barks of the *Taa Gike* and *Toom Gar* trees, were found throughout the *nah*. Like E-Paw, E-Mae also had a healing hand, but her natural remedies came from the teachings of Grandpa La for healing the body's aches and irritations. The holistic teaching of natural remedies had been proudly passed to her from generations.

"Here, this one is for when someone is having difficulty with their pregnancy" or "this helps with a paralyzing illness that has taken over their well-being," she would say after untying the little hand-stitched pouch that Grandpa La had given to her and spreading it out before our curious eyes. E-Mae poured everything on the reed mat we called *sard* and began to examine small pieces of a seashell, deer antler, bark, root from a lime tree, and a stone on which Grandpa La used to grind his concoctions. She then would rinse the stone with the ground-up remedies by dipping it into a cup of water. I stared at Grandpa La's medicinal gift to us, and I cringed at the thought of how gross each of those items could be.

I remembered drinking some of Grandpa La's potions and then fighting the ill feeling of barfing his brew back out. Conjuring the thoughts of E-Mae's pungent brew was just as awful, and the bitter acrid taste of these remedies was not for the faint of heart. After a hard time swallowing her concoction, my stomach wanted to coil up, but it uncoiled, emptying all its contents. We'd all have to brace ourselves for it each time. The red or sometimes yellowish brew was bitter and sometimes would go up my nose.

"It will make you strong and you won't get the worms in your stomach," E-Mae claimed.

Sometimes instead of boiling the potion, she'd chop up the thumb-sized billion-bitter vine and mince it in the clay mortar with the wooden pestle. Then she would roll her remedy into a ball the size of a marble, coat it with salt, and tell us to swallow it. Back then E-Mae made me believe that this one plant with its super-pungent bitter taste and slimy consistency would keep me alive or kill me right then and there. When we got lucky, she would coat it with sugar. I love sugar and often ate it with rice, but even the saltiest or sweetest taste in my mouth couldn't hide the acrid odor or the body's reaction to the bitter with a slimy aftertaste.

One day while vending her goods throughout the village, E-Mae met an old Thai lady by the name of Mae Yai Maa. E-Mae explained that she was the daughter of a medicine man who was medicinal, spiritual, and had even helped the villagers in delivering babies. Mae Yai Maa asked E-Mae if she could heal her from what appeared to be a paralyzing illness that she had been having for years. E-Mae agreed with great zest. At first E-Mae offered the ill woman recommendations. But that wasn't enough for Mae Yai Maa. E-Mae had to return home that day to quickly grab her arsenal of natural remedies in their worn white pouch. She quickly concocted a brew starting out with a hot pot of water that, according to Grandpa La, must be kept separate from other cooking pots. Then she tossed in the bark that she pulled out of the small bag. As the bark was boiling, she asked Mae Yai Maa to sit in a relaxed position, and she began to pray and bless the brew. She repeated this process over and over for Mae Yai Maa, sometimes at our hut, or during her travels toward the center of the village where Mae Yai Maa resided with her husband.

A few months later, E-Mae made a believer out of Mae Yai Maa. Mae Yai Maa, who we had seen crawling around her hut, was now beginning to walk again. She didn't know how to thank E-Mae, except with her deep appreciation.

"Don't worry. Helping each other is a good thing," E-Mae said.

I now saw the benefits of E-Mae's concoctions. What's more, it was her own lively spirit that helped Mae Yai Maa to get up, feel better, and be more active. I realized that this holistic approach of "goodness" and "let's be positive and excited" was a part of the cure.

8

MOVING AGAIN

January 1977

During that dry season, the water had receded, green grass withered, and muddy water faded into dusty brown clay, leaving cracks where pools of water once gathered. Still, there were greens within the tall trees scattered across the open fields, Puk Mek and Pern bushes, and the forest behind our hut, where we gathered wild vegetables, mushrooms, and hunted food. But along with the hot weather came Vung and several large bags of rice as Paw Yai Banh had promised E-Mae. Vung's return marked the end of the rice-harvesting season, as it did with Paw Yai Lerm's nah.

"Vung! Vung!" I jumped up in joy with Nok and Thurng at the sight of our eldest brother.

Vung had a new pair of blue jeans, a red-and-white-striped flannel shirt, and his fine hair was an upside-down dark bowl-top parted in the middle. He smiled at us and hopped off the truck, and the driver helped him unload his belongings. He thanked the driver and tossed the large brown bags of sweet rice in the corner of our grass shanty. The much-needed rice seemed to be enough to feed us for several months.

"Where's Narng?" Vung asked.

"She has been working with Mae Yai Tuu and didn't want to come home," E-Paw said with a half-disappointed look on his face.

"Err . . . " Vung nodded with a reserved smile. "I was in Phibun working with Cousin Vee at the brickyard. I got five *bahts* a day, just barely enough to keep me alive.

"Come in, come in," E-Mae quickly chimed in and ushered Vung eagerly inside the hut.

That evening after we all settled in, Vung recounted his endeavor at dinner. "We worked from dusk to dawn making mortar and bricks, then during the wet season I helped Paw Yai Banh with his rice farm."

While the homemade torch fire burned with a glowing warm smoky yellow fire, it lit up the grass dome. Vung continued to share his stories of concerts, markets, and how he blended in with the locals. We sat almost elbow to elbow with smiles, surrounded by dishes of fish and vegetables and baskets full of sticky rice. E-Paw had been trying to complete our family puzzle but was constantly missing one or two pieces—this time it was Narng.

"Hmm, we have to stay together. The Thai government wants us to leave their land. Soon we won't have a choice," E-Paw said with his brown eyes staring at us and then lowered to the ground.

For a while as we sat in the presence of one another, a silence lingered with the air from his smoke and the smell of burnt sap from our homemade torch. E-Mae sat in her own corner with her usually overly zealous body falling into silence. We kids knew that when she was quiet she was the most worried.

After Vung came home during the dry season, E-Mae decided to visit Narng in Banh Pong. She wanted to know why Narng didn't want to be with us. E-Mae returned three days later to tell us that Narng still wanted to work on Mae Tuu's farm helping with her garden, so she left her girl in the good hands of the kind Thai villager, even though she wanted her to return home . . .

By the end of the drought season, we had been living on Paw Yai Lerm's land nearly half a year. E-Paw was under more pressure, and we were on the verge of moving again. Since we heard the news from Kubar Somdee and Brother Liam, signs of E-Paw's worry came through his restless nights of sleep talking and snoring. Sometimes E-Paw's snores would sound like an elephant gargling water through its trunk. But E-Paw's sleeping habits were no longer a nuisance to me. They were something I expected, something as soothing as the orchestra of insects outside our hut that I would fall asleep to at night. "*Bor Pai, Bor Pai! (No go, No go!)*" E-Paw snorted. "There is no turning back," E-Paw repeated in the middle of a choking breath.

This conversation had surfaced during Kubar Somdee and Brother Liam's recent visit. During their last gathering the men discussed the dangerous possibility of going back home to Banh Dong. Then in a hushed conversation with Kubar Somdee, E-Paw's hopeless expression caught my attention. Sometimes I wished that I didn't understand what they were saying, because I was daunted by the thought of what the Lao Dang would do to E-Paw, Kubar Somdee, and Brother Liam if they ever got ahold of them.

"The old regime is dead, and all those who served the Royal Laos Army who didn't run were taken for mental cleansing, tortured in these seminar camps. It's a way that they were working the foreign influence out of us. Through the lies of the communist party, the men were at first promised a new training in exchange for disarming themselves and taking the trip to these camps. But once they arrived, they were put into hard labor, starved, and some were executed," Brother Liam said with a bitter look on his small dark round face.

"Hmmm . . . don't go back to Laos," Kubar Somdee warned gravely as the warm smile left his moon face.

"Err . . . it's too dangerous now." E-Paw stared at Brother Liam with a warm worried look on his face.

Brother Liam looked up and gave the two men a humble smile. After his visit that day, Brother Liam thanked E-Paw and E-Mae for their hospitality, then bowed to Kubar Somdee with his warm smile. It would be the last time we saw Brother Liam. A month later we learned that Brother Liam died from excessive blood loss after stepping on a bomb. He was sneaking back to the village of Banh Dong to retrieve some belongings. The men who were traveling with him said that they had made it to the Hin Soung's high rock, then "Boom!" he had hit a landmine. One man said he might have made it as they attempted to get him to the Thai hospital with his right leg wrapped tightly. "But he had lost a lot of blood," another man recalled. "What's more, the Thai bus driver didn't let him on the bus. So, he died."

After we learned about Brother Liam's death, E-Paw and E-Mae were having more hushed conversations in their little dark corner of our hut. Their talks about a leap of faith—about going to America—became random conversations during our meals. Nok said E-Paw wasn't going to keep it a secret from us; we had to move again. This time we may have to live with the Farang or "*French*." In my mind at the time, the America the adults spoke of was like a fearful fairytale of some imaginary place.

"There are glittering lights and blonde-haired, blue-eyed people who are bigger and stronger than us," E-Paw told us.

I started to develop a fear of America. At this point in my life, all Caucasians were referred to in our uneducated minds as Farang. I had never seen a Farang or American, and my imagination now grew to a ghostly foreigner with light hair, blue eyes, and white skin, as the depictions from the men had filled my head with images of demons and the *Yuck* or "Monster," who was said to speak a language like a hissing snake. *But if they are so bad, how can we go live with them?* I thought.

Soon signs of E-Paw's worry began surfacing again through his soft conversations with E-Mae.

"We should wait for the war to be over, then maybe we can go back home to our family," E-Mae said.

E-Paw gave E-Mae a sunken look, then said, "The war *is* over."

"What about the Ubon Refugee Camp? What happens there? What does Kubar Somdee say about its conditions?" E-Mae asked hopefully under her own cloud of fear.

"The camp is a poor environment, but the children will get some education. And once we enter the camp, we might not be able to get out. But if we wanted to, we could go to America, Canada, or France when we are eligible and sponsored," E-Paw said, falling back into his silence.

Then one day E-Paw came home, hung his fishing net to dry on the post by the rough wooden stilts of our hut, and gave us the news: "We're moving. We'll be going to live with Uncle Lun on his farm by the water. We'll be closer to the water and the abundance of water would be perfect for a nice garden." E-Paw had been spending his days helping Uncle Lun with his farm and fishing in the Sirindhorn Reservoir to supplement the little income to support the family.

"Uncle Lun and Brother Dang offered to help us put up a grass hut on his land," E-Paw continued.

E-Mae smiled with E-Paw's news. She envisioned the possibilities of the lush green fields and all the fishing in the flooded valley right in front of our new home. But now we were going to be leaving Paw Yai Lerm, his playful children and wife, their little *nah*, the silk farm, and close access to the main road. Although we kids were more excited than E-Paw and E-Mae, a feeling of sadness and loss began to roll into my life once again.

I had a child's sense of sorrow at the realization of something everlasting, such as a goodbye to people who were fond of us. It was then that I'd understood how these separations affected my heart, that each time there was a departure, I would begin to feel the nostalgic loss of a life that once existed in me. First it was for our family back in Banh Dong—I really didn't have a chance to say goodbye to anyone except Grandpa Oosu and Uncle Wan. Next it was Buc Ang, who E-Paw said went to a better home. Then Vung and Narng, whose faces I still looked for outside the window, hoping for their prompt return. But months had gone by, and while Vung paid us two visits, Narng had almost disappeared forever from the family. Everyone's absence made me sad, but the thought of moving away from Paw Yai Lerm and his children made me feel homesick before we had even begun to pack our belongings. Paw Yai Lerm's hospitality saved us from going into the Ubon Refugee Camp, or even worse for E-Paw, returning to Banh Dong.

But E-Paw's news was also exciting and the thought of fishing and swimming in front of our hut fluttered through my mind. More so than Nok and Thurng, who would love to swim in the water in front of our hut, I wanted to go fishing with E-Paw. He had been promising me that when I was big enough he would take me with him on his fishing trips.

With E-Paw's news of moving, thoughts floated through my little mind of fishes tangled in our nets and spearing the *Pa Vuu* fish (the brown fish that floats to the surface of the water at night). After listening to Paw Yai Tut's tales, I too wanted to catch the fish that floats at night like a brown log when E-Paw shone his light in the water. We were all elated with E-Paw's news, and Nok and I couldn't stop talking about how we could swim in the water. What's more, Nok said that she'd help me catch the fish if we had a fishing net.

That night I asked E-Paw with Nok and Thurng, "E-Paw can

you get us a fishing net, so we can help you fish?"

"We'll have to wait and see," E-Paw said. This was E-Paw's common response to telling us we aren't ready yet. Then he took another puff of his tobacco and added, "The water can be dangerous, and people can drown in it if they don't know how to swim." E-Paw was his usual worried self again.

E-Mae was excited about it as well, as it seems her hands weren't quite occupied enough, and she had been wishing for a bigger garden. No longer would E-Mae have to excessively dry herbs and spices for the drought season. Being near the lake she could grow the finest vegetables and herbs throughout the year.

Besides being able to fish and plant our garden, we could still hunt for rabbits, birds, and lizards and climb for the wild fruits in the same woods, which were now only a short walk from behind our hut. The wild mango tree was my favorite; there wasn't anything like the tropical sweet scent of a wild mango, which we used for *Som Tam*, a concoction of shredded wild sour mangoes with the lingering salty and spicy mixture (that became a savory meal when minced together with roasted lizard using a mortar and pestle).

But long before E-Paw's announcement, my mind was flooded with so many stories about the reservoir from Paw Yai Tut. We'd stop to listen, in awe of the amazing tales from his local adventures. Paw Yai Tut said that the reservoir was a great source of life for him. He and his family used the water to cultivate their lands during the dry season and catch all sorts of fish throughout the year. The tale I loved the most was when he and his son were fishing for the giant mudfish they called *Pa Doe* (a fish the size of a man's thigh that looks like a torpedo with a white belly) and the clown featherback fish (the feather-like flat fish reminded me of a black dotted silvery flag fluttering in the wind), some of which I'd seen E-Paw haul back from his fishing trips. Paw Yai Tut's stories of the lake always captivated us as we sat listening eagerly. Some of his tales made my heart excited with the thought of catching a fish myself, and others left my heart stuck in my throat.

Not only did Paw Yai Tut share his riveting adventures with us, but one day he gave us some python jerky. "My son and I snagged it one night," he said as he handed a bundle of snake jerky wrapped in newspaper to E-Paw. I knew that once roasted, the savory meat would go perfectly with E-Mae's warm sticky rice. Then Paw Yai Tut recalled a fishing story with his son.

They were night fishing, using spears and homemade torches for the *Pa Vuu* fish, when they noticed a large python slither by the canoe. Paw Yai Tut quickly grabbed a harpoon that had already been fastened to a rope and threw the spear at the snake, catching the serpent's body and causing it to coil up on the rope he held tautly.

"The python was like a branch from a tree—it was thick, and I thought it might even pull me over and capsize our little canoe. But I held taut on the rope that wrapped around the snake and my harpoon. I told my son to hang onto the torches while he steadied the canoe."

In my mind, I saw Paw Yai Tut struggling with the giant serpent as he was telling his story.

"The snake struggled and immediately constricted itself with the rope and ultimately suffocated itself," he continued. Then he gave out a hard laugh, before telling us about the leeches: "The little bloodsuckers were everywhere in the water."

I knew the black slug-like critters well; they sucked the blood out of me when I used to swim in the ponds of Banh Dong. I hated them. The only time I enjoyed seeing them was by the tip of E-Paw's hot cigar. Their bodies would coil back, slip from my body, and fall to the ground to their death. Sometimes when I was in the water, I searched for their elusive dark and slimy bodies floating in the cloudy water. It was hard to notice them until I got out of the water, and by then it was too late—they had already latched themselves between my thighs, neck, and sometimes under my armpits. Most of the time I was able to pry the slimy creatures off my body with my hands, but sometimes E-Paw would help me out by burning them off with his cigarette, and they always left a bloody mark on my body that reminded me of a bullet wound.

"Are there any alligators in the water?" Nok asked, fearing the tale that E-Mae said was passed down to Grandpa La about the giant alligator that swallowed men whole.

"No, I never saw one." Paw Yai Tut laughed and made his way back to his hut. His stories kept us at the edge of our seat.

E-Mae also had stories of how the lake came to be. Her vivid details of the fables sounded so real—the animals came to life and the distant land appeared to be just like the one we were living in. According to E-Mae, the lake was once filled with a different life, where fish took refuge in the algae-filled burrows and trunks of trees, birds once soared the skies, and other animals lived among them. Then one day the Thai government decided to flood the valley to help the poor farmers with the irrigation of their lands and to create a rich habitat for many species of fish and marine life. And they named the reservoir Sirindhorn or *Kuern Sirinthon* as the Nong Mek Villagers called it, in honor of their princess Sirindhorn, one of the three daughters of King Phumiphon, the venerated king. So, the life before us, E-Mae said, was because of what the king did to help his people.

A few days after E-Paw's announcement, word got out that we were moving, and E-Paw's friends began to stop by for their last visit at our hut. Paw Yai Tut was there with Mae Yai Maa and her husband.

"We came to say farewell and good luck to you, Brother La."

Mae Yai Maa smiled; she was no longer limping in with her cane. She believed in E-Mae's prayer and was still grateful for the healing power of the brew that E-Mae had concocted for her.

"Why don't you stay here with us? Who is going to cure me if I'm paralyzed again?" Mae Yai Maa cried to E-Mae.

"Don't worry, we'll just be on the other side of the forest," E-Mae told her.

"*Err*," Mae Yai Maa said, still with the grimace on her face.

"Remember what I told you: Make the *Kunh Ha* (a blessing-platter offering to Mother Nature) and find the roots of the *An-Ar* and *Taa-Gike* trees—they're all over our yard," E-Mae said, smiling at the old humble couple.

"*Err*, I wish that you would stay. No matter what happens, *soak dee* (good luck) and good health to you and your family. And thank you," Mae Yai Maa said with a soft genuine smile on her face as she walked back to her home along the road behind Paw Yai Lerm's hut.

As soon as our visitors left that morning, we ate a simple breakfast of leftovers: rice, pepper paste, and sunfish E-Mae roasted over the fire. We didn't wait for the food to settle in our stomachs.

"You don't want to be lazy, and your legs will begin to idle before a good day of work. Let's gather our belongings," E-Paw said with a warm smile still on his face. But in his eyes I saw a man on edge from his worries. "Make sure that we don't forget anything." E-Paw urged us to move on hastily.

"*Err, Err.*" Nok and I went happily to the sound of our own laughter.

Before our legs began to idle, we packed the last of our prized possessions: the soft pillow made of *Maak Kanuun's* cotton, some warm blankets, and two reed mats, one for our guests and one we slept on.

Shortly after, we made our way through Paw Yai Lerm's dried-up rice paddies with the morning sun already beating down on our backs. Along the dried-up dike of his *nah*, we kicked the dusty brown dirt over the withered grass. We trailed behind E-Paw in a single file, with Nok in front of me and Thurng and E-Mae behind the pack. Each one of us had something in our hands; even Thurng, who was struggling to keep up with us, was happy to carry our precious bamboo serving trays. E-Paw was hauling our clothes and blankets over his shoulders and his much-needed fishing nets. E-Mae, Nok, and I had cooking utensils that E-Paw had bundled together for easy carrying with the strand of rope he bought from the village store. Before we noticed, we disappeared into the cool trails with trees hovering over our heads. I was relieved that the sun no longer burned my backside. Through the trail the interlocking boughs were dense all around with intertwining vines with thorns like the claws of a sparrow.

"Be careful, don't trip on that twig and keep yourself on the trail," E-Paw's voice echoed from ahead of the line.

I thought of the images of my childhood fears, but being in the middle of the pack, my thoughts were wiped away with the excitement of hopping over the next log. After what seemed to be a short walk through the dark green canopy of trees, the view that opened to me was as refreshing as the blue sky above our heads. It was as if I remembered it; the valley of dead trees stretched across the water and the blue horizon beyond it. Before it was the open farmland with Uncle Lun's hut and our new grass shack out on the open field of his land. It was a glimpse of happiness, even though I was delusional for imagining it to be our permanent home while we were living on borrowed land.

9

THE SIRINDHORN RESERVOIR

The Sirindhorn Dam Reservoir came into view as it stretched wide without a visible distant shore over the water in front of our hut. To the left of our hut, Uncle Lun's land separated the water and groves of forest and thickets that stretched across the plain. Beyond a spreading meadow of yellows, whites, and purples covering the field, Uncle Lun's hut sat on its stilts on the wide farm-land. By the water, brown cows were grazing between the wooden fence and the barn of gawking chickens and quacking ducks. Along the barn Uncle Lun's canoes sat by the shore next to green grass and marsh weeds. Standing there made me feel like a little child standing at the beach, staring out into the great sea as if it was a vast universe. In the middle of the water, the dead treetops pro-truded like dark spears laid out before the open sky. There I began to imagine Paw Yai Tut and his son struggling with the python that I ate delightfully.

I sucked in the warm soft air scented with waterweed and algae that had dried up along the shore. Glancing over the lake I searched for the shores over the dead treetops in the distance, where E-Paw had pointed to the town of Phibun. I was hoping to see Vung and Narng on the other end, but I saw no end, except for the shimmering water touching the blue sky of my own delusional heaven. I envisioned the faces of Narng and Vung just over the submerged valley. In my thoughts, I could see them working the muddy field in the scorching sun, thirsty for water and rest, their bared hands and knees caked with mud and faces soaking with sweat.

I followed the shoreline along the mysterious water from east to west, before my eyes met an island in front of a great boulder—a mountain on the northern shoals of the small water inlets. At the base of the mountain, an inlet separated the small grass huts scattered along the distant shore behind the temple. On the shore, the green bushes of water grass were swaying back and forth with the sparkling waves crashing on them. To the right, vacant huts stood ominously before the water's edge near the temple's dark tombstone leading up to the temple. Here the inlet ran perpendicularly to the main road directly in front of Ku Mai's hut, with the temple ground on my left and the forest along our side of the shore. The sparkling lake drew another magical feeling from within me, as I made another wish to live here forever. But before another thought could occupy my inquisitive mind, I heard E-Paw calling over to us kids.

"*Pai!* Let's go back for the last of our belongings," E-Paw said, breaking my trance.

"*Err.*" I shook off the images that flowed through my mind.

Inhaling the heat that filled my lungs with the dry air, I ran behind Nok and E-Paw. I jumped over clumps of small, crumbled logs in our path before the trail into the murky wood. The air cooled and I was relieved to be under the shelter of the trees again. I continued to look for the *Maak Yaang* above my head while I kept my pace with everyone. I searched for the sweet and slightly "sticky fruit," even though its yellow skin and oozing white sticky sap glued my little fingers together. Along the trail there were orchids of red, white, and lavender that attached themselves onto tree limbs and hung happily over our heads, but the ones I liked the most were the ones that dangled from the vine. I noticed that they were still growing under the shelter of the dark green leaves even in the dry season.

Along the trail prickly vines pinched my shorts and left a little red line on my legs. E-Paw said that these vines belonged to a wild edible potato. Unlike the wild potatoes that E-Paw said he found by canoeing over to a nearby island, these so-called *Goil* potatoes were small and not worth the time digging. What's more, their skin had to be peeled to let the slimy sap ooze out, and then they had to be soaked in water before you could cook them.

It was also here that we could dig up the roots that smelled like dog farts. It was not completely taboo in the village to eat this starchy potato-like treat called "dog fart" wrapped and steamed in banana leaves. The only catch was that you may be surprised that they literally took on the scent that lingered after your dog had relieved itself.

Skipping along the fallen tree limbs and avoiding the prodding branches, I dodged a few snapping branches that were jabbing me. By the time I noticed a scratch on my skin, it was too late and I heard E-Paw saying, *"Buc Shour!* I told you to watch it." Then E-Paw paused and did his quick meditation and blew air on my wounds with the blessing *"Oompang!"* Then, like a child in a playful state, I was healed.

"Shour!" Nok stood there looking at me, her humor expressing sorrow for my injury.

Out through the trail opening of the tall trees, I was hit with the warm air again. There our flimsy grass hut sat on Paw Yai Lerm's land. It was like coming home not to rest but to say goodbye to it forever. From afar, the hut looked flimsy with its grass roof on the verge of slipping off its top, and I thought about how it stood almost indestructible against the monsoon. The relentless rain that pelted against its withered roof and the great gusts of wind that tested its supports.

Once we arrived at the steps of the old hut, the nostalgic laughter and memories came alive in my head. It was as if a part of me was being left there—I began to understand that another stage of my life had just died. I stared over the gray peak that was behind us now, and I saw the faces of Uncle Wan and everyone dear to me meandering about in the old village. I wondered if I would ever see them again. I thought of Grandpa La and Grandma Dao, if they missed us and wondered about our whereabouts. E-Paw hadn't received any news of the village of Banh Dong in months, as many of his comrades had also disappeared.

We followed E-Paw into the hut for the final time. Inside the little dimly lit dome of a grass shanty, piercing rays of sunlight showed us the old pots and pans with rock-dinged bottoms that were blackened from the open fire. We grabbed the remaining cooking utensils and the rest of E-Paw's fishing equipment.

"Nok you take the pots and pans, Boun you take the empty rice basket," E-Paw, said pointing to each item.

Nok and I nodded as we watched E-Paw check the cracks and crevices in the wall and between the wooden floor panels.

"Look at everything before we leave," E-Paw said, scanning the empty hut for the last time.

"*Err*," Nok and I hummed in sync.

"*Pai*, let's go tell Paw Yai Lerm that we are leaving for good," E-Paw made his way down the worn lumber steps after he was content that we hadn't left anything behind. Then he grabbed his fishing gear and clothing, throwing the bag of clothes on his right shoulder and hanging on to his fishing gear with his left. Nok and I followed his lead and headed toward Paw Yai Lerm's hut.

We walked past the fire pit where we'd roasted just about anything from meats to lizards to herbaceous shoots (turning them sweeter or softening their bitter taste), peppers, and even popcorn over the frying pan. We'd also roasted the *Maak Boak*, the almond-like nuts found on the forest ground behind the hut. I thought about how we used to sit by the red-orange fire while the adults entertained us with curious tales of the jungle and water over the smoke and flaming fire.

Now in every corner of the field a sense of laughter mixed with melancholic memories almost like a balloon that had been deflated. Paw Yai Lerm, his wife, and their children were there waving their farewells to us like the day when we said our last goodbye to Uncle Wan and Grandpa Oosu.

"*Soak Dee* (good luck) and come visit us soon," Paw Yai Lerm and Mae Yai said with slight sunken faces.

"*Kolp Jai lai lai* (Thank you very much)," E-Paw said sincerely. E-Paw and Paw Yai Lerm exchanged smiles.

"*Soak Dee!*" Nok and I smiled, tilting our heads to the family as they stood there like they were in the frame of a family picture. That would be the last time I saw Paw Yai Lerm and his children standing there with humble smiles.

"Watch out, you'll fall off the dirt path, you two," E-Paw said, leading us on the straight and narrow path of the dike once used to hold back the water for the rice field.

"And keep an eye out for the tiger in the woods and scorpions at your feet," Nok's humor came from behind me with a twist of seriousness.

"*Err,*" I mumbled with the empty rice basket bouncing off my hips, recalling a time when E-Mae got stung by a centipede at the foot that left her ill for days.

After grabbing the last load of our belongings with E-Paw and Nok, we made our way back to our new home. I ran behind Nok and E-Paw, holding onto the empty rice basket and a bag of rope E-Paw used for trapping birds and rodents. I was excited to drop the last load off to E-Mae, since she was waiting anxiously with food spread out on the reed mat just outside of the hut, so we could have dinner by the water.

Uncle Lun and Brother Dang and his wife, Sister Thong, were also there. Brother Dang and Sister Thong were a young-twenties couple with a three-year-old baby girl and another child on the way. Brother Dang was handsomely well-built, taller than E-Paw, with the strong stout hands of a Thai Isan.

"We can't stay to eat rice and food with you, but we came to see if you need anything," Sister Thong said with a huge smile that stretched across her face.

"No problem, we are fine. We'll have the little holes on the roof patched up by tomorrow." E-Paw gave the visitors his wrinkled smile.

"I also got some long beans, *Puk Ga-Doon*, and *Puk Ga-Dao* to go with your meal." Sister Thong handed E-Mae a bundle of greens.

"Thank you," E-Mae said with a friendly smile.

"Brother La, you let us know if you need anything," Brother Dang said with a big smile.

"And there's more wood over by the pile of timber I have by the barn. You'll find that not all of the wood is rotten." Uncle Lun pointed at his wood pile.

"*Err*, thank you," E-Paw replied.

"No worries," Uncle Lun said with a gentle smile.

"*Dee, dee* (Good, good)," Brother Dang and Sister Thong repeated, with smiles and welcome looks on their faces, as they made their way back to their own hut a few hundred feet from ours.

Soon after our new hosts left, the five of us sat quietly enjoying our meal on the *sard* (mat), and we ate one of E-Mae's finest simple meals: a spread of freshly picked greens, pepper-anchovy paste, and roasted dried fish with warm sticky rice on our own beach for the first time.

"E-Paw, whose hut was this?" Nok wondered which one of E-Paw's friends had left.

"All of what is on this land belongs to Uncle Lun and Brother Dang. Another Laos family was living here and left to join the other refugees in the Ubon Camp," E-Paw said to Nok.

The shack was built on the ground with bamboo posts and a grass straw roof. It needed more covers where the wind had blown off the dried grass attached above it. That evening E-Paw and E-Mae found some giant fan-like palm leaves, then they fastened them over the holes to cover us for our first night at the hut.

By the following day, we dragged in bamboo poles found near the edge of the woods and more *bai* Toong and *bai* Hung, the same huge leaves we used to wrap our homemade wood-sap torches. The leaves were woven with bamboo strips making the covering durable enough to reinforce our little shanty. E-Paw and E-Mae had spent countless hours tying grass straws in strips with bamboo strands for each panel eventually replacing the damaged roof. Although the materials for restoring our hut like the grasses and *bai hung* leaves were found nearby, we also scavenged the forest in search of other huge leafy plants and some of the fibrous plants found in the forest. There was plenty for us to use on our new shelter. The bamboo strips proved to be durable even against the monsoon rain; some even outlasted the man-made fiber strands that E-Paw purchased from the village store.

In the days and weeks that followed, we continued to make the old hut stronger than what E-Paw called a "livable condition." We'd eventually turned that hut into our cozy new abode with a beach-front property surrounded by tropical trees and a vegetable garden with wandering livestock. There were days when I watched the ghostly clouds float over my head, and I listened to the great gusts of wind that howled through the swaying trees in the nearby forest behind the hut. I felt the warm breeze blow through the *bai hung* leaf and bamboo thatched walls. On stormy days, we cuddled together under a thin blanket on the *sard* E-Mae had thrown over our home-made bamboo mattress, and we listened to the rain pelting down on us. Sometimes the gusts of wind became strong enough to pick up the grass roof allowing little droplets of water to get in. This was when E-Paw would make a quick patch, or sometimes he'd place a bucket underneath the drip until the storm passed by. Then he would come back to join us under our cozy blanket.

With the sounds of thunder crackling to the bursting flashes under the dark sky, and rain pelting on our grass roof, we listened to E-Paw's stories from the *Sisavad* Book, a Thai book of fables. Some of the stories were poetic, rhyming words with words that I didn't understand. E-Paw said the tales were the same as the ones that his teacher had him recite in class when he was young. Many of the stories were of animals that had become a great fable in our country, and of a time when our country was at peace. "E-Paw, can you tell it to us again," we would often say to him when his stories were over. Then he would surprise us and say "hmm . . . " with his fingers tugging our ears, and crawly-creeping fingers running up our bellies and necks. E-Paw was full of surprises and would find humor keeping us entertained. From the story of a woman who had abandoned her twelve children in the jungle to survive on their own, to how a tiger got his stripes, before we knew it, we had forgotten that we were living in fear.

One day we huddled together in our little bamboo and grass hut, listening to the crack of thunder and lightning as it flashed across the sky. It rained so hard that the droplets of water fell through the grass roof, and it formed a big puddle on the pressed ground underneath us. We would catch the droplets with a couple of buckets and if the monsoon water was relentless, we'd also resort to our aluminum sticky-rice-steamer pot. When the buckets and pot were full, E-Mae would toss it through a small grass-covered awning that happened to be our windows, two large open ones in the back and one in the front facing the water. And E-Mae would say as she emptied her water on the over-soaked grass, "We are just redirecting the flow of water."

Our main door faced the shore, so we could keep an eye on the rising lake water. Leaving this door open, we could see the waves crashing along with the howling and hissing of the wind. One stormy day, the lake came alive before us and had almost taken away a man's life right before our helpless eyes. It was hopeless as we watched the horrible image of a man drifting out farther into the dark protruding dead treetops in the water. The gust of wind thrusted the water, making waves unimaginable to anyone with a small canoe. The man and his canoe were at a distance, but the dark image of his hopeless body was almost clear to me. The waves were rocking and pushing him into the dark spears; he was leaning and hanging onto one of the dark limbs for life. There wasn't much we could do for the man; everyone sat there helpless. E-Mae prayed, E-Paw stared with his eyes wide with fear for the man, and we kids watched in awe with mouths agape.

It was here for the first time I saw a man in distress being dealt with his fate. It seemed imminent that death was flashing over him in that moment. It had appeared that whether he was going to accept his fate or not, fate might have already accepted him.

Then, suddenly, a hero emerged from the inlet to our right by the temple. From a distance, he was a larger and stouter man than average. His canoe was larger and wider than the struggling man's. He was on his feet at the bow of the canoe chopping at the water like E-Mae digging her garden soil, but with immense vigor and intention. The rough water continued to rock his canoe up and down as he fought through the water with his dark paddle.

His canoe wasn't yielding to the water that came alive, as he was moving urgently toward the hopeless man. Both canoes were still rocked by the white waves, but the distressed man's grip was now on another dark spear and the water bounced his vessel around, as he was trying to steady his canoe from capsizing. Finally, the savior reached the man still clinging to the dead treetop as if he was on the back of a bucking bronco. The stout man quickly tossed a rope over to the distressed man. The two pulled their canoes together and the struggling man boarded the bigger boat. Not only had the distressed man been rescued but also fate dealt him a card of life that day.

Back at our hut, the air was filled with relief as we watched the men paddle toward the inlet to safety. The image of the heroic man risking his life to save the other man that day made me a believer in the true nature of kindness that existed within the human spirit. Even more so, that one man would risk his own life, so another could live. I wanted to grow up and be as strong, brave, and caring as the heroic man whose name I never discovered.

After witnessing the extraordinary display of human triumph for survival, we returned to the warmth of our blanket for more of E-Paw's stories as the relentless rain pelted down on our grass shack. As the air chilled, we huddled, pressing our backs against one another for warmth and we waited anxiously for E-Paw to make the *Sisavad* book characters come bursting to life with the thunder and lightning above our grass roof.

Another rainy season passed rather quickly as we were lost in our daily chores, while we shared our time living in that tight little grass shack. Although it appeared as a flash of time that went unnoticeable, the time filled our days with new surprises. The thuds of gunfights and explosions became far less than the frequent sounds that had echoed from the distant jungles. Still, they left a vibrating sensation through my body like a burst of unsuspecting thunder. One night before we closed our eyes after E-Paw's bedtime story, I asked E-Paw about my jittery nerves.

"E-Paw, why do I hear my heart, and why is it beating in my fists?" I asked.

"You have a smaller heart than Thurng, *Buc shour*." E-Paw gave me a warm smile.

"Aren't our hearts the same size?" I asked E-Paw, knowing that I had never seen a heart other than that of a chicken or rat at that point in my life.

"When you have a small heart, it means that you have a lot of fear," E-Paw explained.

Before E-Paw could blurt out another word, his centipede-like fingers climbed up my neck then tickled down my sides. The more I laughed, I felt other crawly fingers and nails as Nok and Thurng joined in on the fun. Soon I found myself surrounded by prickling fingers all over me until my small heart had forgotten its own beats. This playfulness that involved everyone as we lay in the same bed became our bedtime routine. E-Mae was not as playful as E-Paw, but sometimes she would just go along with our giggles and tugs.

What helped me to displace my fear of death and the unknown were the sounds of laughter and E-Paw's stories and imagining the animals in his fables. I couldn't wish for anything else from our newfound happiness than those comforting moments in that little grass hut. Like the wind carried a new scent of life from its misty breeze off the water, our life appeared to be refreshed. But I didn't understand why E-Paw would be talking about us moving again. In my mind, this was our glimpse of hope here in this plentiful world.

"We're living on borrowed land," E-Paw said to E-Mae one day during one of their soft conversations. E-Paw was now expressing his concerns as many of his Laotian friends who lived nearby were packing up and heading into the Ubon Refugee Camp.

I was six now, and at night when the light of the world was shut to my mind, I'd fall asleep to the waves gently crashing on our shore, E-Paw snoring, and the elusive night creatures singing and droning on outside our hut. Then early in the morning when the little critters fell silent and E-Paw disappeared, we would walk up to the waves crashing onto our shore, and birds would chirp their happy tones in the near distance. I was happy for everything happening around me, because it occupied my mind, replacing my fearful thoughts with a new and intriguing sense of wonder.

Before the sunrise just over the tree line, E-Mae was up tending her garden. Sometimes like little ducklings, Nok and I followed along to help her heave her water to her garden. E-Mae's small garden was about a couple hundred feet from the water, a much shorter haul from the shore than the well at Paw Yai Lerm's *nah*. It was next to Uncle Lun's. Looking at what Uncle Lun had in his vegetable and plant beds, E-Mae was missing cucumbers, yuca potatoes, the long purple and green beans, yellow melon, and hot pepper plants loaded with red chili pepper.

There were no fences along Uncle Lun's garden. "Fences are good only to keep the animals out, but not the neighbors. Sharing is a common virtue," Uncle Lun made clear to us.

One morning we ran into Sister Thong working the garden. She was standing there with her big smile and hard-working hands like E-Mae. Her skin was dark like ours, her hair was long and black, and her sweet smile stretched across her round face. E-Mae said that Sister Thong was happy to have us for a neighbor.

"You pick whatever you want to eat out of my garden," Sister Thong said.

"*Err* . . . thank you, there's plenty here," E-Mae said to the friendly woman with gratitude.

Nok, Thurng, and I were excited at the thought of picking whatever we wanted in the field, especially when Sister Thong planted many of our favorite fruits in her garden. The one I enjoyed the most was the Asian melon cucumber that smelled like honeydew and tasted like candy when it ripened. Although, we kids loved to eat the melon, it was unlike any of us to pick it without E-Paw and E-Mae's consent.

The smell of the sweet melons and working in the garden made me feel closer to Mother Nature. I also loved the smell of the earth, especially as it soaked up the water, and the indelible scent of the *Puk Wan* (sweet plant). E-Mae would steam the crunchy, tender, light green shoots, often entirely with the leaves, under her steamed fish in the sticky rice steamer. Besides the *Puk Wan*, other vegetables that triggered my zesty spirit were Thai sweet basil, eggplants, lemongrass, peppers, tomatoes, long beans, and cilantro. My mouth salivated from the aroma of the raw minced shrimp paste with crushed roasted rice and hot pepper with cilantro, lemongrass, and kaffir.

It was at this moment that I wanted to become one with the earth by planting a seed in the soil—tilling it and watching it grow from below the soil, then seeing it stretch toward the sun. Not only was I excited by these wonderful savory scents but also helping E-Mae with her chores in the garden made me realize how much I enjoyed planting and watching things come to life. So I followed E-Mae around enthusiastically, waiting for her to tell me what to weed, how to pluck the fruits and leaves, and how to water without hurting the plants.

E-Mae's Garden had more than basic Isan vegetables; she was also growing tobacco for E-Paw. The giant leafy and sticky plants were far from my favorite. I wanted to puke every time the pungent smell hit my nostrils. Although the repelling plant kept me away from the tobacco end of the garden, it was a great satisfaction to see E-Paw chopping it into thin slices and inhaling it with enjoyment and a smile on his face. There was nothing like watching the smoke float about his face after he had rolled up the chopped tobacco in the discolored Thai newspaper stack in the corner of our hut.

Seeing E-Paw's delightful smile, E-Mae, who loved to make him happy, would do anything to make the tobacco a lot stronger and stickier. One day she surprised us by pulling out an empty tin can. "We'll make it stronger for your father. Here, pee in this and we'll use it to fertilize the soil." E-Mae would tell us to go behind the bush and pee in the can.

Thurng and I were more than happy to oblige—we got to pee in a can and then recycle it for a greater purpose than we had ever imagined. The bucket of pee was at times pungent enough to make me hold my nose. Then on some careless aim, we would get pee on our hands, and we would say "Oh yucky!" and then run over to E-Mae who already had a bowl of fresh water to rinse us off. Still, the urine odor made me sick to my stomach, but most of the time E-Mae would dilute it with water that we would carry from the reservoir. We worked happily under the hot sun knowing that our soil would be rich in nutrients that would bring us more vegetables and fruits. There was never a time when E-Mae was out of fertilizers. If she was, we would go around and gather chicken and duck droppings from Uncle Lun's yard. At first, I cringed at the thought of picking up animal feces with E-Mae. But soon my little nostrils acclimated to the heat, then the dissipated smelly poop became second nature to me.

When we were done with watering E-Mae's vegetable garden, we'd continue over to Uncle Lun's. His garden covered a wider ground than ours and needed a lot of weeding and watering. Some of the plants like the yuca potatoes that stretched across his field were planted throughout the year. When the harvesting season arrived, we would go and help him gather the starchy brown roots. We kids were asked to pick any yuca that Brother Dang and his wife left behind, since the work of digging and unearthing the thick potatoes required the muscles of adults.

After we were done with helping Uncle Lun's garden, we'd wash up by the shore and return to our hut. But sometimes Brother Dang and his wife would ask Nok to babysit their toddler so they could work in their rice fields. We were told to always help Uncle Lun's family whenever we could.

"It's because' of their hospitality that we can live on this land," E-Paw reminded us.

Sometimes when we returned to our hut, E-Paw was home early in the morning after setting his baits and checking his nets. One of my favorite activities was helping E-Paw weave casting nets. With a spool of nylon and a wooden measuring block, E-Paw would start at the top of the casting net like a spider spinning its web from the center then outward. Then he'd add more loops at the end of each circle, widening the base of his net like the sweep of a woman's dress. The looping knots seemed like they would never end; to complete one knot, several knots had to be looped.

I also loved being out on the water with E-Paw. A few months back E-Paw had hesitated about taking me along on his fishing trips, but now E-Paw said that I was finally ready. On our first fishing expedition, I sat on the bow of the canoe stiff like a little stump as I watched E-Paw launch us out toward the dead valley. The world was floating by me as we glided over the water underneath us. Over E-Paw's head the sky moved, the hut and the forest started to shrink behind him, and the waterweeds gave way to our canoe and the plunging of E-Paw's paddle.

"You just saddle yourself on that wooden board by the stern and don't move," E-Paw said, still mustering the boat with the beaten oar. As I sat there, I remembered that I wasn't to call out anything either: "You don't want to taunt the spirit and the demon of the water." This was something that wasn't just E-Paw's warning; it was the village's tradition to keep from pointing fingers or using profanities that might offend the spirits of the water. This discipline was something that I automatically complied with, knowing what I knew then.

It was at that moment that I went from being a gardener to being a fisherman. I knew that I wanted to be a fisherman like E-Paw—the water, the smell of spoil baits, seaweed, and worms were now in my veins. Even as those floating dead branches still haunted me at night, I stared inquisitively at it, and I wanted to be out there.

Before sunset that evening E-Paw had showed me how to set the hook and wire to catch the giant mudfish that people often spoke of. To catch the fish, we used a hook as big as my bent index finger with a metal leader. We also needed a wire strong enough to fasten to tree limbs sticking out of the water. For our bait, we used live minnows and baby blue gills, along with grass shrimps, these little fishes were found throughout the shore.

"Setting our hooks and bait before the sunset is the best time. If the fish eat the bait and die on the hook at least they won't spoil before we can get to them," E-Paw said. With that in mind, I began to picture how E-Paw would canoe out here early in the morning and then bring home those huge fish like when we used to live with Paw Yai Lerm.

One day when E-Paw and I were pulling up our metal leader we saw the white belly of a *Pa Doe*. The giant snakehead fish was floating with its white belly like a piece of paper in the water. At the sight of the fish, my mouth was agape, as I watched a fish the size of a log floating before us.

"Look at the big fish, E-Paw!" I said excitingly.

"*Err* . . . " E-Paw spoke the words out of his nostrils like a ventriloquist.

"How did it stay on the hook that long?" My mind swirled with the brisky breeze.

"*Err,* don't move," E-Paw said, smiling at me and reaching over the boat to pull the fish aboard.

"E-Paw is it alive? I think he's dead," I said, recalling a story that E-Paw once told us about how sometimes to escape predators some animals would play dead.

"No. Shh, don't talk too much." E-Paw quickly glanced at me.

"*Err* . . . " I replied, knowing exactly what E-Paw meant. In the spiritual world, it was bad luck to mock or say anything about the biggest fish your father caught or if a specter just flew over your head.

My eyes were still wide open as I sat there complying with E-Paw's wishes. He finally plopped the fish onto the canoe, with one hand hanging onto the steel leader and the other on the tail end of the fish. And shortly after E-Paw unhooked his rig from the two parallel branches shooting straight out of the water, he grabbed his paddle, then slowly pushed us away from fields of tree limbs. We headed straight for the lines of foamy bobbers that stretched about fifty feet off the shore. I knew exactly what that was, because I had helped E-Paw fasten those floaters to the fishnet.

With his oar, E-Paw picked up one end of the net then hoisted it vigorously onto our canoe. I was excited again and wanted to jump off the boat when I saw an assortment of fish tangled in E-Paw's net. In a pile before E-Paw were the *Pa Koor* (mudfish), *Pa Toong* (featherback), *Pa Vuu,* and the puffy fish. Others that I didn't recognize had tenacles, prickly scales, and catlike whiskers and fins.

"E-Paw, are you going to pull the fish out from the net?" I asked E-Paw, hoping that he would let me touch the fish.

"Yes, but after we get to the shore. I need to remove the fish and untangle the net if I'm going to reset the net. But I'm going to take these in with us today, because I need to fix the holes in it," E-Paw explained.

My eyes were still in awe when E-Paw pulled up his last net. Now in the middle of the canoe, there was a pile of fish and water weeds piled with the meshy nylon net that looked like E-Mae's bowl of clear noodle soup.

"That's it! We caught quite a bit today," E-Paw said happily.

"Err." I nodded my head still with my mouth open and eyes feeling like they would just fall out of my head. I wanted to tell E-Paw that there was enough fish there to feed us for a month, but I kept it to myself as I watched his body rotate the oar of the canoe from side to side.

On the shore before Uncle Lun's hut, there were other fishermen who had already pulled their canoes onto the grass. In the gathering I could see Ku Mai's wife and the men dividing up their catches and exchanging them for money. Uncle Lun and Paw Yai Tut were there as well, helping Ku Mai's wife load the fish into the two huge bamboo baskets that she used to carry the fish to the market. E-Paw explained that this common practice was a way that the locals could make a few *baht* by selling the fish that they caught. His fishing skills were almost as lucrative as his secret practices in healing people. On a good day's fishing, E-Paw said that he could make more than Vung working at the brickyard all day.

At that moment I didn't think much about the money that E-Paw could bring in with all the fish he pulled up—I was more ecstatic about bragging to E-Mae, Nok, and Thurng about how E-Paw and I had caught the biggest fish of my life.

Once the canoe slid over the shore and stopped on the grass, I jumped off the stern and made my way toward our hut. I ran past the crowd to get the attention of E-Mae, Nok, and Thurng, who were meandering about the hut waiting for our return.

"Come see what E-Paw and I caught!" I yelled out excitedly jumping up and down.

"What is it?" E-Mae asked.

"What did you guys catch?" Nok added.

"E-Paw and I caught the biggest *Pa Doe* ever!" I shrieked with the adrenaline still pumping in my veins.

Everyone followed me to the crowd gathering around E-Paw's biggest catch from the Sirindhorn Reservoir.

"You're lucky today," E-Mae said, staring at the huge *Pa Doe* and the pile of fish as she began to help E-Paw pull it off the net.

"Wow! Look at the size of this *Pa Doe*. I think it's the biggest that E-Paw has ever caught," Nok said, marveling at the fish.

"Is it going to bite?" Thurng asked while running his little fingers down the fish's slimy head.

"No, it's dead, but don't touch it, you're going to get your hand dirty," E-Mae said, hoping that we would stop playing.

"Ho! *Pa Doe Yai*, Big Pa Doe." I heard Ku Mai's voice approaching us from behind.

"Wow! *Err!* Brother La, you are always lucky, how you do it? I fish in the same water, but I have never caught anything like that," Uncle Lun said, joining in the conversation.

"Where did you catch it and how did you do it?" I heard another voice say.

"Just over by those dead treetops, and I used little bluegills." E-Paw gave a wry smile.

"Are you selling the big fish?" Ku Mai's wife asked, staring at the buckets full of fish that E-Paw and E-Mae had just pulled from the nets.

"Well, I think we're going to have this one for dinner. Thank you," E-Paw replied, staring at me, who was still bragging about the fish.

"Thank you." Ku Mai's wife acknowledged E-Paw by withdrawing the money out of her bamboo basket and handing it over to him.

The giant mudfish was a rare catch. E-Paw himself had never caught one this big, so he claimed. Because much of his catch went to Ku Mai's wife, sometimes we never got a chance to see what he pulled out of the water. All we knew was that he drew so much curiosity that the other fishermen stopped by our hut to ask him the secret of his success.

As E-Paw rinsed the canoe and his fishing net, E-Mae, Nok, Thurng, and I marched back to the hut with E-Mae carrying the oversized fish by sliding her hands through its gills. From behind us I could still hear E-Paw, Uncle Lun, and his other fishing buddies inquiring about how E-Paw had been so successful in consistently catching the fish.

"Brother La, I don't know how you do it, you must be putting some magic in that bait," Uncle Lun laughed.

"Hmm . . . No magic, just a lot of patience." E-Paw gave Uncle Lun a modest chuckle.

The men's voices lingered in the distance as I jogged to our clay pot full of clean water. I kicked off my sandals and washed my hands with the little bar of parakeet brand soap that had a strong Jasmine scent. Out of the corner of my eyes, I saw E-Mae sharpen her knife in the bucket of water with a flat stone; then she proceeded to scrape at the fish's body, causing its scales to fly in front of her. Since the fish was fresh, E-Mae didn't have to struggle with the scaling. After the fish was descaled, E-Mae took her blade and opened its belly. By then we kids gathered around her, watching E-Mae clean the innards. E-Mae taught us not to be wasteful. If she thought the fish would spoil quickly, she'd toss in a handful of salt, or even add it to her already fermenting anchovy buckets.

"Eew, yuck, look at that bluegill. That must have been E-Paw's bait," I said.

"Yuck, that looks like a shrimp and a crab, and look, there's even a leaf," Nok said, pointing.

"It stinks!" Thurng said, reaching to touch the ball of rotting slime.

"Don't touch it!" E-Mae pushed Thurng's hands away.

"Come here!" E-Paw put him on his lap and then mussed my hair and gave us a soft gentle smile.

For lunch that day we shared with Uncle Lun and his family one of E-Mae's tasty slightly tamarind-based soup loaded with the Pa Doe chunks. The aroma of the tamarind and its sour leaves stewed together in a broth of head and the innards that E-Mae had split open made my stomach growl. Another one of E-Mae's mouth-watering fishy concoctions was her pickled fish, which she mixed with the leftover chunks of the *Pa Doe*, the steamed sweet rice, and salt, garlic, and MSG, the *umami* brothy flavor that lingered with most of E-Mae's dishes. Beside leaving the fish out to dry, often this is what she would do with fish that didn't make it to the market. Even though E-Mae's preserved fish would be ready within a few days, most of the time it would be gone within a few weeks. Like most of us who have acquired the taste and neglected the smell and texture, I would rip the fish meat off the bone, place it over my ball of sweet rice like some sashimi, and pop into my mouth a hot chili pepper that intensified my taste buds.

That night I went to bed on a full stomach, dreaming about another fishing adventure with E-Paw. The water, seaweed, and the stench of the rotten bait were seeping into my veins. Although E-Paw would never let me out there alone, I watched how he could tell a good fishing spot and the sort of bait and size of hooks to use.

But in my dream, I saw the fishing hooks, string, worms, and E-Paw as we dropped our lines and quietly waited in our canoe so that the fish would take our bait. And we drifted along the dead trees, taking shelter from their leafless limbs like the egrets above our heads and lowering our bait down along its trunk, where E-Paw said a school of fish might be hiding. For hours it seemed that I had been sitting out there with E-Paw in our little canoe, rocking gently to the motion of the waves and pulling up all types of fish out of the water.

10

A YEAR IN PARADISE

year later, we were still living an idyllic life by the sandy
shores of the Sirindhorn Reservoir. Random thuds of gunfire became less frequent and soon faded out from where they had
echoed. Every day was a new day, and E-Mae kept our little hands
busy and happy and E-Paw filled us with the surprises of his daily
catch. Along the sandy banks we kept our eyes peeled for anything
that might have washed up on the shore, and sometimes we'd dig
for crabs, snails, and even insects that lived in the marsh under the
wavy grass. When we couldn't find anything for a meal, we would
turn to foraging the woods behind our hut.

"Nok, what is school?" I asked one day while following E-Mae
to gather wild greens nearby.

"That's where you go and learn, and they give you a notebook
and pencil to write with." Nok and I stared excitedly at each other.
"That's also where they whack you for not being smart enough to
recite your homework," she added.

Nok, three years my senior, was already ten, and neither one
of us were getting an education other than the homeschooling

with E-Paw and E-Mae. But we didn't have the responsibility of going to school either. In my little head that saved me from getting "whacked."

But what could be greater than this lush green world and great stretch of water? For me, everything was here along our shore and Uncle Lun's farm. E-Mae had her garden and all the fish she could dry or turn into anchovies, or ferment into pickle fish. E-Paw had his fresh tobacco, and his Thai friends were fond of him, and oftentimes they would stop by for good laughs and a few drinks. And we kids had our beach that we'd roll around in, soaking up as much sun and water as we could until E-Paw would yell out, "You kids stop playing in the water or else the leeches are going to your privates." There in those lost moments of childish playfulness, we would move at the speed of the leeches during E-Paw's calls.

My favorite time of the day to be down by the beach was just before noon, when the temperature was already scorching. I'd run down to the water, toss my sandals aside on the grass, and then dip my dirty feet into the cool water. It was a relief to lay there on the sand sunbathing with Nok and Thurng, with our backs and feet partially soaked in the water. What I loved the most was flipping side to side, catching the cool rush of water that crashed on me then dissipated into the sand underneath my bare back. We would watch for items to float in, hoping to get rich so that we could live forever on our borrowed land, but nothing monumental ever washed up on the shore besides driftwood and seaweed, especially the foot-long flexible and grassy kind that we gathered with E-Paw to eat with the spicy-hot ceviche of *larb* grass shrimp or *larb pa*. Along with the seaweed that we called *Neer* or *Taow* (the slimy green algae that looked like a clump of green hair), this was my favorite seaweed that he would turn into a floating soup of green slime, with chopped beans, hot pepper, snail chunks, and minced fish. The other seaweeds were far less slimy, although they'd tangle my toes each time I stepped on them under the water. The freshwater seaweed looked almost like crabgrass with soft and slimy stalks that went perfect with the shrimp ceviche.

Still, E-Paw and E-Mae were having quiet conversations about leaving this land for a life that seemed to have been made for caged birds. For me, the only thing that was missing now was Vung, Narng, and the rest of our family over the distant mountain.

Sometimes when Nok and I would watch the clouds float gently by in many shapes that resembled E-Paw's puffs of smoke, we would entertain ourselves by bringing into the light what E-Paw and E-Mae had been talking about.

"You know that E-Paw's Lao friends aren't coming around as much," Nok said to me.

"Where do you think they are going?" I asked.

"I overheard that some returned to Lao," Nok said, shrugging her shoulders.

"Maybe they are all moving to that refugee camp in Ubon," I said.

"They say there's a lot of people there and we have to learn Farang," Nok explained.

"Are you afraid to see the *Farang*?" I inquired as my own image of their faces flashed in my mind like the *Yuck* and the *Pee-Polp*, the demons of the forest that the adults had conjured up.

"I'm scared too, and I don't want to move away from here." Nok cringed. "You know we can go to school wearing the khaki uniform and white blouse, and we can get books and pencils." Nok's suggestions were frightfully intriguing.

Then I thought about how maybe Narng and Vung would join us if we moved to the Uboun Camp, not too far from Aunt Tai's *nah*, where Narng was staying. Along with E-Paw's plans of us moving, Vung and Narng were also a part of his conversation. In my mind I saw them going to concerts and shows at Banh Doo; Vung had spoken excitedly about this during his last return. They seemed to be having the time of their lives.

"I only made a few *bahts* working all day at the Brick Yard," Vung said disappointedly to E-Paw one day.

"Do the best you can." E-Paw stared proudly into Vung's eyes, as if he shared Vung's growing pains.

"I heard it's worse at Ubon camp. I've seen its rusty barbed wire fences and the strings of huts. And I've heard that the opportunity for work is almost none." Vung slumped over the pillow and rested his head on it as he lay on our reed mat bamboo bed not wanting to add more to his disappointing observations of our future.

The next day, after learning more about Vung's travels, Nok and I sat on a wooden bench next to the hut pondering the life that evolved around us. Nok was able to see more than me; in her eyes, a deep dark resentment for the world was slowly seeding itself inside her scrawny soul—she was beginning to put things together and was able to grasp E-Paw's fears that came with the hopeless look on his face. I saw this darkness manifesting itself through her dark eyes and pressed jaw exposing its defined muscles when she talked about our situation. It was a way of not letting in the dark hatred that she was now aware of.

"Nok, why don't Narng and Vung come live with us if they aren't making a lot of money?" I mused to Nok one day, wondering why they didn't want to come home and help E-Paw and E-Mae.

"Our brother and sister send the sticky rice home to us every once in a while." Nok reminded me that our sister and brother loved us and that they were working hard to put the rice on our table.

I didn't know how to tell Nok that day that I didn't really care about the money and the rice—I wanted E-Paw to be happy. I wanted to take the fear and the aching love for them away from his face as I watched the grimace and the wrinkles become a part of his warm smile and earthly brown eyes.

That evening after my conversation with Nok, Uncle Lun strolled over in his sandals and rope wrapped around his thigh.

"Brother La, why don't you come live in our farm hut? My son will be living with me in town since his wife is having another baby." Uncle Lun pointed to his vacant farm hut sitting a few hundred feet from the lake.

"Err, thank you." E-Paw happily agreed to get us off the ground.

The following day, we helped E-Paw and E-Mae with gathering bamboo posts and even shaved off branches to frame the awning of the window to the hut. Our new home now stood high above the ground and closer to the water—so close that we could literally fish right off our balcony when the reservoir swelled up. When the water rose along the shore, it almost touched Uncle Lun's barn that was adjacent to the hut. We would be living in a raised shanty with a grass roof, nestled on the second level of several wooden stilts.

"This is how we can avoid drowning in the rising water," E-Paw said to us.

From the top of the step, a view of green fields stretched farther along the water before the edge of the woods. On the southern side, the field of lifeless tree limbs were still in the midst of the water, as if they were floating on the constant waves that crashed through. Over the dark field, the distant shore was lost to the stretch of heaven and water. To the east over the tree lines, the glittering roofline of the ornate temples beamed like little golden rays of sunshine.

Behind our hut, the sun was ablaze over Uncle Lun's *pore* (jute) crop. During the day a field of the flexible tall green plant swayed with the warm wind. During harvest, the fibrous *pore* plants were cut and dragged down to soak in the water for days until their rotten fiber could be peeled off their stems to dry along the shore. The drawback to farming the fiber was that the rotting plants ruined our beach paradise. And the lingering smell seeped in between the cracks of my toes and fingers. But not all the excitement was ruined by the spoiled odor that left our beach polluted during the *pore* season. Once I was knee deep in the water, the foul odor soon disappeared with my childish laughter as we chased each other with whipping sticks. Once dried, the *pore* would be rolled up like a giant roll of hay, and Uncle Lun would hire a pickup truck and transport it to the local factory in Phibun. E-Paw said that the rolls of fiber would be turned into rice sack and ropes.

Now the vibrant green field was calling me as I thought of us kids running and hiding in it during our inventive games. Then from below, I heard Nok and Thurng giving chase to one another, something we loved to do. Unable to control my own excitement beating in my heart, I quickly climbed down the steps to join them. We chased each other as our childish laughter grew louder until E-Paw ushered us along by yelling out, "You kids stop playing and go help your mother bring our belongings over here."

"*Err,*" Nok said, running toward the old grass shack.

"Ahh . . . I'm going to get you!" Thurng screamed, running along my side.

I stopped to look at the hut one more time, and, once again, I was regretting moving and leaving an old home behind. Like all the other huts we had lived in, our cozy abode proved to be indestructible against the sultry sun, howling wind, and the pelting rain that came with strong gusts of wind to rip it apart. But the beaten bamboo and grass top haven stood strong and indelible in my memories. Sifting through my childhood memories, I could find no other moments so comforting than those close nights that we huddled together under our thin blankets like a packed can of sardines, as I fell asleep to E-Paw's storytelling.

"Boun, come and take this bag," Nok said, interrupting me.

"*Err.*" I nodded as I entered the dimly lit hut.

I was happy to oblige, because E-Paw's sacred *Maak-Lord*

discipline didn't allow women to touch it. I grabbed E-Paw's sacred bag and held it at my chest level as I followed Nok and Thurng out the door. It was the last few bundles that E-Mae left for us to take over to our new place.

On the way back, I was mesmerized by the sparkling waves in the water caused by the wind and beams of sunlight just beyond our new home. I had an epiphany that I wanted to make this place a permanent home. I hoped E-Paw wouldn't reconsider the refugee camp in Ubon and going to live in a new world with the Farang. I couldn't imagine a more suitable place to replace the magnificent displays of this tropical yard that lined our hut and Uncle Lun's carefree-like fences. I looked forward to when the fruits ripened and I would smell the aromatic fragrances of mangoes, bananas, tamarinds, Brussels sprouts, and *Maak Mou* (the little bunch of M&M-sized green fruit tart to the taste like olives) from the green fields. The taste of *Maak Mou* still lingered in my mouth. But each with their own distinct tangy, tart, sour, or sweet taste can be a part of the bursting flavor of our favorite *Som Tam* — especially with an intense sour and slightly tart taste of the green plum locally known as *Maak-kok*. Then there was the *Maak Di Kai* (the chicken spur fruit), a fruit that looked like a rooster's spur, but to me the green or sometimes red (when ripe) hot Thai chili pepper-like fruit was instead sweet and crunchy like candies.

The heat of the day reminded me that we'd have a bigger roof and smoother floors to lay on in our new home. I never got used to sleeping on the bamboo floor that E-Paw and E-Mae had strung together like a raft.

During the hottest months we kids took to our favorite pastime: playing in the water and cooling down from the sultry heat. Here the hottest months began in February and went until July, with April being the most scorching. Since I never got used to the heat, it always seemed to be very hot, even after it rained.

Each morning we woke up early with E-Paw and E-Mae and watched the sun rise over the temple together. Although our chores kept our little legs running after E-Mae as she tended her garden, each day offered us hope from the submerged valley that had now become a paradise to me. Soon our daily routine became splashing water and sand along the shore and caring for our livestock of chickens and ducks.

E-Paw also kept our little hands from idling—like the time he came home with the fishing net we had been asking for. We knew E-Paw had a soft spot and if we asked him profusely, and gave him plenty of enthusiasm, he'd break down. So, the next time he took a trip to Phibun, he came home with it.

"I told you that E-Paw would buy it for us," Nok said to me after we finally got the net.

The nylon net with loops just a little bigger than the size of a pencil was perfect for the needle-nose fish we called *Pa Tot Tong*. The needle-nose fish looked like a doctor's syringe with an elongated needle jawbone lined with tiny sharp teeth that reminded me of the mouth of those gharial crocodiles that were born ready to clamp their mouth on an unsuspecting fish.

Now we were ready for the syringe-like fish that sometimes darted between our legs in the water. Nok and I knew exactly where they were hiding: in the slippery grass-like seaweed by our toes with the grass shrimp and water snails. But to catch them we would have to work as a team; this meant we would have to include Thurng, who was anxiously waiting to help on the shore.

"You have to work together. Now go find two posts so you can attach and anchor the net," E-Paw said.

At E-Paw's instructions, we immediately jumped up and scrambled to search for any piece of wood that resembled a broom stick.

"E-Paw, we found it!" we repeated excitedly as we ran toward him with our sticks of wood.

"Good, and you must tie the net's anchoring lines at the top and bottom of the posts. You see the metal leaders lined along the bottom of the net? That's how you can tell the bottom and the top," E-Paw said as he handed us the assembled net that rolled up around the wooden posts.

"*Err, Err, Err . . .* " We nodded excitedly like a pack of seals as Nok grabbed the net from E-Paw.

We made our way toward our favorite beach spot. When we reached the water, we took off our sandals and Nok handed me the left end of the net. I grabbed the post attached to my end of the net from her, and immediately anchored the post about knee deep into the water. Nok, with the rest of the net in her hands, made her way down toward the deeper end of the water. The water gently rose above her as it moved in motion with her when she got waist deep. She slowly pushed her way outward to the deeper water like a duck swimming in the pond. Then she finally arched the net, making a sweeping motion along her path toward the shore.

"Hold your pole and keep it steady," Nok said when she stopped with water now almost up to her chest.

"Once you set the net, Buc Thurng can chase the fish into the net, but don't go too deep." E-Paw pointed his fingers while he supervised us from the shore.

With the net lined with little white floaters like a volleyball net between Nok and I, Nok waved her hand yelling to Thurng for him to charge into the water. Then at Nok's cue, Thurng frantically flapped his hands as he stumbled into the deeper water, then suddenly slipped on the water grass underneath him. The water level was at his chest, as he quickly scrambled up again, then rushed with all his child's might to stir up the water in every direction, as Nok continued to loop the net, forming an arch before our little beach. From where I was standing, I could see my toes in the water. Deeper in the water, Nok held her stick firmly while hauling her end of our dragnet toward the sandy shore. Thurng cheerfully ran out of the water, as we walked our bundled net out of the water, settling it on the grass with the little fishes flapping back and forth.

"Look, there's the fish!" I yelled out with excitement staring at the wiggly fish scattered along the net.

"Look, there's another one!" Thurng said, jumping up with his shorts soaking wet.

"I think we got a school of them," Nok said, spreading out the net.

"Yeah, we saw many of them over there," I said elatedly after knowing that we finally brought something out of the water by ourselves for E-Paw to see.

"*Err, Buc shour,*" E-Paw said, smiling at me. "Here's how you get the fish out of the net without being pricked by its fins and beak." E-Paw placed his left hand by the loop of the net by the fish's body and with his right hand pinched it through by its head.

We went back into the water many times after that. E-Paw stood there proudly watching us net our fish for a while, until he was confident that we knew what we were doing. Then he left to go back to the shade of the hut to repair his casting net. But before he left, he said that we could do what he did with his nets out by the deeper water: set it like a volleyball net with two posts supporting each end and then the fish would swim into it on their own.

"You kids be careful not to go too far into the water," E-Paw said, concerned with the tangling seaweed in the water, since our little legs weren't strong enough to swim out of them. He was also afraid that the leeches would find their way into our privates. E-Paw had a rule when it came to swimming and fishing in the water: we were not allowed to be near it unless either him or E-Mae were close by.

When we got tired of dragging the net around, we decided to do what E-Paw had suggested by setting the net in the water. We found two long sticks to stake each end. Then we all took part in the job of beating the water by causing havoc with our hands and feet. Now we watched the fish scrambling for their lives as they unconsciously swam right into our net. Together with Thurng we were happy to play in the water by beating and diving into the water headfirst. Then we worked the water just like E-Paw told us until we cleared out what I believed to be almost the entire population of the *Tot Tong* fish that were swimming near us that day. We caught more than enough fish for supper and even had some for E-Mae, who fileted and salted them and dried them out in the sun.

We ended those days of playing in the water with our eyes all red, fingers and toes shriveled up like the wrinkled skin of an elephant's trunk, and E-Paw calling for us to come in and dry up.

"*Shour*, I told you to keep your head out of the water," E-Paw said while wiping the mucus off our faces.

Most days, E-Paw kept an eye on us while he fixed his nets. One day E-Paw was repairing a ripped hole in his casting net the size of my head.

"It was caught on a tree branch," E-Paw claimed.

The casting net hung by a rope on the branch above E-Paw's head and looked like a pyramid of cobwebs. At the base of the net was a circle of metal chains that not only helped E-Paw to hold it and helped it to sink quickly into the water but also allowed E-Paw to cover a circumference of almost twelve feet. The net with the metal chain at its base was heavy. After E-Paw was done weaving, he showed me how to soak it in animal blood before drying it.

"It'll make it more durable," he said.

While his old casting net was sitting in the animal dye, he constructed a new net as a backup. I quickly took on the process of tying the strings, but soon I realized that it was taking us forever. E-Paw would teach us how to make each knot with the rolls of nylon thread. Each loop required me to make two wraps around a guiding stick and two more locking knots around the existing loops using a pointy wooden spool that the nylon was housed in. The traps that used it to catch fish, birds, and even rabbits were made in the same fashion as the net.

When we were done with catching fish with our own net, E-Paw would say; "Did you clean the slime off the net like I told you, so that you can use it again?" His virtues somehow always stemmed around the fact that you should always care for your belongings.

"*Bor* (no), but we're going to wash it up with some well water in a bucket," Nok replied, staring at the algae caught in the loop of the net.

"*Dee, dee (good, good)*. You can wash it in the water, and I'll watch you." E-Paw smiled as he watched us in a collaborative effort cleaning the net.

Nok and I took the collapsed cone-shaped net to the water and shook it in the water until the slimy dark green algae and water weed came free from it. Then we carried it together toward E-Paw so he could show us how to hang it to dry by the swivel end attached to its long pulling rope.

Once Nok and I completed our chores and dried ourselves, we turned our attention to chatting about Vung and Narng. Another rainy season had come and passed, and yet there were still no signs of them except for the bags of rice that the pickup truck dropped off by our hut.

After Narng was done working for Mae Tuu, she joined Vung in Banh Honghee with Paw Yai Banh (the village chief) and Aunt Tai. I missed Narng and Vung. I thought of Vung singing *Thai Luk Thung* pop songs and playing his acoustic guitar. Narng's soft heart-shaped face was still lingering in my mind. I still remembered the expression on Narng's face that day when she left us; she went without much to say. Even then, I yearned to see her as I thought back to the village of Banh Dong. She had been my protector while

E-Mae and E-Paw were long gone, and then she had dragged me across the mountain as if her life depended on it.

"Nok, do you think that Narng and Vung will come back to live with us again?" I asked.

"*Err.* E-Mae is going to see them soon. She plans on bringing them back with her," Nok replied.

By the following week, E-Mae visited Narng at Banh Honghee village. She spoke with Aunt Tai, who told her that Narng was happy and helpful while living with her. During the dry season, Narng had been assisting her at her little village shop, selling small items from soaps to sandals, to an assortment of sweets. When E-Mae asked Narng to come home with her, she became reluctant, then she told E-Mae that she'd be joining the family soon. But before leaving Banh Honghee village, E-Mae gave Narng the news that we were moving to the Ubon Refugee Camp that left a cringe on Narng's face.

"We don't have a choice. This was once my birthplace, but I moved to Laos so long ago they won't recognize my citizenship," E-Mae said to Narng, who agreed.

Disappointed that her teenage daughter didn't seem to want to join the family, E-Mae visited Kubar Somdee in Mukdahan. E-Mae decided to visit him for his blessings on her prayers of keeping the family together in a tumultuous time. Her trip led her to the fallen monument they called *Thaat Phanom,* where artifacts and monuments were said to be laid in gold, and her spirit healed in the presence of ancient relics encased in glasses.

Nok and I helped E-Paw fix his fishing nets while E-Mae was gone on those sultry days. E-Paw gave us nylon lines and cotton strands, teaching us repairing techniques with his hands and showing us how to enclose ripped holes and snagged knots.

"The fish love to be where the fields of tree limbs are dense in the water. I'm not sure how long I'll be using these nets since they are in bad shape." E-Paw took a long draw of his newspaper-wrapped cigarette and let the smoke out of his mouth while he focused on the hole the size of my head.

Nok and I excitedly watched E-Paw work, nimbly twisting and looping the strands together. Even though it took him days, and sometimes months, to make his nets, it became our pastime to help him. It kept our hands from being idle, especially during those rainy days. Inside our hut, E-Paw had already started a new net with something that resembled a little horn at the top end that was attached to the guiding rope end. It was here that the net would start out like a spider's web, then gradually spread out into a tepee-shaped net. Then the weaving and locking of nylon threads into non-slip knots with two wooden sticks began—one wooden spool was used to hold the thread and tie the knots, and the other to keep each loophole consistent. After E-Paw showed us the technique hand-over-hand, I would sit there for hours at a time with the net before me making the twelve-foot casting net.

When we were done making nets, he'd show us how to tie a fishing line to a hook with a special loop, by quickly tucking the fishing line around the hook.

"Look, E-Paw, it's easy for me to hold the hooks with my fingers," I'd say. Then there was a time I slipped and got pricked and I'd bled as the hook slipped out of my fingers into the palm of my hand.

And this is when E-Paw would say, "*Buc Shour*, why did you do that?" Then he'd stepped outside the hut and pinched some *Bai Pern*, a dark green leaf from the bushes scattered throughout the yard. He'd chew it into a paste, then dab it on my wound and say, "Don't do that again."

"*Err* . . . " I said, acknowledging E-Paw's words gravely, only to be jabbed again by many more barbed-hooks several years later.

After getting a lesson on how to toughen cotton nets and tying hooks with E-Paw, I'd go back to swimming and fishing in the water with Nok and Thurng. We kept our promises to E-Paw and didn't dare venture too far out from the shore. Fortunately for us, we didn't have to go past our waist; the school of smaller fishes we were trying to catch were near the shore. By the time Nok was ten and I was seven, we had gained E-Paw's confidence to leave us by the water. Nok would disagree with me and press her little lips together saying, "We kids will always make at least one gray hair grow on E-Paw's head whenever he's not with us."

II

VISITORS

One afternoon after we settled into our new home, Vung came strolling along Uncle Lun's *pore* fields. Vung wasn't alone this time; next to him stood a tall and lanky teenager.

"It's Buc Vung and Buc Vee," E-Mae said excitedly.

"Yay, yay!" We kids jumped up elated and full of smiles. It was exciting to see Vung and Cousin Vee, who we respected as our older brother.

Vung looked the same as the day he left, but his face was darkened by the sun and his hands were dried like he had been working out in the *nah*. His sinewy muscles could be seen in his forearms and biceps. He didn't look like he'd grown an inch—he was still a petite teenager.

Vung and Cousin Vee quickly came to a halt before us. Tilting my head slightly backward, I stared at Cousin Vee's face for any resemblance to the family. Seeing that he was tall with a reserved soft voice and narrow features with big ears, he reminded me of Grandpa La.

"Where did you kids come from?" E-Paw asked them happily.

"We met in Phibun at the brickyard," Vung replied.

"How long have you been living down here at this hut?" Cousin Vee asked E-Paw.

"Just after the monsoon season. Uncle Lun and Brother Dang don't come down here as much, so they said we could live in their farm hut," E-Paw said, smiling proudly at Vung.

"What are you kids doing?" Vung asked us with a soft smile and the demeaner of an adult.

We didn't have much but a smile for Vung. He looked at us and then handed Nok a bag of candies and said, "You guys share it."

It had been months since E-Paw had given us candies. Thurng and I quickly reached out with our little hands before Nok held the brown and yellow candies out from the plastic bag. Then we popped the delightful treat into our mouths, and I waited for the sugary sweet to hit me with a grand delight, as it dissolved into an aromatic flavor on my tongue while the hint of honey went straight up my nose. Immediately, I felt a surge that gave me a rush of sweet running through my entire body. I had developed a sweet tooth for more than E-Mae's gelatin-like green pandan treats—now I looked forward to the sweet flavors of Vung's candies, which seemed to burst not only in my mouth but also my mind.

By the time we were done with our candies, Vung and Brother Vee had already hopped up the wooden stairs and set their belongings on the worn wooden floor in the corner of the hut. Brother Vee was still smiling at us. "You guys are getting bigger. Do you remember me?" he said in gentle tone, giving us a soft gradual smile.

"Do you remember Brother Vee?" E-Mae added elatedly from the kitchen end of the hut. She had been preparing dinner that day.

"Err! Err!" Nok nodded to him, while Thurng and I giggled.

Vung quickly joined E-Mae as he grabbed the mortar and pestle and ground the hot chili pepper with homemade anchovies, lemongrass, and roasted scallions and galangal into a dipping paste.

And Brother Vee helped her with the sticky rice, freshly steaming hot right out from the bamboo basket steamer still sitting on the aluminum pot.

"You kids wash your hands and get ready to eat," E-Mae said.

"*Err*," Nok said, as we kids stood before the clay pot of water sitting next to the highest rung of the ladder at the entrance of our hut.

With the lingering sweet candy still in my mouth, I said, "Nok, will there be more candies like this in the refugee camp?"

"I think so. I heard that the *Farang* loves candies," Nok said with a big smile.

That night we took to each other naturally, knowing that we shared the same bloodline. Sitting there staring at each other with more than just the glow from our homemade torch, as the fire stick burned on its tip and the hot sap dripped sizzling to the bare ground below, we learned that Brother Vee had escaped from the Village of Banh Dong following Vung's trail. As Brother Vee recapped his story, E-Paw and E-Mae said very little.

Then there was a smile on E-Mae's face that came with a soft glow and she said, "It's a blessing to see each other."

Cousin Vee continued with his story with a low humming voice. "I hid between trees and boulders when I saw soldiers and kept my distance from the thuds of gunfire that emanated from the jungles in the distance. Then I went back to Banh Honghee, and eventually I met up with Vung while working at the brickyard."

E-Mae pointed out Cousin Vee's patience and his soft smile. "But don't go getting him mad," E-Mae warned, "he might have Grandpa La's temper—he'll keep it to himself until he gets angry."

There was no visible sign that Cousin Vee was the person that E-Mae had depicted, and shortly after exchanging a few smiles with him, we carried on as if we were under the cover of Grandpa La's bustling roof.

The next morning, I ran along the beaten path behind Vung and Cousin Vee, as they took to the open fields of the farm, then inside the thicket woods behind Brother Dang's hut. For Vung and I, it was a good old time. In my hand, I had an empty tin bucket, and around my neck I had a slingshot I liked to hang as a wooden necklace. Vung and Cousin Vee also had their own tucked in the back of their jean pockets. Along the way we searched the ground for marble-sized rocks that made the perfect ammunition for a quick kill. Since I had been playing with slingshots, E-Paw had given me one when I was able to pull back the rubber string with my hand. I pinched together a small pebble and the leather pouch with my right thumb and index finger.

Vung took us to the old wild mango tree just by the edge of the woods. We picked our favorite mangoes; they were wild, unripe, and just big enough for me to palm with my little hands. It was an acquired taste that kept our hunger at bay, crunchy and tangy with every bite. It was that sharp sour and sometimes tart taste that went with our concoction of *Som Tam*. We could practically turn any sour fruit or vegetable, whether shredded or plain, into this *Som Tam*. For us, the acquired taste required E-Mae's fermented anchovy sauce, hot chilli peppers, roasted ground rice, and pepper, salt, and MSG. And if we were lucky, we'd add sugar to top it off.

After picking wild mangoes, we pressed deeper into the woods, passing our old trails leading toward Paw Yai Lerm's *nah*. Halfway, Cousin Vee spotted a spiny green lizard resting on a limb over our heads. We stopped and watched him gently pull out his pebble from his pocket, load it into the leather pouch of his sling shot, aim, pull back the rubber string, and let go of his rock as it struck the lizard and knocked it to the ground. Vung ran and quickly stepped on the maimed spiny creature, killing it almost instantly.

"See, I can hit anything," Brother Vee said, laughing.

"Yeah, that's an easy kill—even a blind man can do that." Vung chuckled at Brother Vee, who then laughed loudly enough to stop the birds from chirping in our green canopy.

Vung was still the humorous brother who gave me orders that I'd eagerly follow. He knew that when he was around, I would do what he told me—if I didn't, he'd yell the fear out of me. He never struck me when he got angry. His frustration was nurturing, showing me the trick but expecting me to be quicker and faster with my wits. I knew he was kind and was still giving me survival skills for living off the land. But no matter how it was, Vung told me that one day I'd become a man, and I shouldn't be afraid of anything.

By noon, we had foraged the ground and hunted along the edge of the woods until we came to an opening where we found more mango trees and another tree clustered with tiny fruit we called *Maak Moaw*. It wasn't as crunchy as an unripe mango, but it had a herbaceous aroma. What made this fruit good for our *Som Tam* was its tartness and a chewy texture that resembled a Thai long bean.

"Look, they're green and unripe. When they are a darker color, they're ripe and tougher to chew," Cousin Vee said.

"Yeah, Boun, put those in the bucket," Vung added, pointing to some that had fallen to the ground that he twisted at the fork end with a long wooden stick he had picked up from the ground.

"They're the best," I said to Vung as I picked up the soft greenish-yellow fruit with its aroma still lingering in the air all around us.

"Yeah, see through that trail? That's where E-Paw and I set rabbit traps." Vung pointed to a little trail leading toward Paw Yai Lerm's hut and the marsh leading to a muddy pool of water.

After we picked wild fruits, we went back home and Vung had a bucket loaded with what we needed for lunch and dinner that day. I felt proud that I had gone along for the hunt and got to help bring food home to the family. Far more, I had two older brothers watching over me.

One day they decided to gather ant eggs from the red ant's nest under the canopy of trees behind our hut. They'd cut down some banana leaves with the machete, and I'd followed them into the thick woods. There under the canopy they cut down two lengthy branches of some tree saplings. After cleaving off the greens leaves and all the lower limbs of the tree, we walked toward a leafy green balloon-like nest hanging over our heads.

Vung and Brother Vee began jerking vigorously at it with their long wooden sticks. They whacked their sticks at the green ball of leaves like two kids with a pinata. Then they jabbed the nest until it gave way, releasing hundreds of red ants and their precious little white eggs on their banana leaves laid out on the ground like a small tarp.

"Boun, you stand back and keep your distance. I don't want the ants to bite you," he told me.

"*Err . . .* " I nodded as I jumped back after I'd noticed the sharp sting from the ants.

"Ouch, ouch, ouch!" Vung would jump around swatting at the stings on his body.

Vung would let me and sometimes Nok join us for the hunt. Nok had a keen sense of which edible mushrooms and soft greens to pick. The only times we didn't go with them were when he and Brother Vee went to gather honeycombs with handmade torches, and they both came back home laughing about how each got stung.

One day they decided to hunt green snakes to make a tasty soup with the fresh sour green tamarind leaves found next to our hut. We watched them dig holes on Brother Dang's field and pull the snakes out of the holes.

Another warm dry day, they took us along with them to catch butterfly lizards with white speckles and orange bellies that stretched their thin scaly wings, reminding me of the flaps on flying squirrels. We called them our "sand lizards." These lizards were no longer than the length of my feet from heel to toe. They had a network of holes and they moved quickly in and out of them. We smoked them out from their burrows and caught them while they fled for their lives to an alternate escape hole.

"Be ready, keep your net over the holes, and scoop them up with your net when they come up," Vung prepped us for the hunt.

We didn't need to catch a lot, since one or two would go with our unripe green mango dish. Brother Vee whacked the heads of the little critters with the tip of his machete, then showed us how to clean the insides out. And Vung roasted the lizards almost dry and then minced them all together in the mortar and pestle with his mixture of chopped mango, peppers, a drop of anchovy sauce, and a dash of MSG.

"That's all you need to go with this hot sticky rice!" Vung laughed.

My little hungry belly was agreeing with Vung. Once you acquired the intense taste of hot chilis, sour, and saltiness in combination, it was hard not to salivate just at the thought of eating such meal.

Later at night Vung and Brother Vee played their guitars and sang the popular songs that we heard on our crackling radio in the moonlight.

"*Dourn cha, dourn cha* (oh moon, oh moon)." Vung sang his own songs while playing the acoustic guitar. In my memory of him, he's still serenading the moon with its reflection over the water of the dead valley.

The following morning, Cousin Vee, Vung, and I ventured a lit-tle bit farther into the lake, way past the depth of our waists, where E-Paw had told us not to go beyond. As we drew ourselves closer to the tree, its submerged branches were brown and murky green with clinging algae. High above the water its limbs were shiny and smooth, almost as if it had been polished by the elements that left it without any bark. There was other life that existed: Water insects lay their larvae along its trunks, giant water bugs scattered deeper into the water toward the dark base of the tree while water-skaters danced above the water, and a school of minnows fed on the little unsuspecting insects. The limbs extended out in several directions, as if it was still reaching for the sunlight that would have nourished their roots and branches.

When Vung and Cousin Vee reached the tree, they dove head-first into the water through the branches. They dove deep and disappeared for minutes at time. Then they resurfaced like otters, pushing their hands through the water just to hang onto the canoe with one hand while they anchored their feet on the slippery branches beneath the water.

That day they swam until their eyes were red and completely exhausted, and after dinner, they laid on the reed mats, in Vung's own words, "like two satisfied pigs."

A month later, Vung and Cousin Vee returned to Phibun. Disappointed that our brothers couldn't stay longer, we waved goodbye to Vung and Cousin Vee and wished them good luck. E-Mae packed them a bundle of dried fish and fruits, and she even did a prayer to Mother Nature to ensure a safe trip and a prosper-ous life for them.

"There will be some pretty girls waiting for them at Banh Doo,"

E-Paw said jokingly as they made their way to the bus stop by the temple.

"*La gon, Soak Dee!*" We waved them *goodbye* and *good luck.*

"Remember, you need to come in and stay in the camp for us to sign up and go to America," E-Paw reminded Vung after having a long father-son talk in the hushed corner of the hut.

"*La gon*, good-bye, you kids behave!" They replied.

That would be the last time I saw Cousin Vee, until years later when I stood next to him as a middle-aged man, still a foot short of his height.

We also had a great time raising our own livestock. My favorites were the handful of chickens and ducks that kept me feeling like mother hen, especially when it came to feeding time. They would trail us to where we could dig worms for them. One day I almost took the beak off one of the ducklings with my shovel as they were crowding to get the worm I dug up.

We had a lot of ducks and chickens in the little barn next to our hut. I was quite fond of them all, but there was one chicken that I literally bonded with. Well, it bonded with me—by its claws and spurs, sometimes embedding its sharp claws into my legs.

I called him, *Kai Tee*: the fighting chicken. He was a part of the dozens of chicks that E-Paw had given to us as pets. We did the best we could to raise those commercial chicks out in our barn, but only Kai Tee survived. He was a plump chicken and with gray and white speckled fringe feathers. Kai Tee had a special bond with only me, and Nok and I couldn't figure out why.

"I don't know why that chicken chases you down and attacks you like that." Nok laughed. "You ran as fast as you could, and he still got you."

"Yeah, and it pecked and clawed me until I bled." I laughed along with her.

"There must have been something you did to it to make it mad at you like that, maybe it was because you were a little rascal." Nok continued laughing.

One day E-Paw and Uncle Lun had visitors who were looking for some entertainment. Some of the men were the local fishermen and some of the people I had never seen before. E-Paw had told them stories of the chicken that had been attacking me, and that the chicken could fight. And of course, they had a contender, one of Uncle Lun's: Red Rooster. He was a real fighting rooster, not Kai Tee. Kai Tee had a more domesticated plump and round look, unlike the lean Red Rooster. I knew that he was getting ready for the hot boiling pot and his feathers plucked—there was not a chance in hell he would make it through the fight. But there wasn't anything we could do about it. Even E-Paw, who knew that we were fond of the chicken, had to go along with the other men.

That warm evening, the men formed a circle. Some of them were drunk and randomly loud. To my surprise, one of the men took Kai Tee, tautly gripping him with both hands on his gray feathers, as he walked toward Uncle Lun who stood excitedly on the opposite side of the ring. Then both men released their fighters, as they yelled, *"Tee, Tee!* (Fight, Fight!)" There were faces ablaze with the shiny glow of sweat; others had a dark-red-tan complexion like when E-Paw spent too much time under the sun.

I watched the entire scene before me with a childish fear, too young to understand the meaning of hate, the hate of not liking what was happening, and the fact that there was no mercy in the act of cruelty. Through the gaps between the rowdy men, the birds immediately stared at one another, gawking with their necks stretched out and erected toward one another. Then the natural animal response took over, and they launched their spear-like beaks at each other, as if they knew that it was either life or death. Their wings spread wide, their spurs slashing at each other at every advance. I tried not to watch as I heard their feathers flopping in the air. Then I could no longer hear their wings, as the men were shouting louder and taunting them to fight harder.

"*Tee, Tee* (fight, fight), kill, kill, get him!" And every now and then I would see the fight through the cracks of light through the crowd. The fight lasted several minutes as I stood there on the outside of the circle of spectators.

Before I could take in another breath of hope for Kai Tee, it was over. Red Rooster was walking around Kai Tee with his shiny orange chest pumped, holding his red crown high in the display of an overly confident bird. While Red Rooster appeared to be ready for the next contender, Kai Tee was now limping . . . he was done. He couldn't fight anymore, his spirit broken, his plum gray feathers deflated. The circle of men cheered and broke apart. There was Kai Tee, bruised and badly beaten, his crown cut, and blood dripping down over his left eye, which was now completely shut. He looked like a sick chicken, and life was fading out from him; his neck was drooping down as I held him tight.

"Let me have the chicken," E-Paw said to me.

I knew exactly what he was going to do.

That night there were several dishes of food that were prepared to host the group of men at Brother Dang's hut. Some of the meals were raw and still alive like the grass shrimp jumping in the huge bowls of chopped hot pepper, fish sauce, mint, and cilantro. We even served the seaweed grass that we pulled out from the water while we were out fishing for the needle-nose fish earlier in the day. With all sorts of soft herbaceous stems, hot, bitter, spicy, and minty food scattered all over the *sard* mat, some even had a mixture of the animal's blood like the duck *larb*. But everyone was concentrating on the main dish: Kai Tee. E-Mae served the chicken soup and *larb* chicken salad (a mixture of thin slices of grilled chicken in almost a ground consistency with peppers, anchovy sauce, cilantro, basil, ginger, and kaffir with the intense citrus fragrance and a touch of bitter like the peels of its bumpy lime fruit).

Kai Tee's death lingered in my mind, more so the animal-and-man connection during my fleeing moments of running away from his attacks, but knowing that his purpose was to keep me alive for another day. It was here that I had realized that something must die in order for something else to live—in those days, it was the lives of those hopeless animals just like Kai Tee, who were destined for death at the palms of our hands.

One bright morning after Kai Tee was gone, a big bird I had never seen before came to perch on the lifeless tree that was half-submerged in the water before our little beach. At a distance the bird was magnificent and graceful with a wide wingspan stretched side to side; it was a bird like no other to my naked eyes. It began to fan and groom itself, and it appeared to be the size of Kai Tee. It had black feathers and a white crown (I later learned that this bird was a bald eagle). As I watched with E-Paw, the rest of the family soon joined in. A few days later Brother Dang took a bigger interest and watched the bird with us, as the giant bird kept coming back to the dead tree.

Soon Brother Dang and E-Paw stopped staring at the bird and were already nodding to each other "*Err . . . err . . .* let's get it alive." So, within a few days, they climbed the trees and tried to trap the bird using a well-conceived line of thin ropes and fishing lines with loops that might entangle either the bird's feet or neck.

That day, the bird studied the water below, then looked at us as it stretched its wings and off it went into the blue horizon, flying over the boulder of a mountain toward Phibun. The two men wasted no time grabbing their traps with a similar setup for catching field rats with small loops and strings. Then they quickly pushed the canoe straight out to the tall skeleton of a tree partially in the water. We kids and E-Mae watched from the balcony of our hut in silence and with high hopes of them catching the great bird. They reached the tree and E-Paw held one of the dark branches as he steadied the canoe for Brother Dang, who hoisted himself upward to the highest limbs. He pulled himself higher to a height where he didn't dare stretch any further, to where he set the trap—a live mouse strung to a little rope as bait.

After the mouse died and his corpse tossed in the water, little minnows, live grass shrimps, and even our favorite needle nose fish were tied to the trigger stick of their contraption. More traps of both dead and live baits were used on reachable limbs. The majestic bird returned day after day, only to perch and stretch its graceful wings above their traps. They waited for days until they finally came to the conclusion that their efforts to cage the bird were going to continue to fail.

"It's too clever!" Brother Dang and E-Paw nodded their heads and broke into laughter in between their puffs of smoke.

"Let's shoot it!" Brother Dang said, as he strolled over to the hut with a rifle resting on his shoulder.

The two men were anxious to catch the bird; they knew that if they didn't catch it, someone else would. They decided to set up a small wooden box next to E-Mae's garden on the shore facing the dead tree.

"We want to surprise the bird," Brother Dang said excitedly.

Adding to their ambush scheme, they used four wooden posts, tying them together in a teepee shape and threw some grass straw around it. In their little teepee, they made an opening for the barrel of the rifle and enough light for them to see through. They kept vigil with their rifle ready to take the shot when the bird returned. Above their little grass teepee, we kids and E-Mae waited anxiously for the rifle to go off, waiting to see the fate of the giant bird.

The next day when the bird came to sit on the lifeless tree, it perched at the very top limb. We all knew that Brother Dang and E-Paw had a clear shot of it, but they were several yards away. Then Brother Dang positioned the barrel of his rifle, and without any warning there was a loud tap from the rifle that broke the silence that hung in the air. The big bird stood up with its wings even wider than I had ever seen before. It took off in the flight for its life as the second and third shots followed. Then the majestic bird flew into the blue horizon and disappeared over the mountain.

During the last month at the Sirindhorn Reservoir we had two visitors. They were E-Paw's Lao comrades who had been living in Banh Pong, a village next to the Laos border. The men had small frames like E-Paw, and they came with kind words and news. They spent their last two nights with us before making their way to the Ubon Refugee Camp. We helped them gather the bitter *Puk Ga-Dao* leaves with soft shoots from the trees behind our hut, and E-Mae packed them dried minnows and panfish that she had salted and sun-dried.

That day as the sun began to set, they asked E-Paw for his casting net and a cotton bag to hunt birds resting in the bushes by the woods behind our hut. Occupied with getting dinner ready for the men with E-Mae, E-Paw said that I could guide the men to where we hunted birds.

"You don't have to go far, just on the edge of the woods," E-Paw said.

"*Err.*" I nodded to E-Paw.

The men grabbed E-Paw's fishing net and we walked toward the woods that were already dark from the interlocking boughs above. With the men behind me, we followed the trail that E-Paw, Vung, and I traveled many times in the past. For a successful hunt we had to stay quiet, even if it was dark. We were hunting a bird called *Nuk Kum*. These birds reminded me of gray speckled feather quails, but not quite as big, and their meat was a tender morsel after they had been salted and roasted over the open fire.

By the edge of the woods, I quietly pointed to the bushes that one of the men was going to cast the net over. As soon as the sun set behind our backs, the men began their hunt. At almost eye level to the bush, I stayed behind and watched their dark images move around the trees, and I heard the familiar sounds of feathers fluttering in the dark. Without a word, the man with the net on his shoulders cast it over the first bush. In the dim light, the birds fluttered their wings, trying to escape through the loops of the net. Then the other man scrambled toward the fleeing birds, cracked their necks, and tossed the dying birds inside the bag, while they flopped their wings a few more times and then fell silent. The men were excited to have caught a handful of birds to add to E-Paw's dishes and the little bamboo baskets of sticky rice.

When we arrived home, E-Paw and E-Mae were almost done with prepping dinner with spices and an abundance of greens from the young tree shoots and vegetables and herbs from E-Mae's garden.

Before E-Paw and E-Mae inquired about our hunt, I blurted out, "E-Paw, I thought we heard your voice, and we even called out to you."

"*Buc Shour*, that wasn't me. And what did I tell you about calling out to strange sounds or things in the dark?" E-Paw said, staring at me and smiling at the men.

Both the men and E-Paw believed in spirits, but soon the discussion of the *Pee-Polp* (demons) was replaced by a conversation of the news coming from the war front. I cared very little for it, and after dinner I took my exhausted body and lay down. Before I sank into a deep sleep, one of the demoralzied men said, "It's not an option; the Thai government is ordering all illegal immigrants to vacate their land."

"We're going to take our chance in the Ubon Refugee camp," said the other man with the faded red-and-white-striped scarf around his waist.

The next morning I woke up in the dark, and the men were gone. I never saw them again. Like the voices that we had heard in the woods that night, their voices echoed with the gentle wind that carried my memory of such vivid moments. They were the last of the strangers to visit before E-Paw gave us unsettling news.

"We're going to the Ubon camp," E-Paw said, staring at us with semi-sunken eyes.

For the very first time, I couldn't find any comfort in E-Paw's words. E-Mae, Nok, and I remained silent. Thurng, who was covered with a thin blanket, was still asleep on the *sard* mat. Nok and I swallowed our fears, and together we gazed out to the moonlight shimmering over the field of treetops and our beach below, casting countless shadows—shadows that filled my head with images of death and suffering. My notion of "a forever paradise" by the Sirindhorn Reservoir died with the sounds of waves crashing into the shore and the water disappearing onto the soft sand.

By the following week we helped E-Paw and E-Mae pack food that had been dried or preserved with salt, and we squeezed our lunch and dinner in our bags and in E-Mae's carry-along bamboo baskets. E-Paw said that whatever we couldn't take, we'd leave for Uncle Lun and Brother Dang.

After saying our farewell to everyone we called brother, Uncle,

Paw, and *Paw Yai,* we made our way, distancing ourselves from the shores of the Sirindhorn. Nok and I looked at each other, then we looked at our hut, our feral calico cat and our chicken and ducks, and then back to the shore, where the gentle waves of water crashed into the swaying grass by our little beach. One by one they were waving goodbye to me, and I was parting with them . . . this time for good.

By mid-morning that day, we caught our ride in the cab of a large pickup truck sitting at the bus stop next to the temple. We were heading into the unknown: the Ubon Refugee Camp I had only heard of through E-Paw's adult conversations. With the looming Hin Soung Mountain behind us along the Laos-Thai border, the truck sped off gradually away from the mountain and the village of Nong Mek. When it picked up speed, I stared into the blurry images of the huts, banana trees, and coconut trees that lined the road. I smelled the diesel and engine oil fumes that wafted to the back of the truck and lingered indelibly.

As we continued on our journey, huts with tin roofs gradually blended into red brick and concrete buildings that lined the roads with green, yellow, and red signs, oversized images of the King of Thailand, and golden Buddha and naga serpent statues at the entrances of the temple. A concrete and steel bridge stretched frightfully over a body of water called *Nam Mun.* I tightened my grip on my belongings as the truck worked its way through Phibun's bustling traffic. Here an entire new life opened before my eyes: A large crowd of people were bustling along the cha-otic street and the aroma of Thai and Asian cuisine filled the air. Street vendors, rickshaws, tuk tuks, motorcycles, and lories of different sizes whizzed by.

Shortly after we stopped, we followed E-Paw out of the truck and found ourselves by a food stand. The life around us was busy and had a unique yet familiar aroma of cooked herbs and herbaceous stems and the noise of chattering among the crowds of people. There were vendors touting and flashing their goods before ongoers. An assortment of clothing, sandals, and plastic toys and candies of red, green, blue, white, and beyond hung before my amazed eyes. Then without notice, a motorcycle squeezed in between us, carrying greens tied to the baskets at the front and back of his bike. Meticulously, the man worked his way through the crowd inches away from us. To keep us from bumping into the motorcycle, E-Paw changed my direction by easing his hand on my shoulder, sometimes to a sudden halt. E-Mae also hung tightly onto Thurng's hand, afraid that his little feet would take off to the colorful world that bedazzled his eyes.

By the vendor's wheel cart, a friendly petite Thai woman with a gentle smile handed us our lunch wrapped with banana leaves. It was *larb* chicken and sticky rice, and a small bundle of fresh mints and soft green shoots that left the lingering taste of bitter and fresh herbs in my mouth. We quickly sat down on a wooden bench a few paces from the vendor's stand and devoured every little bit of food set before us. It was there that I came to know the life that existed over that huge boulder, sitting on the other side of our shore by the inlet of Nong Mek Temple. It was there that I knew that the modern world was far beyond my imagination.

"*Pai, pai.*" E-Paw hurried us back inside the truck after washing up. In the modern bathroom we were no longer using little sticks to clean our dirty bottoms. Here bowls of water were used for a quick rinse. After E-Mae's quick potty training, we made our way back and sat next to E-Paw, who hadn't spoken much since he gave us the pep talk back at the hut, preparing us to embrace a new life at the Ubon Camp.

12

ARRIVING AT UBON REFUGEE CAMP

March 1978

The two-hour ride came to a halt at the main entrance of the Ubon Refugee Camp. We all hopped out of the truck and collected our belongings. E-Paw and the Thai driver exchanged their gratitude, and the driver drove away. On the ground, we stood looking at one another with unease. Naturally we kids were shy to this new world, and E-Paw and E-Mae were overly prepared for the worst. Nok kept her head low, and E-Mae held Thurng's hand. And as we waited for E-Paw's instructions, each one of us fell into our own silence as we stared at our new home with the sultry sun already baking the backs of our necks.

The camp was surrounded by rusty barbed-wired fences that stretched farther than my eyes could see. The entrance was a wide flexi-metal gate wrapped around brown wooden posts with wire spikes. At the guard post, the *Or-Sors*, the Thai soldiers, interrogated ongoers hurrying in and out of the camp. Beyond the gate there were dark green military vehicles parked along the road at the entrance of another small encampment surrounded by more barbed-wired fences.

Rickshaws and food peddlers rattled by with their creaky bicycle wheels kicking up dirt and sand. Not too far from the lorries, the main road before us disappeared into the left side of the camp. Where the heat appeared to be rising and bending the blacktop, another crowd of refugees had gathered in front of the warehouse across the main road from the military encampment. In the background of the commotion, there were hundreds of grass huts connected to each other—many of them were built around the huge and mysterious reddish-brown mounds of dirt. Through E-Paw's comrade, we later learned that the Ubon camp was once a deployment base for the US Air Force during their strikes against the North Vietnamese during the Vietnam War. And the mounds were for military training and even served as a barrier in the event of an accidental detonation, since ammunition was said to be heavily stored at the camp.

To our right, along the inner perimeter of the fence, eucalyptus and pine trees were scattered before grass huts facing a small tin-roof building just outside the wired perimeter of the camp. Along the stretch of trees, more men pushed their rickshaws and women carried their children (some tied to their hips), standing in line before a pile of rice bags waiting for their rations. Some children were left to run shirtless in their dark dusty sandals, while others were completely naked chasing and screaming after one another. It was like we had woken up from a bad dream and found ourselves in an unimaginable zoo of people.

One of the Or-Sors quickly caught our attention as he stepped toward us with his M-16 strapped on his shoulder. There were three soldiers working the checkpoint that day; they all wore dark green military uniforms. I stared at them in the heat, my mouth dry, and my heart sank into my stomach as my eyes wandered aimlessly along the stretch of the fence.

"*Ma ti nai?* (Where did you come from?)" the Or-Sor asked.

"*Lao, Kup* (Laos, Sir)," E-Paw replied in Thai.

Then E-Paw handed the soldiers his documents: a list of everyone in the family and a black and white picture of himself. The picture shows him wearing his beret with a medical insignia on it from his service with the Royal Laos Army in 1960. Along with other pictures of Grandma Dom, Grandpa La, and Kubar Somdee, it was E-Paw's precious photo.

The Or-Sors scanned through our paperwork and didn't give us a hard time. One officer took down our names, checked our bags, and handed back E-Paw's documents. Then the other said, "You will need to see the camp advisors, *Kup*. The building you need to go to is over there." He pushed the wired flex gate opened and pointed at the open cover of a building with a tin roof with lines of people.

We slouched behind E-Paw and E-Mae as we headed toward the tin roof edifice where the Or-Sor pointed. I felt the hot blacktop underneath my feet bake my rubber sandals. I kept my silence, but I was longing for the sounds of the jungle and soothing water on my toes. Instead, another group of children who were running and screaming after each other caught our attention.

"You need to register with the counselor at the metal roof building ahead," the Or-Sor added.

"*Kup, Kup.*" E-Paw nodded with gratitude.

"*Kup,*" The Or-Sor replied.

"*Kolp Koon, Kup* (Thank you, Sir)." E-Paw immediately zipped up his brown plastic travel case, tucking it deep in the tote bag he was carrying.

"*Pai.*" E-Paw lowered his chin then led us to an open span building with a tin roof. Under the cool cover from the sun, men and women sat next to small tables inside the pavilion.

"This is where we have to announce our names," E-Paw said, as he came to a halt at the end of the line.

We stood in line and waited for our turn to register our names with the counselors. It was here that I saw my first Farang man. Contrary to what was instilled in my head, there was no yellow in his hair and he did not have blue eyes. The Farang man that I was staring at had milky white skin and dark curly auburn hair with hazel brown eyes.

"Buc La!" Paw Chamdee stood up from his chair to greet E-Paw. He was a thin man, slightly taller and with a lighter complexion than E-Paw. They both had a similar happy glow in their eyes.

"Good, you made it!" Paw Chamdee was now gripping E-Paw's shoulder tightly. Then he smiled at the rest of us. Paw Chamdee had been one of E-Paw's Patigan comrades. Far more, the two men had attended school together since childhood. Back in Laos, Paw Chamdee and his family lived in Banh Jik, walking distance from Banh Dong.

"Paw Chamdee! *Sa bai dee.*" E-Mae gave him a humbling smile.

E-Paw immediately returned a happy gesture and placed his hand on Paw Chamdee's shoulder, and the two men exchanged more cheers and smiles. Later, E-Paw told us that he wasn't surprised at all to find Paw Chamdee working with the camp's counselors. After all, he was a high-ranking official among his comrades back in Laos.

Paw Chamdee took out a pen and jotted down our names and birthdates. "I'm going to be here, but make sure your family is here early tomorrow for the rations," Paw Chamdee said, looking at us still with a genuine smile on his face.

"*Err . . . err.*" E-Paw nodded to Paw Chamdee, as he made his way out from the pavilion under the tin cover.

We quickly grabbed our belongings and followed E-Paw toward

the flat strip of bamboo huts. He took a sandy clay path into the dingy alleys filled with the foul odors of the sewer and feces. In the narrow alley entire families huddled together cramped in a thatched bamboo hut. Their eyes gazed upon us like cats in the dark. They were faces of children who seemed to have lost their youthfulness and adults with eyes sunken in despair.

Continuing along the alley, it led us to a crossroad and the barbed-wire fence that encompassed the Or-Sor's barracks in the middle of the camp. Another string of huts along the dirt trail faced the Or-Sor's barracks. At the corner of the road, we came to a hut with two warm faces and the wide smiles of an older woman and man staring out the entrance. Their faces were small and round, and the grays in their hair were a bit more pronounced than E-Paw's. The woman wore a decorative silky brown sarong and short-sleeved shirt, and the man was in his shorts and a pair of flimsy brown sandals.

"*Sa bai dee*. Come in, come in," the happy pair said in sync. They grabbed our hands, touched our shoulders, and helped us into their thatched bamboo hut made of bamboo floors and a grass roof strung together with rusty tin panels.

"*Sa bai dee*, Mae Sei, *Sa bai dee*, Paw Boa," E-Mae and E-Paw greeted them.

We didn't know who they were until the moment their names were mentioned. Paw Boa and Mae Sei were Kubar Somdee's aunt and uncle, and they had always considered us family. Kubar Somdee spoke of them while visiting us in Banh Nong Mek.

"Kubar Somdee said that you were on your way, and we have been waiting for you," Paw Boa said.

"Yes, he told me that you have been living here for a few years now." E-Paw paused and motioned us to take off our dirty sandals.

But before the words escaped E-Paw's mouth, Mae Sei pulled us over and we settled on the bamboo floor slightly raised from the ground. She handed us each a cup of water. "Here *E-Laa, Buc Laa,* you must be exhausted," she said.

"Err, Err." We all nodded together in shyness and confusion.

She gave us kids a gentle touch on our shoulders and then turned to E-Mae. "E-Saan, what happened?" Mae Sei said to E-Mae with a gentle smile on her face.

"We spent three years living in Banh Nong Mek, and it was difficult for us to get ahead. And the children . . . they couldn't attend the Thai school out there. Then they told us to leave the land," E-Mae said.

As the adults gathered, their voices drifted to the far corner of the hut. Nok, Thurng, and I sat in silence by the entrance— exhausted and disconnected from the world around us. The crowded atmosphere was as dirty as it was depressing. We watched men and women draw water from a well to bathe their children next to green puddles of sitting water. Then a woman came running to the public well, claiming that she had stepped on a piece of poop left at the base of the small mountain of dirt.

In our silence, Nok and I tossed each other a confused look about what we had seen.

Then we took our drinks from Mae Sei and remained speechless with no sense of enthusiasm for the camp. I didn't realize it at that moment, staring at our countrymen and the confinement before us and coming to accept our fate, that this would change us for a lifetime.

That night friends of the family crowded in Mae Sei's hut. There were some warm faces that I recognized; most of them came from the village of Banh Dong. Some of E-Paw's comrades who had visited us at the Sirindhorn Reservoir were there. Uncle Taa, E-Mae's cousin who Grandpa La had raised alongside E-Mae until they moved to Laos, was there with his wife, Aunt Tee, who also was Paw Chamdee's sister-in-law. It was said that Uncle Taa's parents died young, so Grandpa La was happy to take in his nephew as his own.

"Chamdee told us that you entered the camp today," he said, standing there with his cheerful, yet reserved smile and fine black hair neatly combed from one side to the other.

"*Err . . . err . . .* " E-Mae gave him her friendliest smile in return.

"I didn't think you were going to join us," Aunt Tee added with a grateful look in her warm brown eyes and black hair hung over her shoulders tucked in a bun.

"We escaped at night. We walked from Banh Hai and followed a trail to Hin Soung; at the high rocks we made our own path through the thickets. When we got close to the border, we didn't know if Thai soldiers or the Lao Dang were waiting for us. We were blessed that the Lao Dang didn't catch up with us. We went to Banh Honghee and stayed with E-Tai for a year. Then the local Thai government warned us of our fate—they told us to leave the land if we didn't have the proper paperwork. If we didn't die that day we ran away from home, then we'll live," Uncle Taa said, looking at E-Paw. We later found out that Uncle Taa and his family of seven lived on the other side of the Or-Sor's encampment.

Cousin Gun and his friendly reserved sister, Cousin Bee, were there too. They were happy to see us. Cousin Gun gave us a huge smile with fine black hair slightly receding away from his glowing round face. He was still a jokester, singing Thai music, and making sexual innuendoes to women who would just laugh along with his silliness. He told us that he had escaped from Laos in his military uniform and was arrested by the Thai soldiers when he crossed the border. But he was released from the Thai prison by the end of 1975, shortly after the communists took over Laos.

In his own mix of humorous sarcasm, he said, "The communists made people run scared for their lives. In killing you, they'd rather cut your throat than waste their bullets."

Then there were E-Paw and E-Mae's lifelong friends, Paw Seel and Mae Seel. It appeared that our families were inseparable. E-Paw told me that he had been friends with Paw Seel since they were young. Paw Seel would often walk from Banh Bok to visit Uncle Wan and Grandpa Oosu. But E-Paw and Paw Seel quickly bonded into a lifelong *Seel* friendship, where two children are said to be bounded for life by a religious and spiritual ritual. Since then, we kids respected them like our own parents, and we had always called them Mae Seel and Paw Seel.

"You're not dead yet, huh?" asked Mae Seel with a bright cheery smile under her dark curly hair.

"Good fate and fortune would have it—we get to see each other again," E-Mae said with great joy.

The garrulous group chattered with flat and nasally loud tones in their voices distinctive of the Village of Banh Dong. They reminisced about the old times and spoke of the demoralizing acts of the Lao Dang and how some of their fallen comrades had been taken to the Seminar Camp for re-education, some had died from hard labor, and others had been executed for their association with the westerners.

"Did you hear about the monks that were accused of helping the *Lao Khao Patigan*? They tortured the five monks in Banh Jik to death. They made them dig their own grave, roped them together, shoved them in, and buried them alive."

"You could even hear their pleas and their last gasps for air when the *Lao Dang* threw dirt on them and beat them with their shovel," someone said from the far end of the corner of the bamboo thatched hut.

"And what about the old couple from Banh Usoo? Their daughter was walking behind them, and she stepped on a bomb. Her limbs were blown out from under her, and she died almost immediately. The couple screamed as they ran to her. She was their only child. The group urged them to move forward, but they didn't want to leave the dead girl."

"During our escape through the mountain and the jungle, E-Laa, my youngest, got her legs stuck in between the roots of a tree. We pulled her out and did everything to keep her from crying, but she didn't stop. We were afraid that the *Lao Dang* would hear us. We almost died that day," said Mae Seel.

"I've been in the camp for almost a year now. I was waiting for my brother. He escaped with seven others. The *Lao Dang* caught up to them and killed five of his friends. He was lucky that evening— he had nowhere to run, and he had taken a bullet in his leg. He crawled and hid in a dark bush. If they had dogs to sniff him out, he was done," said the sunken man still concerned for his maimed brother.

Then the long dark-haired woman with chapped lips and a gap tooth recounted her story: "During the previous year, we were living with our Thai relative in Banh Doo. Then one day the official came and told us to leave. So, we moved here to Camp Ubon. After we crossed the mountain, we thought we could take shelter with the Thai villagers. We never thought to go to America. We hoped that one day we could go back home and live with a sense of freedom. Before we thought of escaping Laos, we waited month after month, and year after year, then the communist officials started claiming our property and land. We didn't have the proper documents to prove that it was ours for generations. So, they took all our land. They told us without any paperwork, there was no point contesting them. It was then we feared for our lives and escaped with everything we could carry over the dark mountain that night. Now we aren't sure of returning since we don't know if there'll be a home to go back to."

I fought to keep my eyes open as I listened to the rising tempo of excited voices and random laughing that was common during those gatherings. I cringed at my own frightening images from the disturbing accounts that kept drifting into my ears. I listened to the stories while lying next to Nok and Thurng on the *sard* mat, as my mind sank to the drowning stories and the reality of Camp Ubon. As I faded out into the darkness, I wished for the sounds of waves crashing on the shores, with chickens and ducks quacking and birds chirping in the woods behind our hut, and the comforting cool breeze of the Sirindhorn Reservoir.

13

LIFE IN THE CAMP

The next morning, I woke up to shafts of sunlight on my face, and the Thai national anthem blaring on the loudspeaker. I had heard the national anthem broadcast before on our little prized possession, the brown leather-cased radio. The national anthem was highly regarded by the Thais and even the Laotians had a similar version of their own. E-Paw said that it was the way of respecting the kings and the land that we were living in. It was more than just the national anthem, somehow it was the law that people had to respect by standing in silence during the broadcast.

"You have to respect the image of the king. It's dangerous to burn a flag or step on money, each *Baht* and *Satang* has the image of the king. You can go to jail if someone sees you stepping on it," E-Paw reminded us.

Heeding E-Paw's warning, each day we got caught out and about, we stopped with our little bodies stiff and our hands flushed against our thighs, standing in respect of the national anthem blaring on the loudspeaker twice a day, once during the morning and another before sunset when they hoisted the Thai flag. But the national anthem wasn't the only thing that was played on the loudspeaker; there were announcements made in Vietnamese and Cambodian, and sometimes English or French. We often broke into senseless laughter, especially when we first heard the sharp pronunciations of the "Sh, Ch, S, and Z's." To my childish ears the foreign words became a part of our childish amusement, because they sounded like someone peeing. To Nok it sounded like a snake hissing, but to Thurng and I the sound reminded us of peeing. *Shu Shee* repeated. But the slight sign of caution coming from E-Paw's eyes was enough to remind us that we ought to keep out thoughts to ourselves.

"No matter how funny or depressing the situation, we shouldn't make humor out of it. We must find goodness in it. If we bring bad thoughts to our head then it will lead to our hearts, and we'll never be at peace with ourselves," he said.

Soon after a breakfast of sweet rice and a few hard-boiled eggs minced together with a few droplets of fish sauce, E-Paw took us to see the camp's advisors. He hurried us along the same beaten path that we had taken the day before, and we found ourselves by the main entrance once again. E-Paw was worried that we wouldn't make it on time for the day's early rations and other governmental aids. He was still the overly suspicious man who sometimes made me paranoid.

"Be on your guard—we're surrounded by many people, friends and strangers collectively," he said. "Don't trust anyone. You must look out for each other and yourselves." He wanted to sink deep in our minds that in the world of desperate human beings, they fought, they cheated, and they stole.

Even if the situation looked overwhelming, I felt safe under the protection of E-Paw, who was still fighting to get us a little more in life, even along the dingy strung huts and beaten alleys. At that moment, as he stood waiting for our turn with the camp counselor, we could see that in his brown eyes he was planning his next move.

Inside the building we met the counselor who was scribbling in his notebook as the fan blew gently at his pile of paperwork on the table. There were many people inside and outside the crowded building in the heat. Outside the cover, men were chattering along the wooden rails and others were smoking. Many of them meandered along with a soft smile and sunken eyes just like E-Paw and E-Mae, avoiding the heat of the midday sun.

Across the street there was another commotion taking place. A crowd formed on the dirt road in front of the food storage warehouse. Under the hot sun, men and women stood in lines hovering over a huge pile of brown rice bags laid on the ground. There were rations in barrels, bags, buckets, and metal canisters. E-Paw told us that the supplies came from the United Nations. Not too far from the tall and sappy *Hung* tree, children were playing with marbles in the dirt and sand. Suddenly, a rickshaw with a man on a bike went whizzing by with squeaky wheels, carrying food and passengers. The three-wheeled bike zipped in and out by the entrance where Thai vendors stood with their woven bamboo baskets of vegetables and fruits.

Thurng was standing next to me, his ever-wandering eyes now fixed with a child's glee, watching the amusement of other children playing on the hard dirt. Before us a group of kids appearing to be no older than us knelt on the ground, shooting marbles with their fingers and aiming at their opponents' marbles. Some waited patiently in line, and one by one they would pitch their coins into holes in the ground the size of a coin no bigger than a golf ball. Other children were making shapes and drawing lines with sticks in the sand.

"*Pai, Pai!* We have to register with our group leader, over there." E-Paw guided us farther along the road, leading to the entrance to a second layer of fence that circled the Or-Sor's camp.

We came to a halt and stood in another line with people. We exchanged looks; E-Paw and E-Mae smiled in the friendliest way, eagerly waiting to have words with them. Then the men behind the small wooden table took E-Paw's information and handed him some papers to read. We learned that the huts were in groups. Several families residing in our group were people from the village of Banh Dong, and E-Paw wanted to be a part of the group. We also learned that the Or-Sor soldiers oversaw the refugee camp, and the men at the registration table were there to help keep order and assist us.

When the registration was over, E-Paw took us across the street to get our handouts. He handed the paperwork he'd received at the front desk to the leader of group 116. The leader of the team and his men stood guarding the bags of rice piled on the dirt road about twenty paces from the open warehouse. Some of the men were short and had straight jet-black hair with tattoos of ancient symbols with dark ink written in cryptic Pali language like E-Paw scattered from their upper arms to wrists.

The short little man with straight black hair and a round face gave us our once-a-month allotment, consisting of sticky rice, fish sauce, corn oil, salt, pepper, a small bag of charcoal, and five small mackerel fishes we called *Pa Tu* for our perishable weekly rations. E-Paw took the needed charities that was intended to sustain us daily with warm gratitude. He told us that everyone in the camp had a number and group leader. The group leaders determined how the rations were to be divided based on the number of people in each family. The leader also told E-Paw that trucks of rations also dropped off food to groups of refugees who resided farther within the perimeter of the camp. So, we needed to follow our group for rations once we settled in a hut.

After our food was given to us, we returned home and had to cook our fish, since we didn't have a refrigerator or electricity. We helped E-Mae start the fire with the small clumps of charcoal in the backyard of Mae Sei's hut. Then we grilled the five *Pa Tu* mackerels on an open fire with thick smoke filling up a small area behind the grass-roof hut. The uncontrolled flame of E-Mae's fire would leave an uneven texture on the rationed fish, burning its fins and scales almost charcoal black. Worse, swarms of flies would blanket our food; they were as hungry as we were, even daring enough to quickly land on my hand for an invisible morsel. The food rations held our hunger at bay, and we didn't have anything left to spoil since there was hardly anything left by the next handout.

E-Mae quickly learned to salvage our rations whenever she could, stretching them into many savory meals for us with vegetables she was able to pick at the community garden. She jumped at the opportunity to join the women who worked diligently on the small plot of land next to the Or-Sor's fence.

"We can use all the bits of the vegetables for a meal," she preached to us while grinding up the vegetables in a mortar and pestle and tossing in her salt, creating a spicy porridge and dip that complimented our sticky rice. E-Mae's warm mushy meals with a few drops of fish sauce were indelibly delicious. That day we ate her concoction with the gluttonous sticky rice that filled my stomach like a rock, giving me the urge to pass out. Then I slipped away for an afternoon nap, dreaming about the sweet rice with hot grilled fish that complimented a dish of hot spicy papaya salad.

While staying with Mae Sei and Paw Boa, E-Paw heard that their neighbor was moving to America. The Laos family got sponsored by a church organization of *Pra Yay Su* (Jesus Christ). Since E-Paw wanted to live near the people we knew, he bought their hut for an amount of money kept within the adults' hushed agreement. We would also be three huts down from Cousin Gun, and we'd be next to our old neighbors from Banh Dong and friends, since many of them settled in the string of huts next to our new home.

The hut was a small dinky place, a third of the size of Mae Sei's hut. It was barely enough to stack fifteen people elbow to elbow. But it was the end unit of the string of huts, which had room for us to add on to the ten-foot backyard at the bottom of the mound and an open space to our left. It had the number 16 on its entrance, and it was a part of the group 116, so our address was 16 by 116. E-Paw was thrilled to be surrounded by the same neighbors from the village of Banh Dong, although we also had neighbors from Cambodia, China, and Vietnam.

By the end of the first week, we forgot the misery and smell of feces (sometimes rolling down our oversized dirt hill) and open sewers as we acclimated to our new home and naturally rejoiced in other children's playfulness and laughter. The neighborhood was also full of children who were left to the care of their older siblings. When E-Paw and E-Mae were gone looking for more food, Nok oversaw us. Nok was now eleven years old and was attaching herself to some of the neighborhood girls who were older than her.

Even though Nok was in charge, Thurng and I were free to our own entertainment. Sometimes we got lost in our own adventures, which led E-Paw to yelling and pinching our ears, because of his belief in the *Ga-Taar* (spiritual relic). The *Ga-Taar* can only be bestowed on the believers with a *strict discipline* they called the *Ka Lum*. Kubar Somdee had told him that if he believed in accepting his *Ka Lum* discipline, then slapping a child might cause the child to die.

There were many kids around our hut, and making friends was something E-Paw had always been preaching to us, so we took it to heart. Nok befriended Bai, a long-haired petite Laos girl who lived next door to us. Bai and some of her girlfriends were a few years older than Nok. I was worried about Nok, because a few times I had caught Bai coming out of the public bathroom with a huge smile on her face and a trail of smoke behind her. After my encounter with Bai, I told Nok that I was keeping an eye on her, and I'd rat on her if she was smoking with the other girls.

"You stay out of trouble yourself!" Nok pointed her little fingers at me one day. Then she gave me that impish smirk on her face. After that incident I'd never caught her or Bai in the act. I had also taken on my own troubles with Thurng and forgot that the girls were good at keeping their clever secrets hushed.

In the meantime, I discovered that Camp Ubon wasn't a complete prison confinement, and not all refugees within the camp were poor. Some were operating a little store right out of their bamboo huts like Paw Seel and Mae Seel. Some ran rickshaws, sold food and goods at the refugee open air market, or offered services such as haircuts and tailoring clothes.

Soon Thurng and I began playing with Nhe from Cambodia and Lyn from China. They were our neighbors; Lyn lived a few huts down to our right near the Or-Sor's camp, and Nhe's hut was directly across from us. Nhe, Lyn, Thurng, and I played in the little hill behind our hut, sometimes stepping on unsuspecting pieces of semi-dry turds that someone had left overnight by the dark green *Pern* bush that we played in. Although neither Nhe's nor Lyn's family originated in Laos, I was impressed by their fluency in Laotian.

"There are refugees from Vietnam, Cambodia, and China living in the camp," E-Mae told us. "It's the disposition of life. Like us they were children of the stars, and now they're displaced, and on the whim of chance, they're waiting for the help of miracle hands just like we are."

It didn't matter where they came from to me, since our childish games were simple hide-and-seek and games we mutually made up. We nodded, gestured our fingers, and played with each other, especially by the sandbox in front of Nhe's hut across the alley from ours. But we had the most fun during a little game we called "Playhouse." It was simply us kids throwing an old blanket over the little bush behind our hut and then crawling underneath it. For days we played inside our little playhouse, and when we got bored, we snuck through the barb-wired fence of the Or-Sor's camp and played inside the paved black road that ran along their barracks to the housing offices where E-Paw had registered us. E-Paw said that paved road was once an airplane tarmac.

On some occasions when we'd play near the fences by the tarmac, grasshoppers would land nearby in the sweltering heat before us. Like little kittens, we quickly observed their exact location and then began our childish chase of the fleeing critters. On the rare times when Thurng and I would catch one or two, we'd bring them home and roast them on a bamboo stick over E-Mae's charcoal fire. The crunchy and tasty morsels were split three ways with Nok and Thurng. Then we would pay a price for such delicacy, for eating grasshoppers sometimes came with an allergy that left us with itchy bumps along our lower belly, ribs, and back.

Since we had met Nhe and Lyn, we had been good playmates and became good friends for many dried months. As a matter a fact, Nhe and I were still playing in the sandbox in front of his hut when his father carried him away. His hands were still full of sand, clutching onto it like any child who wasn't quite done with the playground. He was held by the waist and put into a military truck full of men, women, and children parked by the entrance of our alley. I stood there watching Nhe, shocked to see that he was still crying when the truck pulled away. It was the last time I ever saw him.

After the truck disappeared beyond the string of huts in our alley, I ran home to E-Mae who was sitting there watching us play in the soft sand.

"E-Mae why did they take Nhe?" I asked.

"They wanted him to be with his people, and they are going to another camp only for the *Kahmaen* (the Cambodians)," E-Mae said.

A few months after Nhe was yanked from our little playground, Lyn, Thurng, and I heard a thunderous sound as a helicopter landed next to the Or-Sor's barracks just outside the camp, not too far from us. We yelled out to each other, threw on our flimsy sandals, and scrambled down to the barb-wired fence to get a glimpse of it. When we finally got to the fence, there were other kids and adults standing along the fence watching it land. It was a dark green military helicopter, like we had seen flying over our heads before when we were in Banh Nong Mek.

We could feel the wind and the thud of the helicopter as it had landed on the big white cross that had been painted on the ground. The propellers were still spinning as three military men stepped out, and one of them was still wearing his helmet. Thurng was so excited that he kept on inching closer and closer to the fence. When the dust settled and many of the spectators had left, Thurng was still standing with his little hands hanging onto the rusty wire.

"I wish I could get a ride on the helicopter," Thurng said.

"You see how much dirt it was picking up, and you can get your head chopped off by those propellers if you get close to it," I said, trying to instill some fear in him.

"Err . . . I still want to ride it," Thurng said as we raced each other home with Lyn trailing behind us.

A few days after we saw the helicopter land, the Or-Sors were having their training in their camp right behind Lyn's hut. A group of soldiers had staged what seemed to be an all-out training. From the base of our dirt mound, we were being entertained right over the fences of the Or-Sor's encampment. Along their paved road, dark green military trucks were parked facing the opposing team. Each team member flanked each other in their own group as they moved along the vehicles.

Then out from nowhere we heard a big boom. There were sparks from smoke canisters tossed on the grass of the Or-Sor's camp. Above and before us, clouds of white and pink smoke blanketed the green field next to the blacktop running through the military encampment. From behind their camouflage army trucks, two teams came together, and they started firing blanks at each other. They all had their M-16s, and when they got hit, they would fall to the ground. Some would even play dead as their opponents poked their bodies, picking at them to see if they were alive. It was the first time that we had ever seen an explosive live display that shook the ground under our brown sandals. The excitement made Thurng want to crawl through the fence that he was hanging onto with his little hands between the spikes. I was thrilled to see the entire action taking place right before our eyes, and for a moment I was beginning to forget about our former life living gloriously by our beach at the Sirindhorn Reservoir.

After we had settled in our new home and acclimated with our neighbors, a fire broke out on the other side of the Or-Sor's encampment. In the middle of a hot afternoon, shrouds of brooding dark smoke bellowed over the whirling orange flames and the fences, adding to the hot and hazy air. Just around the bend from the open-air market there was a fire. We stood there before the barbed-wired fence watching from a distance with E-Paw and the other adults.

Horror could be felt that day as people scrambled to put out the fire that was consuming the very little they had left. They were trying to get each other out. The young and old dragged their elderly and disabled away from the fire. Some people were screaming in fear. Others ran with buckets of water, some ripping off grass roofs to keep the fire from jumping onto the roofs of the next alley of huts. Their faint cries of loss, fear, and despair lingered on the horizon over the thick smoke below.

"Go gather our documents and belongings." E-Paw gave us that same look the night we ran from Banh Dong, the grave direct stare with his vigilant brown eyes.

"*Err, err,*" we said along with E-Mae who happened to be on the same wavelength as E-Paw.

But before we sprung our little legs to E-Paw's instructions, we halted at the sound of Paw Bai's chuckle. He was literally laughing at both E-Paw and E-Mae while pointing at the smoky air that hadn't gotten to us yet.

"Buc La, it's so far away. Besides, if you already escaped the communists, this fire is not going to kill you." Paw Bai tossed another laugh at E-Paw.

We stopped and didn't move from our spot, helplessly watching the fire while it ravaged and wreaked havoc on our fellow refugees. It was here that I realized that each of us has our own fleeting moments of life and death. For me, that moment sank deeper in my ever-developing child's mind. It was seeing those who had very little hope fighting to hang on to life. I understood that if it wasn't my hut that got burnt to ashes, I could only have sorrow in the rubble I saw with my eyes, but not the actual grief of the poor losing everything to a fire.

Paw Bai was right, the dark smoke and orange flames never reached our grass roof that day. At supper that evening, the five of us gathered over E-Mae's simple meal of sticky rice, fish porridge, and steamed garden vegetables. We said very little to one another; E-Paw was the only one talking.

"You kids keep away from that charred area of the camp. Officials will comb through the remains. We don't know if anyone lost their life. If they did, they're no longer suffering in their sins. Let their spirits rise to the heavens and be free to reincarnate."

14

A BRIEF RETURN TO PARADISE

On a bright afternoon a year after we settled in at our new address (16 by 116), Vung came strolling in to live with us, but reluctantly. He was by himself and there was no sign of Narng. When we went to greet him, Vung had very little excitement on his face. His face was dark tan, sun-dried, and weathered. His hair was still parted in the middle and his hands looked rough. There were gradual signs of wrinkles in his soft smile that resembled E-Paw's. He wore dark blue jeans with a black comb stuck in the back pocket and a flannel shirt with the sleeves rolled up to his elbows.

"Narng didn't come with you?" E-Mae asked anxiously before Vung could reach in his pocket to pull out some candies for us.

"No, I was in Phibun working at the brick factory, and Narng is still in Banh Honghee. I saw her a few weeks back, and she said that she'll be joining us soon after the rice harvest," Vung said calmly. Then he pulled the candies out from his pocket and handed them over to Nok and I, which we excitedly accepted. We could see that he was tired and ready for a nap after his trip. But before he lay down to rest, E-Mae had already prepared lunch on the reed mat. We formed a circle around the two bowls of *Pbon pa*, a mush and water mixture of boiled fish, salt, hot pepper, and anchovies. Scattered around the *Pbon pa* were Thai eggplants, red chili peppers, and blanched morning glory picked from the refugee garden. This meal was something that we had been sharing since we were little. E-Mae was still the food fanatic when it came to feeding our family.

We kids and E-Paw were content to be sitting next to Vung for another family meal. E-Mae was straight forward, staring quietly at Vung, then she said, "Keeping you and Narng together is like trying to put little frogs in a bowl. While we cover you kids with one hand, one would jump out, and with the other hand, we try to put you back in so we can stay together."

"*Err . . . Err*, we stay together," Vung glanced at E-Mae with his usual soft warm smile of reassurance.

For the next few days, Vung took a tour of the camp, met up with Cousin Gun, and they went to the marketplace and saw a scarce mix of Thai and Laos food. He saw a movie at the theater by the camp's entrance, he sat on the bamboo benches of the English school, he walked by the medical clinic in front of Paw Seel and Mae Seel's hut, and at the open-air market he saw condiments, candies, and rice shops erected inside people's huts that were facing the road.

"There's no work and no chance of a better life here in this death trap," he'd expressed to E-Paw after his disheartened course about the camp that left him bewildered.

"I know, but I'm planning to take us all to America and start a new life. They say it's like heaven over there. It's far more than what we could ever imagine," E-Paw pleaded.

"I can get work out in Phibun and Udorn and make some money," Vung argued.

"You can, but the *Or-Sors* are tightening the confinement, and getting in and out of the camp is going to be tougher. I'm going to put in an application to get someone to sponsor us to America. Buc Gun is already eligible since he has been living in the camp for a year. So his sponsorship to America can happen at any moment. We don't have a choice; other villagers like Uncle Taa, Paw Chamdee, and Paw Bai are applying for sponsorship." E-Paw's persuasion then turned to a father's urge to save a son.

"How do we know if we can ever come back to our home once we go to America? What if we can get our land back?" Vung asked.

"There's no talk of that right now. Although there are people I know who are returning home like Paw Boa and Mae Sei, who are old and have no desire to go to America." E-Paw put a cigarette in his mouth took a short draw and let out a puff in the semi-lit hut.

"And you know it would be very difficult for me to return. Kubar Somdee and I have enemies. Besides that, the Thai government wants to shut down all the refugee camps in their country. They want us to decide soon whether we're going to another country or returning to the communists."

"*Err*, include me in the sponsorship *Tor Mor* application," Vung disappointedly agreed with E-Paw.

A week after Vung joined us at the camp, E-Paw decided that we should return to the Sirindhorn Reservoir one more time. He said that we could fish, hunt, and gather fruits and vegetables, and retrieve anything that we could bring back to the camp with us. E-Mae and Thurng were to stay with our belongings at the camp.

"E-Paw didn't want everyone to go. He didn't want any trouble with the *Or-Sor*," Nok said to me as she packed our flimsy bags for carrying goods when we returned to the camp.

"We'll tell them that we're going out to the big market, and we'll return soon. They'll grant us the permission," E-Paw told us that night.

So the next morning, E-Paw told the Or-Sors that we were going to the big market and we got permission to leave the camp. We took the bus to the Sirindhorn Reservoir. The bus ride took us across the Nam Mun River once again. It stopped at the Phibun market for gas, and this time I wasn't so frightened by the men running rickshaws and peddling their passengers along the alleys, or the lorries racing tightly along the busy streets. But I was still intoxicated by the diesel that was pumping out from the bus.

When the bus took us through the open farmland, seeing the blue sky and the pools of water along the verdant rice farms refreshed my soul with a sense of peace. It was something that I now missed dearly. The gray mountain out in the distance and the fields of treetops in the middle of the familiar submerged valley made my heart beat faster as we drew closer and closer to the lake.

When we arrived at the Sirindhorn Reservoir, Nok and I ran to our little beach, and I let the soft breeze cool my face. The water was inviting and calm with glittering sparkles from the hot sun. Shortly after, Uncle Lun and Brother Dang came by to see us. They missed us and asked us about the camp, living in its confinement, and where we would move to next. E-Paw told them that there was very little hope for us, and we were running out of places to run, except for America.

The notion of going to America left a cringe on Uncle Lun's face, and Brother Dang sympathized with us. They wanted us to move back to their vacant farm, but they understood our situation. Uncle Lun was saddened that no one was living in our old hut. He said that he was not so sure that the next resident of the hut would be as grateful as we had been to him.

As Brother Dang and E-Paw conversed, we stared at the vacant hut, saddened by the notion that it sat empty before the water and lush field. It seemed not long ago that a mist of morning fog could be seen and the sound of the waves could be heard through its open windows.

"Nok, I miss our old hut. Do you think that we can come to live here again?" I asked.

"This was never our hut," Nok said with disappointment.

After we climbed the familiar steps and dropped off our bags inside the empty hut, we ran after Vung to the water and allowed the cool and gentle surge of water sooth our feet. I splashed and Nok let out a big smile as we watched Vung swim toward the barkless tree. We rinsed our bodies with the water and lay on the little beach for hours, before we pulled out our nets to catch some fish and grass shrimps for dinner.

The next day E-Paw and Vung went to do more fishing. But after they were done, we had a craving for something sour and spicy. Vung was our leader as we headed into the woods behind our hut toward the old wild mango tree with dangling green fruits no bigger than the size of my fist. It was a mango we called *Gaa Sor*, a type of mango that grew wild with a stronger scent of mango than any other mango I had ever eaten. Unripe, it made a perfect treat for our sour and hot spicy craving. But when the mango ripened, it was so sweet that I used to eat it with sticky rice. Sometimes I would suck out the meat of the ripened mango with the pit and the skin of the fruit still intact.

Each day at the Sirindhorn Reservoir, we'd put in our best effort to wake up early so we could take advantage of the day's gathering and fishing. E-Paw and Nok gathered fruits and vegetables to dry, and I ran behind Vung into the woods behind our hut for the very last time with a bucket in my hand. Vung climbed the trees and tossed the mangos down to me. The green mangos were still young and sticky, especially where Vung had broken them off from their hanging vines. We filled our little plastic bucket and headed home to make our thick, hot, spicy anchovy sauce. We rinsed off the sappy mangoes with the bucket of well water that Vung had hoisted up for us. And shortly after we cut the small mangos into thin slices perfect for dipping in the sauce. We filled our stomachs with the hot, sour, and salty concoction and then we all paid for it the next day.

"It was so good that I almost died eating it," Nok said the following morning.

"*Err, err,* it was worth it, and I want to eat some more," I agreed with Nok.

On our final day at the Sirindhorn Reservoir, we gathered all the paraphernalia that we had left behind. They were small items such as string, wood spoons, bamboo skewers sticks, dried mango, dried bitter *Ga-Dao* leaves, and even the batch of dried minnows that we had caught and left out in the sun when we first arrived.

Before vacating the hut for good, we said our goodbye to Uncle Lun and Brother Dang and his family for the last time. They were sad that our stay was short. But Brother Dang said that we were always welcome in his home. We nodded our heads, wished them farewell, and thanked them for their hospitality. Then with our bags full of goods, we headed toward the path that ran along the mouth of the river and woods toward the temple and the bus stop.

As we passed through the temple, we went to say our farewell to Kubar Peng one more time. He was now a monk with the *Kubar* title, who had settled into the monastery and had no plan of renouncing his practice at the temple. He wished us good luck and good fortune and I never again saw the cousin who helped carry me over the mountain.

At the bus stop in front of the temple ground, we grabbed our load of goods and settled into our seats on the metal bench of an oversized cab of a pickup truck with other passengers. Nok and I were flushed against each other with our backs against the open window, while E-Paw and Vung were closer to the tailgate. I leaned against the open window where the exhaust of diesel fume began to crawl up my nose. As the humming truck took off, Nok and I searched for Buc Ang along Ku Mai's land, but he was nowhere in sight. We looked at each other, kept our memories of him in silence, then watched the view outside the truck as it started to make its way toward Phibun, and the linear images before me slid by with blurring huts with tin roofs sitting on wooden stilts with banana, coconut, and palm trees in collective green fragmented memories of the village of Nong Mek.

The truck stopped at Phibun and we hopped out with the other passengers. Nearby we walked through a crowd of vendors and people who filled the open market. Assortments of clothing hung along our path with plastic toys, colorful candies, meats, and a countless variety of vegetables and fruits. E-Paw quickly found a vender and ordered lunch; the scent and taste of larb chicken with warm sticky rice filled my nostrils and belly to a satisfaction that seemed to have lingered a lifetime. The chopped savory chicken with spicy pepper and herbs hit me quickly, relieving my hunger.

No more than three hours later, we were half-excited to find ourselves at the guard post at Camp Ubon. We stood in silence while we watched the Or-Sors flip through our carry-on; they saw our bags of dried vegetables and minnows. They gave us a sympathetic stare and let us through without any problem.

E-Paw and Vung nodded their appreciation to the Or-Sors, as Nok and I stared at the bustling life of food rationing, with people who appeared to have been there before we left, patiently waiting in lines with their buckets and bags. We quickly gathered our goods, then walked past the main entrance paying little attention to the commotion. When we arrived at our hut, E-Mae stood with a gentle welcoming smile upon seeing our faces. Thurng ran to E-Paw, who quickly threw the anxious child onto his shoulders, then happily held out candies from his pocket. Then he gave Thurng a toy that he had bought from Phibun's open-air market. It was a little plastic monkey affixed to a drum with a set of sticks that were fastened to a little rubber hose, so whenever Thurng would press the rubber pump, the little monkey would beat his drum, which lit up the ever-so-excited child's eyes.

Vung opened the bags of food that made E-Mae smile with great excitement. There wasn't anything that made her livelier than her bitter roots and vegetables, even the ones that were as dried as cigar leaves. E-Mae took everything and spread it out and about on our bamboo floor. Later that day, she went around handing the little bundle of gifts to Mae Seel, Uncle Taa, Mae Sei, Mae Kem, and Paw Bai.

"That's how our people used to be; we'd share just about every-thing with each other," she said with zest.

Soon after our return from the Sirindhorn Reservoir, Narng came to live with us. She found her way to the alley leading to our huts. She was lugging her bags, which dangled off her shoulders to her hands. She was wearing a bright blue shirt, white pair of jeans, and dark sandals.

"It's E-Narng!" E-Mae called out catching our attention.

"Narng! Narng! Narng!" we kids yelled out as we ran over to her.

"E-Mae! And you kids, what are you kids doing?" Narng gave us a wide bright smile, as she reached in her pocket and pulled out candies for us. Then she gave Thurng and I a pat on our shoulders. "Buc Thurng, you're getting big!" She picked up Thurng and squeezed him tightly in her arms.

That evening, we learned that Narng had been working at Aunt

Tai's store, and during the wet season, she worked in the rice farm in Banh Honghee. She spent days in the mud helping to grow and harvest rice with Aunt Tai. Her skin was still white, and her dark eyebrows still arched like a rainbow. Her straight fine hair was cut into the shape of a round bowl.

Narng was excited to see us, but her heart was now in Banh Honghee. She told us that she had met a friendly Thai man she called Ai Vin. When she went to live with Aunt Tai, he was still a young monk at the village's temple. After he rescinded his monk-hood from the monastery a year later, he would visit Aunt Tai's little shop where Narng worked.

"He'd stop by frequently at the store just to say hi. So I got yelled at a lot by Aunt Tai. And I told him to go away but he just didn't listen," Narng said.

Narng lived with us for a month, and then we were visited by Ai Vin and his father.

"Come on . . ." The Thai man with a cheerful smile pleaded with E-Paw, pressing his case to give Narng's hand to his son in marriage. "Come on, they love each other. My son can't go on without your daughter. We can be in-laws."

"We are leaving to America," E-Paw said. It was the first time E-Paw and the family met our to-be brother-in-law.

"She's still young."

"I know, I know." The man who was at the same place in stature as E-Paw continued to plead for his son.

"I don't want her to be caught up with this circumstance of a refugee," E-Paw said humbly and gently as a good host.

"Paw, we'll take care of her and make her legal," Ai Vin added with his hands together in a *wai* (prayer) for E-Paw.

"We're going to America," E-Mae added to E-Paw's thoughts with a smile. "I don't want her to be stuck on her own."

While E-Paw and E-Mae held their stance on the marriage,

Narng listened quietly from the corner of the dimly lit room. She put on her sincere loving smile for us, but the notion of coming with us to America was far from her heart.

E-Paw tossed a look over to Narng and saw the disappointment in her face each time he was trying to talk everyone out of the engagement. In the end, he went against his own word and told the men that he'd talk to her, and that she would have the final word.

"*Kolp Kun Kup!* (Yes, sir, thank you!)" Ai Vin already knew the answer to Narng's decision. He gave E-Paw and E-Mae another kind, loving *wai*.

After Ai Vin and his father left that evening, E-Paw and E-Mae made more attempts to show Narng the benefits of a life beyond the hopeless camp.

"Come with us, our family belongs together, you'll be lost among the Thai. Let's go together," E-Mae sobbed. But Narng just stared at E-Mae and didn't say much.

15

AMERICAN DREAMS
AND THAI SCHOOL

The next day Cousin Gun stopped by our hut with more developments about going to America.

"We should all go to America. We'll have a better opportunity and a better life there," he said, stirring up the crowd in his attempt to entice Narng to take that leap of fate with us.

But she wasn't hypnotized by what Cousin Gun had to say about America's glitter and glory. She looked over her shoulder to the bamboo thatched wall, smiled, and said nothing.

"We should go together as a family," said E-Paw.

"*Err . . . Err,*" agreed our cousins, nodding their heads, knowing that they too would be moving far away from Aunt Paa, their siblings in Laos, and Cousin Vee.

"I've already submitted my *Tor Mor* application in case they won't accept us as one big family. If I get sponsored first, I will go, and I'll see if I can get the sponsors to sponsor the rest of the family," said Cousin Gun.

"*Err,*" E-Paw agreed. "We have to leave our options open. I really want to see if we can go to *Ar-May-Lee-Gar*. If they won't sponsor us, then we will see if we can go to *Farang* or Canada."

E-Paw paused to look around the dimly lit room with all eyes staring at him. Our silence lingered—we had more fear of the unknown than curiosity about a glorious new life of paved roads, glittering lights, soft beds, and the opportunity for work.

"They say it's like heaven there in America," Cousin Gun repeated with a smirk.

"Err, it has to be better than being in this situation," E-Paw added. "I'm still waiting to hear from the letter I sent to Paw Somsee who got sponsored by a Catholic Church in California; maybe they will accept us to *Ar-May-Lee-Gar*."

At the time of this conversation, Vung and Narng agreed to be a part of the sponsorship application. E-Paw and E-Mae were sure that they would stick with the family plan, the plan that would take us all to the so-called "Land of Heaven."

A few days later, E-Paw failed to persuade Narng to go to America with us. Instead, he saw only her brooding in her silent sorrow. It was then that both E-Paw and E-Mae yielded to her wishes. E-Paw said he didn't want Narng to resent a lost love, that she was old enough to be a woman. Besides she had been on her own since fifteen.

Then he justified his reasoning further by adding, "Being poor is a life's burden, but to die without love is a sin that I couldn't bear."

We walked with Narng to the main entrance, so she could pick up her ride to Banh Honghee.

E-Mae gave Narng a blessing for her travels: "Take care of yourself and good luck and good fortune."

Then we kids saw Narng's spirit rise to a gleaming smile, as we jumped up and down, waving farewell to our sister, who was once a mother to me. On the way home, we followed E-Paw along the familiar alley.

Trying to keep us moving forward, E-Paw told us, "It's like a natural part of life; she's in love, the love that grew from her own heart." He had accepted his first casualty as a refugee: losing a daughter to the unforeseeable circumstances in a borrowed land.

When we got back to the hut, E-Mae sat in her lonely dark corner while I lay on the reed mat, counting the rays of sunshine cutting through small openings in the thin thatched bamboo walls. It would be one of the few times that I had ever seen tears streaming down E-Mae's face—this time appearing like raindrops in a sunshower.

Before the end of that hot season, E-Paw and Vung prepared to leave the camp to work at the brickyard in Phibun. But the notion that the camp was closing and the tightened confinement of being a refugee lingered in E-Paw's thoughts.

Before leaving to find work, they gathered with the villagers of Banh Dong. Going to America was the main topic of conversation within the hopeless circle. As we kids played outside, their concerns were still heard as they discussed options, and "what ifs."

"We can't go home, and I refuse to be given to a man as a concubine in a harem," said Cousin Bee with shyness in her voice and youth on her side.

Mae Kem and Mae Bout agreed, and said, "Maybe they'll be good to us and maybe they won't be, but let's go, do it until our hearts are settled, and see America. Besides, the Thai government is telling us to leave—they want their land back. Adding to the situation, we no longer have a farm, so what else is left for us?"

But there was no light of truth for Vung other than the glimpse of hope he saw in the Phibun brick factory and life at the *nah* in Banh Honghee. At that point, E-Paw suspected that Vung too had given his heart to a Thai woman in Phibun.

"You can leave the camp and work," said E-Paw. "I've applied for sponsorship to America, and within a year the family will be eligible. You are still a part of our sponsorship application."

"*Err, Err . . .* , I will be back in the camp when someone sponsors us to come to America," said Vung.

Now going to America became more than just a routine conversation within our hut. What a frightening place it must be— perhaps the people are even more cruel. How would we live with them, speak their native tongue, and stand next to them without the fear in our heart, and what if we weren't able to return to our family back in Laos? These questions were still a huge part of those debatable conversations.

Before Vung left, E-Paw told us that he wanted to see if he too could work at the brick factory with Vung to save up some more money before the monsoon season arrived. So that summer E-Paw left with Vung and Cousin Gun to Phibun.

A month later E-Paw returned without Vung. Then Kubar Somdee made a surprise visit to the camp, and our hut was enlightened again. His presence was still beyond good karma and candies for me—it was magical. The hut was filled with the scent of candles, tobacco smoke, and the whiskey-based potion of bitter roots, liz- ards, and even dried insects. Underneath the smoke, a blissful crowd of men surrounded Kubar Somdee. While E-Mae and the other women set down food and drinks, more men politely squeezed themselves through the crowd toward the center of the hut. They lowered their heads while apologizing to anyone they'd bumped into until they came to settle on the bamboo floor with crossed legs. By the entrance more visitors stood anxiously with candles and cotton strings ready to receive the *Ga-Taar*, the magic and spiritual belief from Kubar Somdee.

The magic works only when one truly believes in its true power and self-disciplines (the *Ka Lum*), which would be lifelong. The disciplines had to do with respect, from something serious as not committing adultery to something as simple as walking under a clothesline or eating ginger.

One man whispered that Kubar Somdee could disappear and shorten his distance to travel with a few prayers. Then he said that Kubar Somdee's life had been spared by his own *Tum* (spiritual belief), escaping the barrel of his assassin as he stood at the top of the staircase in his father's hut in Banh Dong.

People said that Kubar Somdee found himself face to face with a man name Van Hai, a Laos Dang member who wanted educated people like Kubar Somdee and E-Paw dead. Witnesses said that Kubar Somdee was staring down a barrel of a riffle—tap, tap, tap—as shots went off. The thud of the gun went off with nothing but smoke. After the smoke cleared, Van Hai was shocked because he did not believe in the magic and power that Kubar Somdee possessed. Van Hai was a devilish man, people would say, daring and taunting something as sacred as the harmless spirit of a Buddha monk.

E-Paw would often tell his tales about Kubar Somdee and the *Ga-Taar*, and some of them E-Paw possessed within his body. But one day E-Paw told a story of when Kubar Somdee had visited us in Banh Nong Mek. E-Paw and Brother Dang were escorting Kubar Somdee across the inlet of the Sirindhorn Reservoir next to Banh Nong Mek temple.

"It was getting dark as we returned home in our little canoe. Halfway across the water, the canoe started to leak, and I was worried about Kubar Somdee. But Kubar Somdee said, 'don't be scared.' So, when the boat finally sank and flipped over, Kubar

Somdee was gone. Brother Dang and I swam around the capsized vessel and found no sign of him. We ditched the boat and swam to the shore; then there he was, Kubar Somdee, standing by the sandy bank."

E-Paw thought for sure that wrapped in the layers of his orange robe, Kubar Somdee wouldn't be able to swim. That day, E-Paw said that it had to be magic that saved Kubar Somdee.

Although, I was too young to be receiving the *Ga-Taar* relic and practicing the *Ka Lum* discipline, it was a magical time in my life. But as I watched Kubar Somdee and E-Paw practice the magic in them, I too became a believer, and the relic of the magic was running through my veins.

On another night, during Kubar Somdee's unexpected visit to our hut, he was standing there on our beaten path with a *Jour.* The young monk was meticulously wrapped in his orange robe, with each bundle of the orange cloth neatly tucked into grooves and delicate intertwining layers, and his brown satchel hung on his shoulder. He was slightly taller than me, so I assumed that he was older by a few years. There was a glowing harmony in his smile, his eyebrows were shaved, and his smooth face looked like a white pearl under a full moon.

"*Sa bai dee Arjan, Sa bai dee Jour...*" E-Paw and E-Mae greeted with humbling *hello*, then we added our bows, lowering our heads as we followed E-Paw like a choir with the tips of our fingers in a *wai* at the sight of the monks. E-Paw would quickly usher them inside the hut, while Nok would help E-Mae prepare food. As with all of Kubar Somdee's visits, he would hand us more candies and bless our spirits and tie cotton strings on our wrist. Then Thurng and I would step outside to play while people quickly filled the hut, even spilling outside.

Later that night, the *Jour* discovered that he had relatives living on the northern side of the camp past the medical clinic. And the young monk wished that he could spend the night with his family.

"Boun," I heard Kubar Somdee calling from the crowded hut.

I went over to Kubar Somdee. I was honored by his request, and I immediately leaned forward, tilting my head with a humbling bow. Before I could say, "*Doi (your holiness)*," Kubar Somdee said, "Can you take the *Jour* to the other side of the medical clinic? He'd like to spend the night with his family."

"*Doi*." I gave him another w*ai* and waited for the *Jour* to pick up his satchel.

Before I escorted the *Jour* to his family's hut that evening, E-Paw stopped me and said, "Be careful. Don't wander off, and stay on the paved road."

I told E-Paw that I would do it. I felt a sense of strength in the *Maak Lord* that Kubar Somdee had given me for protection and bravery the last time he had visited us. E-Paw knew that Thurng and I wandered through the camp when he told us not to. And he was now letting me go in the dark—it was his way of telling me that he was confident in my ability to take care of myself. Then he touched me on my shoulder and gave me a soft and wrinkled smile, and in his eyes, I saw that he was proud of me.

About half an hour walk through the dark alleys, the playground behind the medical center, and dimly lit streets, we found the home of the *Jour's* relatives. They gave the young monk and I a *wai*, and I felt out of place; I obliged and gave one back to them. They handed us a cup of water and I gladly accepted it with a smile.

I thanked them and gave the *Jour* another *wai* before walking back along the paved road toward the clinic and sandy playground. Then I stared at the empty volleyball court, the cast of my own shadow next to me under the silvery moon. For the first time, I was completely alone on an open field of my own vast desert. I scanned with my peripheral vision, left and right, then quickly picked up my pace, running with my own shadow chasing me toward the clinic.

The sand underneath my dark rubber sandals quickly filled the gaps of my toes, heaving them up in the air with each stride.

In that moment I realized that no such magic existed in me, that fear got the best of me, and I would have broken the discipline of the *Tum* and been haunted by the sacred belief for breaking down its principle. I couldn't follow E-Paw and accept the sacred belief and tattoos or *Ga-Taar* bestowed on to his body and soul. I had the belief, but I lacked the bravado to be a true believer of such magic. That not a single drop of black ink from the needles of a bamboo stick infused with Kubar Somdee's sacred relic would make me as brave as the guerilla tactic: *Patigan*.

I didn't see anyone out on the field that night, and when I got past the clinic, I slowed down and came to a hut on the corner where Mae Seel and Paw Seel lived. Their lights were out and their bamboo thatched windows were shut as I walked past their home.

When I reached our alley, our hut was still glowing from the flaming candles before Kubar Somdee. There were silhouettes of people outside making their merriment; even Thurng was up running around the bushes with the neighborhood kids. Kubar Somdee was surrounded by the lingering crowd of people. This time, in the middle of the circle there were the *Mor Lam,* (the *lam thae* singer from the *south of Laos*), and the *Mor Khaen,* the free reed instrument player. And the sound of Brother Bounchanh singing the *Lam thae* came alive as the *Mor Khaen* followed along, blowing in the bamboo instrument that often reminded me of a man making love to a bamboo machine gun, with his hands cupping its magazine and blowing through its firing chamber.

The Mor Lum style of singing was a combination of opera and rap music with the yelping interruption of drunken men, as if they were trying to forget the atrocities that they were going through. I caught Boun Chanh as he began humming and elevating the notes out his nose, his jaw clinched with anger and cynicism for the communists in every word that he sang.

"*Oir, oir, oirrrrrrrrrrrrrrr . . . Jang wa . . . jai sang wang, wang pan saay maow laow, wang pan larb thaow, wang pan paw yai banh . . .*

Oir, oir, oirrrrrrrrrrrrrrr . . . Clear as my heart is, clear like the drunken-ness, clear like the algae soup, clear like the village chief . . ."

Before another monsoon season came rumbling with its relentless rains, the Thai school was open for enrollment, and E-Paw was eager to register Nok and I since we were ready for formal educa-tion. The school was just outside of the camp toward the forest of Banh Gick, where E-Mae, Nok, and I had once snuck out through the prickly fences to pick wild bitter plants and berries. On the outer perimeter of the school another layer of barbed-wire fence stretched parallel to the road that ran along the camp. In front of the main office a red, white, and blue-striped Thai flag undulated in the warm brisk wind.

On the morning of our first day of school, we woke up with great enthusiasm. We quickly fixed our pillows and folded our shared blanket, and E-Mae helped to put on our best clothes. Nok wore her dress, a white top, and sandals, while I had on my white button-up shirt, pairs of khaki shorts, and sandals. E-Mae also reminded us to put a dab of honey from the little glass vial bestowed to us by Kubar Somdee on the tip of our tongue.

"Magic honey vial!" I would say proudly to Nok. Even if I didn't have the strength to receive the *Gar-Taar*, and the power of magic, those little drops of honey on my lips from the small glass vial that was blessed by Kubar Somdee was enough to get me even more excited for school each morning. Inside the vial rested a small rolled-up copper sheet written in cryptic Pali script, but to us, it was sacred. And just like all the sacred gifts bestowed on us by Kubar

Somdee, we were to protect it with honor and discipline. With the disciplines, the magic and power were instilled in the person who had accepted its beliefs. There was a system of belief and *believing* was power.

"First think of Kubar, he gave us the magic honey vial. Second, bring the vial to your head, then pray that your mind will flow as fluid as water, after you have received the blessed honey," E-Mae reminded us of Kubar Somdee's words.

Nok and I quickly followed her instructions and then said, "*Sa tuu!* (Amen!)"

After our little blessings at the hut, E-Mae convinced little anxious Thurng to stay home with her and E-Paw escorted us to school, where I found myself standing in a crowd of fidgety kids from all over the camp. A nervousness filled my body, but I was still excited as the morning sun was beaming gloriously in my eyes, while I waited to be assigned to a teacher. Then the crowd of children moved like a group of chickens looking for a pecking order. I felt lost again, but I stood amongst scuffed-up kids just like me. Some had their best combed hair, other had snots wiped dry from nose to cheek, and others had dirt and sand caked in their sandals. Nuuk, Nu, Noy, and several kids from the clinic playground shuffled along in the crowd with me. We made sure that we washed and polished our hands, faces, and the grime around our neck since we'd already joked about how we could avoid being cracked with the ruler for being filthy.

I watched the teachers gather their students by their age group and form single-file lines. Along the inner fence leading back toward our hut and the medical clinic, I could see E-Paw standing with other parents waiting anxiously for us kids to be assigned to the Thai teachers.

I soon discovered that the teachers spoke Thai Isan and were going to school to learn Thai. Thai alphabets and Laotian had some similarity; there were variations to each recognizable character. I had to pay more attention to Thai since there more consonants, vowels, and extra characters in the alphabet that sounded the same but symbolized something else. What helped, were those days of home schooling with E-Paw and E-Mae, who kept our interest flowing with basic letters of the alphabets, math, and stories with animal characters that came to life under the thundering sky of the Sirindhorn Reservoir.

Before the sun rose over our heads that morning, all the children in the crowd of kids were sorted out from the dusty field. In the confusion, Nok had also disappeared with her group of kids. When the dust settled, the crowd of children finally gathered before their designated teachers. They formed several lines like little ducklings following their teachers, and one by one, they disappeared into their classrooms of one-story concrete edifices without windows.

The edifices appeared to be military warehouses converted to offices and classrooms. From the middle of the line, I counted a handful of buildings and smaller mounds of dirt slightly bigger than our classroom. The units ran parallel to each other with the main office building on the northern side of the camp.

In the crowd, I followed the other kids on the teacher's command, sometimes raising my hands just for the sake of going along with my baffled classmates. When I finally got to our classroom along the small buildings that ran like quads within the school ground, my teacher was Ms. Air, a short Thai woman in her mid-twenties. Her hair was straight and jet-black, cut in the shape of an upside-down bowl that she parted in the middle with hair clips. She dressed like she was a Thai official with her white buttoned-up shirt, and a few pens tucked neatly in her shirt pocket. She assigned us seats and handed out our textbooks, notepads, and pencils. My desk was right next to a window with two wooden boards plopped open to the side like a small set of dilapidated swinging French doors.

Outside the window in the distance there was another set of barbed-wire fences that ran along the road that stretched around the eastern side of the camp. In front of the school a Thai flag hung as high as the palm fronds fanning a tall coconut tree. Behind me was the northern gate and the road that led to our hut, which was about a twenty-minute walk.

It was easy for me to be distracted by the warm breeze drifting in through the open window, but our teacher was a strict woman who would often remind us to pay attention to the class with the edge of her wooden ruler. One day I came home after getting the ruler, and I told E-Paw that the teacher had whacked my knuckles. Cousin Gun was visiting our hut with his voice humming and eyes gleaming.

"What happened to you?" He laughed. "You got the ruler! That's nothing, whenever I couldn't recite my assignments, the teacher would make me stand in the corner of the room and have my classmates erase the blackboard with their hands and then wipe it on my face." He snickered then pointed his finger at me, "Don't let a cracked stick get the best of you, be a good student and listen to your teacher!"

"*Buc Shour!*" E-Paw added, and E-Mae laughed along as if getting cracked by a ruler would take the stubbornness out of us kids.

After a couple of cracks on the knuckles, I'd made sure to avoid having Ms. Air get the best of me. By the end of our school session the first year, the strict teacher was fun-filled, and the memorable straight edge on the back of my hands was no longer just a mark I'd bring home to show E-Paw. It was a reminder of such a wild time that kept me going back to school, even knowing that I would get a cracked ruler. I loved going to school—we had things to do and other kids to play with.

"It's better than sitting here watching each other drool," E-Paw would often say.

When the school year ended, everyone in the class had forgotten how Ms. Air had made the class so nervous that everyone was sitting stiff in their seats. Somehow, we all got used to watching her stroll up and down the classroom with the ruler, tapping it in the palm of her hand just enough for the beat to be rhythmically indelible in my mind. Sometimes she would even bring in candies to treat the class if everyone was behaving and had done their homework. And for our last assignment, we were to sing for the class. Each one of us would have to pick a song that we heard from the radio and share it with the entire class. I shied away from the idea at first, but when I arrived home that day my favorite song came on the radio. It was the song of Sa Yun, one of the Thailand popular pop artists at the time. His songs were constantly on the radio and Vung used to sing his songs frequently back by the Sirindhorn Reservoir. I wrote down the song and recited it over and over, until it was planted like a stubborn weed in my head. And when Ms. Air asked me to go up to the front of the classroom, I became nervous and felt my heart bouncing off my chest, but I sang the song with my heart. The song was about the sun setting and how two lovers had parted and how their love sank with the sun. For me, it was a lasting image of my first teacher.

We had to learn French and English whenever the lessons were being taught at another school inside the perimeter of the barbed wired fences. The school was across the Or-Sor's camp on the other side of the fence next to the big wooden cross in a thatched bamboo church, not too far from where we saw the image of Jesus.

"We have to get the basics of each language, since we don't know if we're going to be sponsored to *Farang* or *Ar-May-Lee-Gar*," E-Paw said.

Sometimes Nok and I would take a shortcut by sneaking through the inner perimeter of the barbed-wire fences that surrounded the Or-Sor's camp. We'd quickly trudge across the inner road that formed a circle around the grass field. During the weekends the market was lively with vendors, as we passed through the market and huts scattering along the other end of the Or-Sor's encompassing fence. The aromas of the fried noodles captivated me each time I passed by the market, and on an empty stomach, it was downright self-torture. The yummy scent of grilled chicken, pork, beef on a stick, fried noodles, and even the flattened salty fishy squid kebob stick left my mouth salivating.

But the more English I learned, the more I was curious about the Christian Church of Christ and the Farang. The Farang, the blond-haired and blue-eyed people that I had run from the first time I saw them. Occasionally they were seen walking around the camp, in the church, and in the children's medical center that E-Paw had taken us to.

But the adults had been talking about them and making mockeries of their features: "You better be careful of *Buc Nun* (that guy). They could kill you with their pointy nose and steal your spirits like a ghost sitting in the Bo tree." They spoke of them as if they were hordes of insects that devoured everything in sight.

I didn't care much about their ghostly images. Now I was in awe when I heard the pronunciation of their sharp "Sh, C, and Z," and all the words that came out of their mouths like a soft whisper. I just knew I wanted to learn English and that E-Paw had been planning to take us to their land and we were going to live with them.

"Hello, and how are you?" Mr. Pun, our Lao-English teacher, would often say to us before he began his class. He was Laotian, but the Farang man who handed Mr. Pun our lessons was a light-skinned friendly man with big dark-rimmed glasses, a brown mustache, and a big warm smile with brown hair slightly receding to the back of his head.

"I want to learn to speak English so that I can speak to the *Farang*," I said eagerly to him one day.

"You mean the *American*?" he asked, laughing along with me.

"Yes," I said.

"You will if you just keep on trying," he said to me while turning to the bamboo hut-turned-English classroom.

"What is your name?" He asked the question in English, which threw me backward to how the Lao people would ask each other *Jao suer yang?*, or *Your name is what?* The very sentence had been the first formed English sentences that Cousin Gun and the entire family had been reciting.

"My name is Boun." My answer uncoiled through pressed lips.

During one of our lessons, Mr. Pun challenged the class to see who would step up and read a few sentences written in English, and the prizes were little red English-Laos books. It was a small saddle-stitched book no thicker than twenty leaflets, but it would be the perfect English-Lao pocket pal for me. *I have to get one*, I told myself as I mustered up all my brainpower. So, I did. From that day on, I'd proudly carry my little red flimsy booklet along with me wherever I went, hoping for an encounter with the Farang.

By the time Mr. Pun's classes had ended, I was able to say, my ABCs, "Hi, how are you?" and "Where are you from?" My curiosity grew with a need to be closer to the Europeans, so it became my secret mission to have direct contact. I wanted to communicate with them, and I often wondered why they were so different from us. It was common to see them at the advisor's office and the clinic, but a close encounter would offer me a face-to-face conversation. I wanted to know what the "*S's* or the *Sh*" really meant. I became fascinated with the strangers who I had once feared.

One sunny morning, I saw a tall Farang with bright, light skin walking toward the hut. I recognized it as a chance to break the ice. My sense of curiosity took over, and I grabbed on to the opportunity to do something scary: go up and talk to the Farang. So, I waited for the man whose name I had never learned and threw in my very first few sentences.

"Hello, how are you? And where are you going?"

I did it. I was thrilled knowing that I was using the sentences I had learned.

"Hello. How are you?" replied the tall Farang man with a cavernous voice and wide jolly smile.

"I am fine," I said, staring at him.

Then he threw me more of what appeared to be words beginning and ending in *"Sh, Ch, shhh."* It was beyond the phrases I knew, and I stared at him like I was verbally handicapped. He was still smiling, as I returned a blank gaze of complete aimlessness. Overwhelmed, I gave him the only thing I was able to produce—a big cheesy smile—then I spun around and dashed toward the *Pern* bush next to our hut.

The next time I went for my English lesson, I passed a Catholic church. Half-curious, half-daunted by the man on the cross, I took a glimpse at the holy image. I was immediately taken spiritually; it was then that I felt my own connection to the spiritual world. Like the English school, the small church was set up in a simple thatched bamboo hut. Along with the cross, pictures of Jesus and angels hung close to the window where just enough light brightened the images for me to look at them with a world of curiosity.

"E-Paw, what is the image of a man on the stick at the *Farang* temple?" I asked after I returned home one evening.

"It's *Pa-yay-su, Jesus,* he died on the cross for people."

"E-Paw, is he like Buddha?"

"It's for the mercy and miracle of mankind like Buddha. It's there to remind us that goodness comes from our heart."

"*Err . . . Err*" I nodded with curiosity as I peered through the open window to take another gander at the image of the man who E-Paw said died for people.

I continued to learn more English with Mr. Pun and by having close encounters with the Americans and the actual French, "our true *Farangs*," passing through our corner. E-Paw also encouraged Nok and Thurng to come with me to the school, hoping it would encourage someone from America to sponsor us.

"We have to be ready and prepared to live with them," E-Paw reminded us.

Nok often joined me for the English and French lessons. Sometimes we'd run late for class, and we'd sneak through the rusty barbed-wire fences of the Or-Sor's camp, and I'd say to Nok, "Nok, aren't you afraid to get arrested by the *Or-Sors?*"

"They would've arrested a handful of rascal kids like us who sneaked in to play in their circle by now if they were going to. We're running late, and besides, we can tell them we're going to school," Nok said.

When she was occupied with helping E-Mae, and Thurng wasn't interested in learning English, I would go alone. I'd tuck my little green notebook and pencils to my side and make my way through the open-air market and turn the corner of the bend by the image of Jesus Christ and the divine angels. More so than learning English, I was filling my curiosity with the wafting sweet aromas of fried food, pastries, and candies that enticed my ever-hungry mind and belly.

16

A NEW HOME IN THE CAMP

Two years later, after we had settled in the little bamboo hut in group 16 by 116, we packed up again to move to Paw Seel's old hut (20 by 195). E-Paw told us that Paw Seel's hut had become vacant because his family had been sponsored to America. The hut had more rooms and a far better view than our former one in the dingy alley at the base of our little mountain of dirt. It was big enough that even Cousin Bee living next door said that she would be moving in with us.

Paw Seel's old hut had three bamboo thatched rooms: a living room that we'd also use for dining, a small storage room, and a bedroom we all would share. There was also a communal outhouse in the backyard. But what I loved the most about Paw Seel's old hut was being in a busy corner. There was never a dull moment there—it seemed that everything that happened within the heart of the camp would pass by our hut. It was the first time in our lives that we were living by a paved road.

From ambulance to sewer truck, to a parade of people celebrating marriages and holidays, to *Blood-Turr* puppet shows, elephant rides, Thai movie stars, and a crowd of people carrying their dead out to the cemetery beyond the gate and the Thai elementary school, we had front-row seats. The best part of it all was that it gave Thurng and I the first shot at the soymilk truck, instead of chasing it down from the far end of our old alley, where we'd sweat a little more for our cup of the warm sweet milk.

"Grab the biggest bowl!" I would yell to Thurng whenever we'd spotted the big soymilk tanker.

"Run faster!" I would tell him as he was trying to catch up with me.

We would see Nuuk, Nu, Nitt, Joy, and other neighborhood kids running alongside in a frenzy. It was as if we were chasing a maimed bird trying to escape death.

Thurng and I were always hungry; everything that we'd put into our mouths tantalized our taste buds. From the sugary sips of soda shared by the family to the sweet spicy dried squid on a stick, to bread and condensed milk, to a can of sardine in tomato sauce, everything was excitingly fresh and flavorful to us. Even the warm soymilk poured into our cups by the men hanging off the side of the tanker truck passing by our new hut was enticingly delicious.

On some mornings, I'd wake up to the rays of sunshine filtering through holes in our thatched bamboo walls, roll about in the corner of the hut, and hear the breadman. He peddled by on his silver bike with a backpack full of bread, condiments, and sandwich meat that we had never heard of before. I'd hear him say, "Bread with condensed milk, bread with ham, bread with vegetables." His repeated words hypnotized my mind, and I imagined the wheat aroma running up my nose making my mouth water for the sweet taste of baked flour that the adults said was the Farang's staple.

Our new home was now directly across the street from the medical clinic, where E-Paw had been working. Although E-Paw had been the village doctor in Banh Dong, he was now happy to be the maintenance man, and if the medical team needed help, he was the nurse's assistant. But E-Paw also had other benefits with the new job at the hospital: Besides extra cottons, and a bottle of iodine, we had access to extra cans of sardines. On some fortunate days, Thurng and I were eager to share a can of sardines in tomato sauce, especially over a bowl of hot jasmine rice, keeping us licking our lips for more.

The Farang doctors at the clinic said that we were all lacking complete nutrition, but Nok was so skinny that E-Paw and E-Mae were afraid she might die of starvation. They gave Nok extra crackers and watered-down powdered milk that became a wonderful treat whenever we got our little hands on the crumbly morsels. Nok didn't care for the crackers that much, and she'd share them with Thurng and I, since we didn't get enough of them.

The medical clinic office had concrete flooring and its outside walls were planked with reddish-brown wooden boards. In the front of the building a wooden entrance door swung slightly off the ground. Above the door the name of the clinic was written in both English and Thai with two red triangle logos. In front of the clinic there was a thatched bamboo waiting room with a grass top like most of the extensions to other structures at the camp that were partially finished. It was also a place where the neighborhood kids, including Thurng and I, would play hide-and-seek on the weekend when the hospital was closed. Thurng and I even housed a family of cats, well, until one day one of the little kittens got out and was run over by the hospital's ambulance. The kittens were eventually taken away and given a new home.

While working at the clinic, E-Paw also became good friends with Na Ma Som, the director of the clinic and Na Somchai, the tall, dark, wavy-haired, and troublesome Thai ambulance driver. The three men had similar interests: They drank whiskey, made jokes, and talked about women, although that was mostly Na Somchai.

"Your wife is going to kill you," I heard Na Ma Som saying to Na Somchai, as I lay there under the bamboo awning in front of our hut pretending to be napping, while E-Mae left with Nok and Thurng for the open-air market.

From that chat-filled bunch, I began to understand the intimate acts between a man and a woman. And it was there that I realized that even a good man will break the laws that confine him to his own happiness.

"Did you buy it?" I heard Na Ma Som saying to Na Somchai.

"Of course, I did." Na Somchai pulled out a liter of whiskey.

"Just make sure you don't get caught with that," Na Ma Som said. "I know that alcohol for normal consumption isn't prohibited within the perimeter of the camp, but I'm not so worried about the *Or-Sor*. I'm more worried about your job as an ambulance driver."

"I'll be fine. I've been doing it for years," Na Somchai said cheerfully as the men each took their turn pouring their desired amount into the glass that was passed around.

That day after I had heard tidbits of the adult's intimate details, like the encounter of Na Somchai with a Laos woman on the previous night, I shyly hopped over the bamboo bench, and I ran across the road to our playground by the clinic. Then I quickly joined Thurng and Nok playing marbles next to the tree near the main entrance, not too far from the bamboo-thatched waiting room. It was here that Thurng and I spent countless hours playing marbles on the sand, jumping in the waste ditch, and stepping on shards of broken glass that had been buried when the aircraft base was in full operation, long before the big holes in the ground had been dug up for garbage in front of the clinic by the open sewer.

There were a few ways to shoot a marble. Sometimes you could lock it in with your index finger and shoot it out with your thumb. My favorite was shooting it with my catapult hand and thumb planted on the ground at the spot while tucking then pulling and releasing the glass marble with my left hand. Nuuk, Nu, Noy, and Joy would join us, and since we looked alike, we often told other people that we were brothers. Noy and Thurng were both the spitting image of two kids from the clinic ground; they were skinny with dirt and grime that formed on what we called "a natural dirt ring around the neck," nails filled with dirt and sand, and snots smudged across their cheeks. Nuuk was a few years older than me. He was good with shooting marbles on the sand.

"Boun, you always give me good luck," he said one day after robbing the other neighborhood kids of their *satangs* playing marbles.

One hot day, I cut my right foot badly, and I hobbled and skipped over to the clinic. A Thai doctor with a grave face swung open the swinging wooden doors, and then he told me to sit on the wooden chair and quickly started cleaning my foot.

While he was fixing me up by dabbing the cotton swab with iodine, he looked at me directly and said, "I saw you jumping in and out of the ditch. If you don't stop playing in it, I'm not going to be here to patch you up the next time."

I immediately looked up at his face, respectfully, and I let out through my nostrils "*Err, Err,*" while holding the stings in my cuts. From that day on, I never saw that stern doctor again.

Our second year of the Thai school came with another wave of the relentless monsoon rains. During that new term Thurng was old enough to attend the school with Nok and I. He was already itching to get his hands on a sharp pencil and notebook paper of his own. So, E-Paw eagerly registered him for his first year of school.

Nok and I were excited to have our little brother tagging along with us to school. Together we'd watched flash floods quickly filled the open sewer overflowing into ditches. We kids would muse about how much we missed the Sirindhorn Reservoir, while we watched ducks and ducklings swimming in the pool of water and jumping out, making splashes with their wet wings. But the most excitement we had were those wet days I huddled under Nok's bamboo umbrella with Thurng.

Although Thurng was anxious to join us at our school, he loved to wander off aimlessly. On some occasions when he had early dismissal, he'd stroll by the perimeter of the camp with Putt and other meandering kids. I worried about Thurng, his curiosity was taking him beyond my own fear. I'd scan the school ground for him during recess, hoping that he would be outside playing in the dusty playground with his classmates. One day he'd taken a dangerous escapade out to those places where we'd once sneaked together by the *Chae Ra Mae* stream past the western fences. Those were forbidden places that E-Paw had told us not to venture to, and when he found out that we did, he'd yelled at us. Once he yanked our ears when he discovered our secret of the little fish. It was our so-called "fighting fish" that we were after, and we had found many of them under the cracks and crevices of rocks along the stream. It was not too far from the hut just beyond the camp's perimeter that caught fire one day.

Thurng and I had another pastime: catching fish and keeping them alive in a big glass jar we found in the garbage. To feed them, we'd cut up a net-like piece of a discarded brown rice bag we found next to the clinic's trash. We then borrowed E-Mae's sewing needles and stitched it together in a small net on a bamboo loop and attached it with several strands of cotton strings to a pole long enough to reach our net into the open sewer across the road from our hut for mosquito larvae.

When we got caught, we'd stand before E-Paw like two obedient children. But E-Paw had his keen eyes on us. He'd give us a serious blank look while mustering up the urge to be angry.

"I told you not to go outside the fence. And the water, it's too dangerous, you can slip into it and drown!" He warned us not to go back unless he came with us.

"Err . . . err" We nodded happily. We played with our little red betta fish until one morning it floated to the top of the glass. E-Paw said that the fish had died because the water in the glass was too warm and the fish suffocated. So, we took it across the road to drop it in the open sewer water, then we both disappointedly watched our lifeless fish float away with the mosquito larvae.

Each morning before school, we'd dab a little bit of the honey with the *Maak Lord* still submerged in the glass vial, and we promised E-Paw and E-Mae not to skip school and learn. On our way to school, Nok and I would remind Thurng that during recess he was not to go beyond the fences over the outer perimeter of the school.

"You know that if someone had kidnapped you, you'd never see us again," Nok said with a grave stare into his dark marble eyes. "And do you want that? And do you remember what E-Paw and E-Mae said about how kids would be abducted and then have their livers and their heart sacrificed to the demons?" She reiterated to Thurng what the adults had used to frighten us kids from all conceivable evils.

"Err, err," he repeated with the zest of a curious child.

"You listen, or I'll tell E-Paw if you don't." Nok added more deterrence for Thurng, knowing that E-Paw pulled his ears for joining a group of kids in their adventures beyond the fence toward the woods of the village called Banh Pa Pak.

I was hoping that Thurng would like school, especially when he had mentioned to me how exciting it was when his teacher had handed out their school supplies. Thurng said that he loved the smell and the colorful pictures in the new textbooks. And the pencils that were given to him looked edible; as a matter fact, he would often try to bite the eraser off the tip of a pencil, because he thought that they were good enough to eat.

During the weekends Thurng and I would wander the camp like two curious and ever-so-hungry kids. We were opportunists; with a few heavy-duty elastic bands we had fashioned our own slingshot, which we would always carry with a handful of pebbles in our pockets. We wandered through the camp looking for birds and small insects to hunt. One day we tried to shoot some house wrens and finches that perched on the beams of the rice warehouse. It was tough to get a few shots off, because we were afraid that our rocks would ricochet off the tin roof and hit ongoers. But we worked as a team: Thurng would be the lookout and I would be the shooter. We avoided shooting at birds perched near the tin roof of the building, because we were afraid that the Or-Sors would arrest us for just having the slingshot.

When Thurng and I chased the birds out of the warehouse with no luck taking anything home, we'd continue to keep our eyes open for grasshoppers or crickets—they were the more feasible prey.

"Grasshoppers are a tasty morsel, as crunchy and creamy as a cricket. If we can catch enough of them, we can roast them in a frying pan," I said to Thurng, knowing that catching one was considered pretty lucky. Most of the time we went home licking the salty sweat off our lips, but we were always on the prowl.

One day we were out with a handful of neighborhood kids, beyond the fence near where dirt bikes raced. We watched them with excitement in our eyes as they spun up the reddish dirt, then turned along the curved dirt course, and then launched up in the air over the dirt mounds. We had slingshots hanging from our necks as a toy, and we also considered them our protection when we ventured beyond the perimeter of the camp. It was still considered dangerous, especially for Thurng, who was still working on his aim.

"I told you not to point your slingshot in the direction where someone is standing, *Buc shour*!" I yelled at him as I ran over to inspect Joy, who Thurng had pegged in the head with a rock after it had ricocheted off the ground, completely missing the little grasshopper as it sprung itself into the air.

"Are you okay?" I quickly looked for signs of blood on the skinny kid's head.

"*Err* . . . " Joy stood there silently scratching the knot on his head, holding back his tears, and wiping the snot across his cheeks with the back of his grimy hands. Then he nodded and gave me a sign that he was fine.

Then I blurted out at Thurng, "I told you to be careful!"

"I didn't mean to do it. I thought the pebble was going to stick to the ground, not bounce up," Thurng said as he exchanged a similar frown with Joy.

When we got back into the camp, Nok saw the mud and dirt caked on our faces. She knew it right away each time we went beyond the rusty fences where E-Paw warned us to stay away.

"*Shour!* It's too dangerous for you two. What did E-Paw tell you?" Nok said with sharp futile words.

Since Nok was more inventive, she added another level of excitement whenever she joined us with our made-up games. From cans to jars to coconut shells or sticks, anything we could kick around, we made our pastime. One game she was good at was Elastic Band Bowling. Having elastic bands was like having status on the sandy playground and around the clinic. It wasn't always cheap to get a bag of elastic bands. The bag of red, blue, and brown elastic bands had flexible bands that could be strung together into jump ropes. Thurng and I even crafted the thin rubber band into strands for our little slingshot. Aerodynamically, it didn't work as well since the strands kept snapping with the pebbles, often pegging our thumbs and the back of the anchoring hand holding the slingshot. But the most fun we had with our string of elastic bands was to take them off our wrists and play elastic band bowling with them.

Elastic band bowling required the good hand-eye coordination of a boomerang handler with a bowler's touch. When Thurng and I lost our bands to the other kids, Nok would get them back for us in a couple of direct tosses on the concrete along the clinical building. Sometimes the stacks of bands were piled to a height where they wouldn't topple over. To participate in our elastic band bowling, each player had to put down the same number of bands as the other. Then a line was drawn in the sand. To win, you had to stand behind the line and swing your sandal hard like a boomerang and knock the pile of bands clear off the stack, separating them from the rest. If there were bands that weren't separated from the others during a direct hit of the sandal, then the game continued outside the original stack until each one of the bands broke apart into an individual band. The person who had a hard direct hit and separated the elastic bands won.

If we were lucky, we would beat the neighborhood kids out of their elastic bands, and turn them into jump ropes. And sometimes we were daring enough to play coin throwing and lose our money, which was a few *satangs* that were hard to come by. We would learn from the older kids as they played coin throwing; of course, their stakes where much higher than ours—sometimes they used *bahts* at a time. We kids would mimic them whenever we could, and sometimes when Thurng and I got lucky, we'd buy candies with our winnings, then bring them home to share with Nok.

Thurng and I would play on the hospital grounds until the dirt covered our feet and sandals. Sometimes E-Mae would call us for lunch, and we'd quickly dust off the dirt from our ashy knees, then kick the sand from our sandals, and race across the road to our hut. I'd always leave Thurng in the dust each time, except for the day I had lost my right toenail to a rock the size of my fist. To my surprise I had left a trail of blood behind me and Thurng was almost ready to cross the street as I was hopping behind him. When I got to the hut, E-Paw was watching the two of us, already mad at us for being so filthy. I knew that E-Paw wanted to yank me by the ear, but when he looked down to the ground, he saw my dangling bloody toenail.

"Why didn't you look where you were going?" He yelled at me as he opened a bottle of iodine, then dabbed it with a cotton rag on my bloody toe.

I didn't cry that day, because I was used to stepping on broken glass shards by the camp's clinic, and some with waste littered along alleys.

On some early mornings, we would follow E-Mae to the food market at the center of the camp. We would help her flip things like clothing and vegetables she bought from the Thai vendors. The Thais would come by the camp and E-Mae would buy a basket of Chinese cabbage and mustard greens and used clothing and sell it at the market. When E-Mae had to run home with Thurng and I for more supplies, she'd leave Nok sitting by herself. E-Mae said that Nok was old enough to exchange money with the customers and keep an eye on the goods.

Next to E-Mae's spot there were other refugee vendors with their bamboo skewers of salted fishes and sweet teriyaki and honey glazed kebobs with grilled chicken, beef, pork, frogs, and flattened dried squids. Others had a collection of what was found in the rice paddy like snails, crickets, assorted insects and beetles, small mud-fishes, eels, and even bowls of small live jumping grass shrimps. Some vendors had edible dried leaves; some leaves were used for chewing the pasty *Maark* tobacco. Tree barks and roots were used as natural remedies for our healing.

From day to day, we'd watch the sun rise and set, knowing that there was so much going on outside, but we were stuck behind this barbed-wire prison, watching and waiting to see who they would bring out to the cemetery next.

One day a half-blind girl came by as I was helping E-Mae extract oil from sesame seeds using the mortar and pestle on the bamboo bench in front of our hut. I was kneeling on my knees and mincing the oily seed with the wooden pestle when the shadow of someone made me look up.

"Beg of you for food and rice," a young girl said, catching me by surprise.

Instantly, I jerked away from the downward mincing motion and suddenly stopped. I looked up to the sky and saw this girl who appeared to be younger than Nok. At first, I didn't know what to say to her, so I gave her nothing but silence. Then I quickly looked down into my own shadow. She didn't move, as I looked up again, this time our eyes were fixed on each other. I stared at her with shyness, curiosity, fear, and my own shame for being poor. She was blind in one eye with a scar that stretched horizontally over her closed right eye. Her uncombed hair was dark and curly, and her face loomed over me.

"I don't have anything," I said as I immediately refocused my eyes to the pasty sesame seeds I had minced into a thumb-sized pool of oil in the center of the mortar.

I didn't dare look at her face again and hoped that she would just pass by like the shadow of a bird flying over me. But she stood there for what felt like forever, and then she pulled her dark shadow away from me. To some degree, it was the truth. Then I thought I should have asked E-Mae.

She looked at me again, and we locked eyes long enough for me to hold her indelible image in my mind. I watched her pressing her lips as she turned around and made her way along the string of huts lining our road, and I never saw her again. It was in that moment that I realized that I didn't have to beg for as much as a bowl of rice each night. That even in the dirty abyss, we were living just above the level of completely poverty.

One night from the dark corner of the hut, E-Paw reminded us, "We just have to make it through until we go to America." E-Paw was still hanging on to the meager work at the camp's clinic, knowing huts were becoming vacant and lucky refugees were being sponsored to America.

E-Mae continued to buy food and clothing from Thai vendors to flip at the open-air market. When her goods disappeared, and we needed a little more money, she took on a new endeavor that led her to heaving bamboo buckets with goods on the thick bamboo stick and balancing them on her shoulders, as she vended her noodle soup as we walked through the camp. On one hot humid day, the weight on her shoulders of the bamboo stick ripped her cotton T-shirt. The heat was searing over our heads and all around us, and I felt like I was going to pass out as I walked behind E-Mae. Looking at her exhausted body and thirsty mouth left me in shame for our condition.

"Do you want anything to eat?" E-Mae asked me. She was determined to sell all her noodles.

"I'm not too hungry, but I want to go home," I said as I tried to persuade her to go home and let us eat the rest of the noodles. I really wanted her to go home to take the load off her shoulders.

"I have a little bit more and we'll be done," she told me. "We should walk this way and I'll see if anyone wants to trade a bowl of rice or buy some more of our noodle soup on our way home." She was persistent, and when her customers didn't have money, she'd smile and say, "That's okay, we can trade this bowl of soup for rice, and more noodles can be made with the rice."

On our way home that day, we passed many huts. Some were empty, while others had little faces peering through the open windows with no more than hunger in their eyes.

"E-Mae, let's go home," I insisted as I dragged my reluctant feet behind hers.

"Okay, I'm done, can you help me carry some rice?"

"Yes, I can, and are we going home this time? I'm getting hot."

As E-Mae reached inside one of her bamboo-woven baskets and opened the cover, I saw how much weight she had been carrying that day when we both walked out of our hut: almost two gallons of water for our customers to wash their hands and her large bowls on one side of her basket and bags of shredded long Thai string-beans, Brussels sprouts, hot chili pepper, mint, scallions, Asian parsley, and chopped up crunchy banana buds on the other side with her chicken coconut curry and noodles.

When we were almost out of money, she sold the last pieces of gold that Grandpa La had given to her—gold earrings that she proudly wore dangling off her ears like two golden pearls. I knew that she didn't want to part with them. She told us that Grandpa La handcrafted them for her in Banh Dong before she got married. But she told us that we needed the money, and we couldn't just sit around.

"We have to help each other," she said.

So, one day she waited for the gold vendor to come by with his rock and a jar of sulfuric acid to test for the purity of the gold, and she sold him the earrings for 300 *bahts*. She then took the money that she received for the gold and bought some used clothing, fish, and vegetables from Thai vendors, who would often stand by the main entrance of the camp with all sorts of goodies: anchovies, sesame seeds, sour fish, and sour vegetables. One of E-Mae's specialties was the pickled Asian mustard greens, and it was also my favorite. Although it smelled like someone had polluted the air in the room, she was selling it by the bucket. Sometimes her customers would even chase her home when she was out.

"Once you acquire the taste for the sour funky pickled vegetables and the hot pepper, you are hooked," Nok said, laughing along with me. Nok helped E-Mae to sell it at the camp's open-air market and turn it into a few *bahts* here and there to keep food on the table.

One day we gathered in our hut, and Cousin Gun came to visit, telling E-Mae that he wasn't feeling good. He had the ache in his back, and he felt like a weathered old man. E-Mae had the answer for promoting good health.

"Eating a live gecko will make you strong and healthy," she said happily.

"Yes, I heard it too, it's old Chinese medicine," E-Paw added excitedly.

This natural method of better health took on a different perspective to us kids. We all would have to eat the little geckos jumping around the bamboo post inside our hut.

"Yes, but its medicinal value comes from eating it raw, swallowing it whole," E-Paw said to all the curious eyes fixed on him from within the hut.

Cousin Gun started laughing and said, "Really, *Na Baow*, *Uncle*, are we really going to eat the gecko? There are certainly a lot of them jumping around in the hut, but I have never heard of it."

"I'm not going to bother trying," Cousin Bee shook her head with a gentle smile pressing her pointy little lips. "You can eat it and live forever, but you can count me out." She gave out a short chuckle and tucked her arms together on her chest.

"What you have to do is catch the little gecko alive," E-Paw said as he spotted one of the many geckos that had been climbing the post around us.

With one hand on the post below the gecko and the other just above the gecko, E-Paw made the small gray alligator-like lizard jump on his arm as he quickly covered it with his other hand. The gecko moved its tiny tail, whipping it left and right, but it was no use with E-Paw's strong grasp. Then E-Paw did the unthinkable and rolled up a blank sheet of notebook paper, making a round tube like a bamboo stick and he put the little gecko inside the tube. He covered both ends of the tube and brought it closer to his open mouth. With the tube in his mouth and the gecko anxious to escape into the dark tunnel—in this case, E-Paw's throat—E-Paw tapped its tail with the other hand. The gecko ran for his life into the dark pit of death and then it was all over for him.

I feared the gecko wouldn't run down my throat, but I went along with E-Paw's instructions. Filled with nerves and the eagerness of a curious child, I wanted to see if E-Mae was right—whether I was going to be stronger and healthier. My first attempt was a success. The gecko ran into my throat, into something I had imagined even darker than the gecko's own dark shelter. Then I felt little wiggles as the little creature ran into the back of my throat and down in my stomach as the gecko went to its demise.

Everyone tried to make the gecko run down their throat except for Nok and Cousin Bee, who stood in the corner of the hut grossed out by Cousin Gun's failed attempt. Cousin Gun's gecko did what I had expected: Instead of running through the esophagus, it was trying to go down his air pipe, then it stopped before spinning around and bit cousin Gun's tongue, making him quickly spit the little critter out of his mouth.

"*Yud! Yud!* (Stop! Stop!")" Cousin Gun laughed as the gecko jumped out of his mouth with spit all over its body. "*Sao, Sao* (No more), if it's going to be that bad, I'd rather be sick." He chuckled some more and added, "I'd rather drink a bottle of liquor-based potion of dried lizard tail and bitter roots instead!"

We all laughed at Cousin Gun so hard that I had tears in my eyes. And Thurng and I ended up rolling on our bamboo bed.

"*Hmmm . . . Shour Tair!* (Really stupid!)" E-Mae said sarcastically to Cousin Gun who shook his head in disbelief as to how he got persuaded to swallow a gecko. Then she recalled a time in Banh Dong when the yellow of what appeared to be jaundice all over her body almost killed her. "When I was 30 years old, my bile leaked after losing my first child during infancy, and your father saved my life by shooting me up with vitamins B1, B12, and B6. And your father and Kubar Somdee injected me with an IV. Some of the villagers came by to visit me on my death bed, and they would say, 'E-Saan, you are dying this time.'"

"I was there," Cousin Gun added. "Your father was making money with his medicine; he would help many people. Sometimes his patients didn't have much money to pay for his services, so he would just ask them to pay for the medicine. That's what he and Kubar Somdee were doing for the villagers."

"Your father didn't care about money as much; he would throw it all over the mosquito tent in our old hut in Banh Dong. He was helping many people and then there was that doctor, E-Taa Puu who hated your father. He was jealous and was always accusing your father and Kubar Somdee of taking away his business. So, during the communist uprising, he turned on your father and Kubar Somdee," Cousin Gun said pitifully.

In the following months, Cousin Gun got sponsored from a church organization in the state of Arizona. He said that as soon as he got established he would work on getting some church organization to sponsor us to come live with him. Then Paw Chamdee stopped by to tell E-Paw that he too got sponsored, to the state of Ohio, and had decided to take his family to America. Cousin Bee, who had been planning to come with us, fell in love, and she told E-Paw to take her off his *Tor Mor* Sponsorship Application. Cousin Bee and a Lao man who she married also got sponsored to the state of Minnesota.

One by one our little village within the refugee camp slowly diminished, while E-Paw became more anxious without any word from any of the applications he had submitted. But he was still hopeful that there would be some miracle hands that would reach out to us during those uncertain days.

17

E-PAW JAILED—
CONFINED IN A CONFINEMENT

Spending time playing marbles at the clinic playground became our pastime. It was there that the misery of poverty didn't bother us; it was also by the volleyball court where we played with kids our age and watched the teenage boys and men play adult sports. We continued to spend hours playing marbles, sometimes until E-Mae came to get us for dinner.

One evening, we saw a crowd of people congregated by our hut at the corner perpendicular to the clinic. At first, we didn't care much, because adults often settled their own personal disputes, besides, E-Paw had told us to stay away from any assembly of men or any crowd in general. One day the neighbors would have personal disagreements, and the next someone was getting arrested by the Thai soldiers for not complying with their orders.

We looked at the crowd again—this time it was growing larger. I feared the worst, since it wasn't moving away from our hut. The anxiety made my heart palpitate in my throat, and an ominous feeling of something happening to the family came over me. I quickly grabbed my glass marbles, with Thurng, Nuuk, Noy, Joy, and other friends who followed my lead, and we scrambled like we had done on several occasions in the fight-or-flight mode. We quickly jumped to our feet and sprang our little legs, kicking up sand and dirt between our sandals through the playground, running past the clinic, and then hopping over the open sewer to the perpendicular road by our hut. When we arrived, the crowd of people grew into a bigger ring that surrounded E-Paw and E-Mae.

At the sight of what was happening to E-Paw, I gasped for air and tried to understand the scene that was unfolding before me. Thurng and I squeezed farther through the crowd of people for a better view. We stood there staring, completely shocked at the violent scene taking place with E-Paw. E-Mae was by his side. Two soldiers and one cross-eyed man all dressed in military green were yelling and one landed a fist on the back of his head. He dodged the pummeling, but like running away from a swarm of bees, the fists were landing on his body randomly. Then the cross-eyed man joined in by yelling and trashing E-Paw.

Then their interrogation grew louder. "Where did you put the rest of your liquor?" one soldier repeated with anger.

E-Paw replied with the white in his eyes brighter than ever before, "I don't have anything else, and you had better keep your hands off me!"

"You're going to jail!" the Or-Sor barked at E-Paw.

E-Mae sobbed, then she begged: "Don't hurt him, he didn't do anything wrong!"

The Or-Sors didn't bother looking at her, and one of them told her to get out of the way. The crowd began to move away from our hut, heading toward the main entrance of the camp. One of the soldiers ordered that E-Paw be locked up until they could figure out what to do with him. It was another moment when we stood feeling helpless; our world was once again mad. But what could I do for him? What should we have done? Up to that point, we had been nothing more than pacifists. All E-Paw and E-Mae ever taught us was to make peace. No guns, no war, just simply make peace.

The soldiers continued to torture E-Paw along the road. I heard another shout out of E-Paw: "Don't touch me! I've done nothing wrong." This time E-Paw snapped at the cross-eyed soldier throwing another punch at E-Paw's head.

We walked with E-Paw to a building not too far from the main entrance of the camp. There was shame in his eyes and anger in his voice.

Then he yelled out to us, "Go home!"

When the soldiers and E-Paw arrived at the small edifice with windows facing the main entrance, they pushed him inside. They said it was the jail.

Unable to interfere, E-Mae and Nok made their way back to the hut sobbing. "Go home, leave him be, he'll be okay!" E-Mae said to Thurng and I.

"We will, soon . . . let us see more," I said to E-Mae and Nok with a little defiance slowly simmering inside me.

As soon as E-Mae and Nok were out of sight, Thurng and I became two curious boys. We tried to go around the building and see over the windows, but they were too far above our heads. I wanted to see E-Paw, to know what they were doing to him. Thurng and I stood there next to E-Paw's confinement, tossing each other blank looks, leaning against the outside wall, listening for sounds of recognizable words. I was looking for a sense of bravery from my little brother, but I didn't see any in his dark marble eyes that evening. Instead, I saw a child lost like me, left with only an innocent look on the face of a little boy in the world of men. I began to realize a darkness simmering with hatred growing inside my own heart.

That night, Thurng and I meandered home from the prison as if we were mourning a loss. We didn't look at one another. In my silence, I'd wished that we were back in Banh Nong Mek once again. I just wanted to live in peace, to watch the sunrise and sunset and have so much to look forward to when we woke up every morning.

The next morning E-Paw came home in the front seat of Na Somchai's Ambulance.

"Na Ma Som was livid at the *Or-Sor*," E-Paw said. "He told them that it was his liquor bottle that he had bought to share with me. And they apologized for making such a mistake. They wanted to make sure that everyone followed the order of not having too much alcohol, whether for consumption, or the intent to sell."

By the evening that day, we learned the cross-eyed man was in fact a Lao man, an Or-Sor's informant. He came with a gloomy look on his face to ask E-Paw for forgiveness, after he learned that Na Ma Som was very angry and had ordered for E-Paw to be released immediately.

"Oh, I'm sorry, please forgive me!" He said with fear in his eyes.

"Nothing happened," E-Paw said gently, repeating his words, forgiving the man who'd punched him in the head.

"Sorry, sorry . . . " The man pressed his hands in a *wai* to E-Paw and we never saw him again.

In the gloomy hut, E-Mae sided with E-Paw on forgiving the man. To soften the blow, E-Paw added, "Letting go and forgiving him is a way to free ourselves of the sin."

Behind E-Paw and E-Mae, Nok and I watched the entire scene unfold right there at the entrance of our hut. While I was still trying to grasp my own feelings of love and hate, good and bad, Nok stared at the Lao man from her own darkness without a drop of pity in her soul for him. From her little pointy lips, with heated words, she said, "I want to kill that cross-eyed man."

The months came and went after E-Paw went to reapply for a new *Tor Mor* application with the counselor under the tin-covered pavilion. This time he told them that Vung and Narng wouldn't be joining our family. E-Paw didn't tell them that both had married Thais in Ubon. He told them that they were adults with decisions of their own. By now E-Paw's urgency for someone to sponsor us had increased. He told them, "Yes, my family will go to America, France, Canada, or wherever good faith was willing to receive us."

While we waited to be sponsored to America, Thurng and I hungered for more excitement—and food. Now living by the clinic came with new aroma that lingered from the women's infirmary just behind the clinic where there was a soup kitchen. The smell of fried onions, cilantro, roasted peppers, and lemon zest in the rice soup from the kitchen often drifted across the street to our hut. I hated when the aroma teased me until my stomach growled and mouth salivated. Thurng and I would immediately be drawn to it whenever the food was being served, mainly to pregnant women. We'd stare through the glass at the food like two hungry wolves staring down on a herd of sheep. Sometimes Thurng and I would cling on the outside ledge of the glass windows like orphans, and we would wait for the scraps. And sometimes we got lucky, and the server at the infirmary would fill our bowls with rice and noodle soup, and we would bring it home to share with Nok. Most of the time Nok would just let us enjoy most of it. She was skinny, but she was still getting her extra powdered milk and crackers from the clinic.

But the hunger Thurng and I felt during those years went beyond the craving for food—we also longed for adventure. It was curiosity that got us into trouble with E-Paw, as we roamed the refugee camp together, sometimes sneaking out of the camp through the rusty spiky fences to chase bigger grasshoppers, birds sailing over our head to their haven in the tall trees, and even to catch little minnows and frogs.

We'd also collect metal, bones, and glass bottles to trade with the Thai junk recycler. For our efforts, the friendly dealer would trade us for the tiny candies that people called "the Gecko's eggs candy"—a tiny egg-like candy half the size of an M&M. Some of the candies were little like eggs, some were like Lifesavers that looked like a ring, and some even came with a whistle. The whistle was a piece of metal that was the size of a US quarter, which we would often tuck between our lips and tongue, then force the whistling air out through the small opening in the middle.

Thurng had a sweet tooth that made him salivate over the delicious treats. His little gleaming eyes would light up when we walked by vendors with candies dangling in the open windows of their huts. One day E-Paw gave us five *satangs* for candies at the candy store ten huts down from us. But Thurng and I gambled with our *satangs*—"it would be more candies for us to split," we said, laughing with each other. We met the local kids who were anxious to play marbles; they had been out on the clinic ground all morning. No more than a half hour later, our great idea backfired: We'd lost our candy money to the neighborhood kids, leaving us with one *satang* each, enough for only two pieces of candies. So, we stopped playing and walked together to the candy store—a hut by the corner before the open-air market.

"We can still get a piece of candy each," I said to Thurng, who was disappointed that we lost our *satangs*.

"I'm going to get us more," Thurng said as we strolled side by side.

"What are you going to do?" I came to a complete stop. I was almost ten years old then and I feared getting caught for snatching an extra piece of candy.

"Just watch me. When the lady is not looking, I'll snatch the candy," he said convincingly.

"Don't do it! You'll get in trouble and our dad might go to jail for you, and besides we both have a *satang* each and we can get at least a piece of candy to ourselves," I pleaded with him.

"I'm not going to get caught. I did it before when her daughter was there, and she wasn't looking," he pressed.

"I'm going to tell our dad if you do. Don't do it," I repeated, as I saw his disappointment.

When we got to the store—the hut with a bamboo awning over the colorful candy jars displayed on the counter—we marveled delightfully at the sweets before us. The wooden awning was held up by two bamboo sticks on each end. The colorful candies reminded me of our first sip of Sprite, and how surprisingly wonderful it was to feel the carbonated gas escaping through my nostrils. Staring at the candies was like waiting for a new experience with the expectation of a new sensation in my mouth.

I was excited to get my candy with the *satang* that I had in my hand, so I picked the affordable option, where I was limited to only one piece of the brown sugar-coated tamarind candies. I wanted Thurng to have his turn; he had been standing next to me anxiously. So, I took my candy, then stepped aside, watching him running his hand through the candy jars. Then he picked up an extra one while the store owner's daughter was watching him. She was a young girl who was no older than Thurng. She'd kept her eyes on him, but Thurng quickly hid the other candies in his other hand. Swiftly switching the candy with the coin from the pocket of his khaki shorts, he handed the *satang* to the mother. He was able to fool the little girl, but her mother had her keen eyes on him.

With a quick lunge, she snatched Thurng by his little wrist, jolting the candy that he didn't pay for out of his hand.

"Let go! Let go of my brother . . . he didn't do anything!" I repeated fruitlessly to the woman, while Thurng was struggling from the clamp of her taut grip.

"You're going to jail for stealing! Where are your parents?!" She was yelling so loud that even E-Paw, who had been napping eight huts down, heard her. She dragged Thurng to our hut as I followed along, fearing what was to come for him. I wanted to do something, but what? We both knew that it was wrong to steal, and worst, E-Paw would pinch our ears with his sharp nails. The "oh no" moment was upon us right then and there. It was too late . . . we were both in trouble. I was an accomplice to Thurng's sinful act, the sin that filled my head with punishable consequences.

"Let me go, let me go!" Thurng cried, pulling himself from the curly dark-haired woman's strenuous grip.

"You're a bad kid, and you're going to be punished for this," she yelled with a fury in her eye.

E-Paw and E-Mae came running out, along with Nok behind them, shocked to see Thurng being pulled by the lady as she wouldn't let him go. E-Paw's face morphed from sleepy to completely alert as the store owner's voice grew loud enough to grab the attention of curious neighbors who poked their faces through the bamboo windows.

"What is the matter with my son?" E-Paw asked with anger in his voice.

"He stole some candies from our counter!" the woman exclaimed.

"Did he pay for them? I gave him some money to get some candy earlier." E-Paw disappointedly grabbed Thurng's hand from the ranting woman. "I'll pay for them," he promised the lady.

The woman finally let go of Thurng's left hand and nodded to E-Paw as she walked back to her hut by the corner. Then she glanced at me with her dark eyes shrinking to almost closed and pinched lips pressed tautly, giving me a warning my fate would be no different if I dared pull the same stunt. I'd wished that she had let Thurng go. I felt bad for him, because a few days before that incident I had unknowingly enjoyed a few pieces of gum that Thurng had pocketed from the same store.

"Why did you have to steal? Didn't I teach you that you have to be good?" He pinched Thurng's ears then pulled him inside our hut.

E-Paw's anger was short-lived. Like most parents who spoiled their children, he was loaded with guilt for each whack. For Thurng and I, it was pinching our ears—just enough for us to feel the sting. Soon after the guilt filled his soul, he'd turn to consoling us with more mussing of the hair and light tugs of the ears.

That day, Thurng let out a shrieking cry as he was beaten for the two pieces of gum, rubbing his eyes then adding to the slime on his cheeks from his nose. While E-Paw strolled down along the string of huts toward the flea market to pay the store owner, E-Mae rinsed Thurng off with a couple of bowls of water. She wiped the tears and slime off his cheeks and nose. But before sunset, Thurng was out playing with Nu and I by the sandpit in front of the hospital.

After seeing Thurng beaten that day, I was ashamed. I felt guilty for the price he paid for my piece of candy. Fear became my friend, it kept me within the lines, and it planted a daunting seed of punishable consequences. I couldn't see it then, but I learned that poverty somehow sows the evil seeds that can push a kid like Thurng to steal from hunger. I hated the pity I had for him for committing such an act and then being punished severely for it. I saw in his gleaming eyes that my little brother wasn't thinking about being innocent, when the hunger was growling in his belly.

After three years of living at Camp Ubon, we were becoming long-term refugees. Adding to E-Paw's stress, more news surfaced of the Thai government's plans of tightening its confinement and closing Camp Ubon—this announcement sealed E-Paw's fate. His dreams of returning home to Banh Dong narrowed like the dark dingy alleys to no more than wishful thinking. He was still worried, Vung was reluctant to join the family, and Narng had already started a family of her own. A year after Narng married Ai Vin, she had a baby girl. She came to visit us with her baby wrapped in a white cloth and an orange hat.

"This is E-Yupin." Narng showed us her baby with a bright happy smile on her face. "You can touch her, just don't touch her head, she's still soft."

Nok, Thurng, and I surrounded our new family member, our first niece. Soon each of us got to squeeze and hold her. The best part of all was when we'd gum her little soft feet and toes by tugging our upper and lower lips over our teeth and she would let out a smile. We hugged and kissed the baby until her brief visits were over. E-Paw saw no solution to keeping all of his children together.

During an evening of happy chatter, while E-Paw and our neighbors sat on our bamboo bench soaking in the sinking sunset, we overheard more of their friendly debate about the land of heaven.

"Ah, did you hear in the letter from America that it's like heaven there?" said the wrinkle-faced gray-haired man next to him.

"Yeah, but if you go to China, you might be able to walk back home," said Paw Dee next door, who had ten years on E-Paw and no intention of starting over in a land an ocean away.

"I heard they can't grow sticky rice in America. Aren't you afraid your family will eat bread and apples for the rest of your life?" Another man chuckled so hard that he stopped the conversation's casual debate.

"I've already submitted my application and I'm looking for a sponsor in America," E-Paw said, glowing with hope.

"No matter where you go, as long as they don't kill you, you're lucky!" Paw Dee said as he stared at the sinking sun over the roof of the refugee clinic. Then he got up and left with his final thoughts, "Hmmm . . . *maen, dee* (right, good) . . . "

The other neighbor stood up with him, as some gave out a deep sigh, some still laughing as they dispersed to their dark huts. In the months to come, they too diminished in number like the sunset as nearby huts became empty, with only a memory of our former neighbors' humbling humor that often masked their disheartened faces.

America was so fixed in E-Paw's mind. I knew it was the country that he'd bet on for his family. If E-Paw wasn't dissecting America with his friends and neighbors, he was gearing us up for a life there. I can still hear his words echo: "We have to know more, learn about where we're going, and find out how we can live with them." If he wasn't talking about it to us, then some nights he'd continue talking about it in his sleep.

We kids didn't talk much about America, besides, it was overwhelming for our undeveloped minds to imagine a country that was glittering, yet frightening. Our biggest fear was leaving to America for good—it was a one-way ticket to a place with the Farang. It would be up to our fate and destiny, and E-Mae believed that our fate was already written.

E-Mae had her own moments of silence about America. One night in her own dark corner, she asked E-Paw, "If we go to America, can we return home to our family?"

E-Mae's question about America left E-Paw wondering if "The Land of Heaven" was as good as his friends who had taken the great leap proclaimed. Then to mitigate any fear of further notions about America, he said, "We have to be cautious with glitter and glory. It can be as dangerous as receiving an insincere kindness from a stranger."

E-Paw continued to entice us with his developments of going to America; it appeared that he was counting the grays in his fine hair and had a deep sense that we were on the verge of being sponsored.

Then one night in his puffs of smoke, he told us, "Dying without any hope would be far worse for me. I'll do anything to give you children a better opportunity to grow and prosper—and in the refugee camp surrounded by barbed-wire fences, we don't have a chance."

18

CAMP PHANAT NIKHOM AND CAMP LUMPHINI

A few weeks after Narng's visit, E-Paw came home and said, "We got news from our sponsorship application—we got sponsored to America!" It was Paw Seel who asked his own sponsors: The Jewish Family Service. They were miracle hands reaching out to us when hope was dwindling down to a dim light.

That night we kids sat with E-Paw on the ledge of our bamboo bed, elbow to elbow, extracting the little we knew about America from our mind. We should have been jumping in jubilation from E-Paw's news. Instead, there was a long hesitation that hung with the hot humid air inside our hut.

"E-Paw, are we really going to *Ar-May-Lee-Gar*?" Nok asked.

"*Err* . . . We're going to stay with Paw Seel and his family," E-Paw said, tilting his head forward staring at the ground.

"What are we going to do? We don't have other choices. We're going with the crows," E-Mae added from her own gloomy corner nearby. Her face was slightly pale, long, and blank.

There was a frown within the shadow of Nok's face, and Thurng had his indifferent expression (still grasping the turning world of a child), but I was already missing Baby Jupin, Narng, and Vung.

Days after E-Paw got word that Paw Seel's Sponsors were going to accept us, E-Paw's brown eyes glowed with a bittersweet glimpse into our future. The exact opposite happened to Nok and I. The thought of Nuuk, Nu, Noy, and my playground by the clinic held me at the camp even if we were leaving for a land they called "Heaven." Nok didn't say much in those days; I'd already known that she was going to miss her best friend, Jip—they were attached together like dry sticky rice to a bamboo basket.

For whatever it meant then, I hung on to those few dwindling days like they were the best time in my life.

Then it actually happened. The next time E-Paw took a deep draw of his smoke and blew out the steaming puffs, he said, "*Pai*, we have to be ready and pack our belongings."

This time E-Paw told us to leave our smoke-coated pots and pans and dinged-up cooking utensils that we had hauled into the Ubon Camp with us from the Sirindhorn Reservoir. E-Paw, who was worried about what was going to happen to us, was now concerned about more than his belongings. He was still crushed that neither Narng nor Vung wanted to come with us and had been looking for solutions to make sure that they were well cared for.

"Vung will stay with Paw Yai Banh, and Narng will stay with her husband," he sighed, releasing puffs of smoke from his mouth in the semi-lit room.

E-Mae didn't say a word as she neatly folded our hand-me-down clothes. She appeared exhausted . . . with heavy heart. She had been questioning her own judgment of sending Narng off to live with her relatives in Banh Honghee, worried that Aunt Tai had persuaded Narng to marry our brother-in-law, Ai Vin. In her quiet moments in her dark corner, she fell silent, feeling remorse about her decisions and now leaving both Vung and Narng behind.

But the decision was made for us—our perpetual motion was moving us forward. No more envisioning America and perfecting our basic French phrases. In a matter of days that followed, we walked to the main entrance and took our individual and family photos next to the edifice where E-Paw had been confined for having a bottle of liquor. E-Paw also signed a Promissory Note to The Hebrew Immigration Aid Service for our travel loan in the amount of almost thirteen hundred US dollars. When we returned home that day, E-Paw laid out his handful of typed documents written in English on our thatched bamboo floor, and hand-translated underneath in Laotian was highlighted that all males between the ages of eighteen and twenty had to be registered for enlistment in the US military as well as a litany of requirements, such as illegal drugs and paraphernalia—not limited to opium and heroin—and weapons were restricted by all means to enter the country. Still, E-Paw clutched on to those documents with both excitement and tentative consideration, as we waited another three more months.

One morning after E-Paw signed the travel repayment documents, he said, "We need to be examined and proven disease-free to enter America. So, we have to go see the doctor at the refugee clinic."

While Nok shied away with discomfort from exposing her naked body, Thurng and I quickly obliged. By then, we had been standing in plenty of lines for rations, donations, and vaccine shots at the clinic, and they sometimes came with a piece of candy, so we couldn't refuse the needles that promised us better health.

"*Err*, they need to know if we have any disease, they don't want us to bring it to *Ar-May-Lee-Gar*," E-Paw said. "Your mom will be with you."

After we had a good rinse from the cool water at the outhouse that day, we trailed behind E-Paw and E-Mae to our familiar clinic right in front of our hut. The two of them were already concerned about the eczema that had spread throughout Thurng's legs.

"It reminds me of what my mother had," E-Paw said.

"It looks like that, but all we have to help him out is just the ointment that the clinic gave to us," E-Mae said.

"I just hope that they will let us get on the plane. I've heard that they can hold you there for so many days or months if they discover your family members are carrying some sort of infectious disease," E-Paw pointed out.

At the examination office, a tall Farang doctor spoke Thai to E-Paw. "Hi *La*, I'll need to see your paperwork."

"*Kup (Yes)*." E-Paw returned a smile, then handed the man our sponsorship document.

"Okay, I'm going to examine everyone and make sure that you have all your shots before you board the plane to America. You and your wife will need to have a chest X-ray for tuberculosis. But the children are still not of age for the test," the blonde doctor explained to E-Paw in his best Thai.

E-Paw and E-Mae were in almost silent stiffness with their concerns about the eczema that spread throughout Thurng's legs. Now as I stood ready to be probed I thought, *I wonder what they'll find in me, and will they just keep Thurng and send only us to America?*

Several minutes later, we received our results. "Okay, you're all set!" said the doctor with the soft probing hands, smiling at us.

"Thank you." E-Paw sighed as he looked at the doctor and E-Mae. There was almost an immediate relief on both E-Mae and E-Paw's faces soon after we exited the examiner's office.

Finally, the day arrived when we'd be leaving Camp Ubon. We

packed up all our valuables and memories: a photo of Narng, Ai Vin, and Baby Jupin; Grandpa La's stone and bark and medicinal white cotton pouch; and Grandma Dao's small woven sticky rice basket. We checked every nook and crevice of the thatched bamboo hut that had been our home for the past year. We finally picked up our bags and marched behind E-Paw with his luggage to the main entrance of the camp. There were buses parked along the fence with a crowd of people already in a line under the stinging heat and warm dust; some had already boarded the bus with their bags and luggage. Some had smiles on their faces like a man with long hair who was dressed in a blue top and bell-bottom jeans. Then there were others, dressed in their best orange, white, and green, carrying more of a heavy hardened look of sorrow and ambiguity on their faces. The expressions on our faces were of a "forever goodbye."

On top of the blue and orange bus, a large silver carriage held the luggage and bags on its roof. The bus was gleaming in the sun, with its diesel fumes filling the air, and its engines humming and hissing. E-Paw went first, then E-Mae climbed through the door with Thurng hanging on to her hand, and I followed. Nok was behind me, stumbling up the steps with her bag of clothes in her hand. Underneath my feet I could feel the engine vibrating up into my knees and thighs.

"You can sit there," E-Paw said to Nok, and I pointing at the seat behind him.

I immediately took the spot next to the window, and I looked for Nuuk, Joy, and Noy, as they'd happily walked with us to the bus. They were still standing there on the ground just below our windows next to Nok's friends, waving their happy farewells. I could see Joy's smile with his upper tooth missing, while one of Noy's arms was leaning on his shoulder like the best of friends. Nuuk remained his cool reserved self, smiling cheerfully in black shorts and flimsy brown sandals. I waved to them, they saw me, and they jumped up returning my farewell with their hands swaying side to side. I didn't dare to knock on the glass window; I was afraid that if I broke it, E-Paw could go to jail again, the prison edifice still lingering with its glistening glass windows just beyond the lines of people still waiting to be seated on the bus.

Then the bus hissed sharply, slowly moving toward the entrance and the movie theater. A rush of warmth came over me as I realized what was happening. Like my Cambodian friend, Nhe, I felt like a child at the playground with a fist full of sand, not wanting to let it go. In what the adults had called hopeless, I still had my family, my friends, and what I thought to be my land. The weight of it all filled me with great sorrow, as the gravity of my own universe created an avalanche of warm tears that rumbled down my cheeks, landing on my beige-and-white striped shirt. I tried to wipe away the tears that swelled up in my eyes, but they kept coming like the monsoon water. No one, not even E-Paw or E-Mae, could hold them back as the bus gave out another hiss and started to roll us out by the rusted barbed-wire fence to our left and the crowd of faces on my right.

In that very moment I came to know who I was and will forever be. The tears that stung my eyes and clouded my vision that day made me aware of the kindness that can still exist, even in the dilapidated and stench-filled camp. That it was still important to be a part of the world. And that the little things we had shared mattered as much to me as others' treasure troves full of glitter and glory.

In the Sirindhorn reservoir we found paradise by the water, and at the dirty abyss of the Ubon Camp, we found happiness and made it our home. The thought of leaving the camp that had been our home for over three years, the friends I'd made in the sandy playground, the teacher who had given me my first English/Laos book, Narng and Vung, and our grandparents and relatives left me with a feeling of melancholy. It was as if I once had them in my hand like the dirt and sand at the clinic's playground, and then with a gust of warm wind, they were gone.

I just couldn't completely process all that I had lost, and where we were heading—America . . . the unknown. I wiped the tears with my hands again, and I noticed E-Paw looking at me with his sad eyes. He knew that I was at the age where I was old enough to understand what was going on and that I no longer wanted to move.

The sidelined faces gradually slid away from view, and I waved again to my playground friends as the image of them standing there began shrinking with the narrow bus windows. They ran with the bus, waving their hands elatedly from side to side with their mouths opened to the hot sun, yelling *"la gon, la gon, soak dee, soak dee!* (goodbye, bye, good luck, good luck!" before they disappeared with the main gate behind us. I never saw them again, except in my own mind, when I thought of us kids running together on the dusty playground by the clinic under our happy sky.

The bus finally exited the rusty-wired camp, leaving me only with lingering memories. It was a place we came to know, a place where families huddled under small, thatched bamboo huts, a place where the human spirit could be as bright as the sun above our heads. Neither the stench of the open sewer or the decaying feces left on our giant mounds of dirt ever kept us from laughing and soaking in the glorious sunshine.

Inside the bus passengers stared silently through the windows. Like us in our own trance, people held their own reveries of open fields, tin roof huts on stilts, tall grass, and banana and palm trees. As the bus took us out farther into the *nah*, shambled huts scattered along the plain became homes and bridges, making paths over streams of water. My eyes were now open wide to lanes of cars, trucks, bridges, and a landscape that kept me fixed to my seat with a child's amazed curiosity. Along the way signs in an assortment of colors were painted on billboards, cars, hotels, buses, and buildings. We were heading toward Phibun in the direction of the Sirindhorn Reservoir. But E-Paw said to get to America, we must go south in the direction of Bangkok.

After a long bus ride through scenic routes carpeted with rice fields, mountains, bodies of water, and skyscrapers I had never thought existed, we finally arrived at Camp Phanat Nikhom, slightly east from the heart of Bangkok. We had been traveling for what seemed to be from the early morning to almost sunset, as the bus took a turn into the road toward the ominous camp. Camp Phanat Nikhom looked like a level four maximum prison facility with tall barbed-wired and metal razor-sharp fences running along its perimeter, and guard towers overlooking the compound. From afar, the isolated encampment stood before scattering trees and shrubs, on what appeared to be a dried and barren land where the dust of brown dirt could be seen swirling with the random gusts of wind.

As we approached the entrance, I noticed the loudspeakers were hung on the posts along the fence like Camp Ubon. I was still looking for America; the naive thought of reaching America in a bus before sunset had been secretly seeded in my head since we left. Nearing the secured fences and groups of concrete camp buildings, another truth about America was discovered: It was going to take us more than a day.

Inside the camp there were concrete houses with tin roofing. The buildings looked as if they were used for small concrete storage rather than living quarters. Although Camp Phanat Nikhom looked a lot smaller than Camp Ubon, the taut barbed-wire and razor fences that surrounded its perimeter made Camp Ubon look like a child's playground.

There were guards with their rifles hung at the shoulders patrolling a road that ran along the fence before the wooden tower. There was no chance of Thurng and I sneaking through these fences to catch frogs, grasshoppers, or the betta fish that we so much enjoyed keeping as pets.

The bus let us off and we walked past the main gate, hanging on to our belongings. A Thai male counselor approached us, and E-Paw handed him a document with our names and a photo from a big plastic bag with a red and white ICM logo that was given to us back at the Ubon camp.

"Follow me," the Thai man in his jeans and short-sleeved shirt said with a warm smile.

Like chickens being herded into the chicken coup, we followed the group of people being designated to a shelter within the camp. In another quad of concrete and bamboo-thatched housing, we stood before an open single room structure with tin roof and windows with wooden shutters. The room was just big enough to accommodate the five of us. The concrete building was one of the many buildings that made up the small quadrant scattered throughout the camp. In the middle of our quad, tents had been set up next to a square concrete basin filled with fresh water for cooking and rinsing. Inside the adjacent quarter from ours lived a Laotian couple with their infant child, a little boy. The woman reminded me of Narng with her fair skin and her short black hair bouncing on her shoulders. The man was kind and spoke with friendly gestures, so we took to each other right away. They adopted E-Paw and E-Mae as their own. From the time we met the couple, we looked out for one another. We learned that they had arrived a few weeks before us, and they gave us insights on where to find some resources during our stay.

Before we settled in that day, an announcement—a call to gather for food—echoed over our heads through the loudspeakers in Vietnamese, then in Laotian. Shortly after, the next call came from the servers standing in our quad prepping food for us, and E-Paw ushered us out of our concrete box, which we had nestled in together.

"*Pai, gin khao vai vai!* (Hurry, hurry, let's go eat!)" E-Paw made his own call for us not to miss our meal.

We quickly marched out of the main entrance to an area where a line of people stood before huge pots of food and rice that was still steaming on a table. With long silver ladles in their hands, the servers stood tending the steaming metal pots of rice and vegetable soup. We were each handed a bowl with two big scoops of jasmine rice, which provided us with enough starch to rest our bodies for the night. We also got a large scoop of whatever happened to be floating up at the top of the pot with fish balls and cabbages to go with our bowl of rice.

After our meal, we quickly washed up with the water allotted to us, then we returned to our sleeping quarter. Inside the room E-Paw and E-Mae turned our bags and luggage into pillows and laid some blankets over the concrete floor. It was another warm night, and we lay side by side again with E-Paw and E-Mae in the middle. E-Paw cuddled Thurng in his arm, and meanwhile, Nok and I were on the outskirts on the opposite ends of the blanket. Before the night became completely dark, E-Paw was snoring again. The ever-conscious man appeared to have finally laid down his guard and closed his eyes. But before dozing off, he mumbled, "Be ready, our door and windows don't have locks, so we're vulnerable to thieves." The rest of us fell silent, listening to the sounds of crickets outside our new home.

During the next morning, we were acquainted with all the bathroom facilities and recreational areas. That afternoon E-Paw, Thurng, and I decided to take a tour around the camp. "Have you seen or heard the news?" E-Paw asked each time he encountered someone who appeared to be friendly or familiar.

We walked through short alleys of concrete buildings that resembled the edifice used for storage at the Ubon camp. Trailing E-Paw, I stared at the barbed-wire fences that encircled the camp.

In between the two fences where we stood, there was an unpaved road that the Or-Sors drove up and down. On the outside of the fence next to scattering bushes and trees, Thai vendors sold their goods wrapped in newspaper and banana leaves. As we moved closer toward the inner fence, we noticed a man had wrapped his coins in a piece of cloth with elastic bands, then he quickly threw his cloth ball of money over the fences. In response, the vendor tossed a small bundle over the fence to him, landing a few feet shy of the inner perimeter where he stood. Shocked to see that his good had landed on the gravel ground on the Or-Sor's road, he quickly pushed his way through the inner barbed-wired fence with immense effort to fetch his bundle of fish. Little did he realize the Thai soldiers with M-16 rifles strapped to their arms approached him quickly from behind. Without a word, one soldier raised the butt end of the gun and struck the man's head to teach him a lesson and set fear into others who were watching that they'd have the same fate, if they'd dared to violate the camp rules. The man was surprised and ashamed that even with money to feed his family, his dignity was stripped from him. He looked back at all of the people staring at him with discomfort, as the soldiers confiscated his fish and left him empty.

The week stay at Camp Phanat Nikhom felt like months. E-Paw met people, but many came from other Thai camps. In most cases he was acquiring news of our family back home in Laos, then he also tried to gauge our future by learning "what lies ahead on our way to America." E-Mae was itching for some way to make money and keep herself occupied, but with so many restrictions and what we had told her about the incident with the Thai merchant and the Laos man, she did very little with her busy hands.

Thurng and I were longing for a game of marbles at the quad with other kids in the camp. Some were still running with snot in their nose, screaming in *Lao*, and what appeared to be Khmer or Vietnamese. If their faces weren't so fresh and our shyness didn't get the best of us, we'd be jumping and hollering with them on the sandy ground. So, we stayed inside our little bunker playing and scribbling and never did join the kids on the sandy playground.

But after a week of sleeping on concrete floor, we got lucky to be moving once again. The big, noisy bus came rolling and I listened to its engine humming and hissing—this time with a sense of comfort. Before the bus, we formed a line with the people who were waiting anxiously to get on board just like us. As I boarded the bus, I gazed out through the huge glass window and saw the cluster of concrete buildings with aluminum tops. For the first time I was excited to leave a place and find a better home. I wanted to forget everything I saw in this place; the awful image of the man with a small bundle of fish cupped in his hands and kneeling before the Or-Sors was still lingering in my head and heart. I took my seat with Nok and E-Paw, and E-Mae and Thurng sat in a seat across the aisle from us. Besides a few "*err, err* and *bor, bor,*" there wasn't much that was said among us as we watched the bus turn away from the highly secured camp.

Then the thought of us moving farther and farther away from our family crept into my thoughts again. I felt warm inside, but this time I didn't let the tears sting my eyes and slide down my face. Instead, I sat there in awe of the new sounds of another open-air market, rickshaws hauled by men and their bikes, *tuk-tuks* (reminding me of a motorcycle attached to a chariot) squeezing between the lorries, colorful billboards, and the smell of Chinese food drifting through the gaps in the windows of the bus. I was anxious to see America at our next stop.

Our bus took us through more glittering buildings and bright streets that bedazzled our eyes with colorful monuments and over-sized billboards. By late noon, we were traveling closer to America—based on my own assumption that the rice paddies and scattering of coconut and palm trees along the open plain had completely disappeared. We were surrounded by cars, streets, and towering buildings that loomed even higher than the tree canopies in the jungles. Throughout the busy streets, vendors displayed all sorts of goodies like the ones I saw in Ubon, many of which had flashy gold and red plastic wrappers. Through the opening of the window next to me, more aromas of Thai and Chinese food and fish sauce drifted in, invoking my curiosity and hunger. Like the days when I didn't dare ask E-Paw to buy them for us, I imagined the delightful tastes of the colorful fruits and candies that left me salivating. By the time we left Camp Ubon, my favorite treat was the "golden junk food," the Chinese version of the flakes of sweetened processed fish meat sprinkled with sesame seeds.

Parallel to the street vending stands, an entourage of trucks, buses, *tuk-tuks*, mopeds, and motorcycles squeezed their way through the traffic congestion with incredible steering agilities. We all moved in sync like blood flowing through the veins of streets' arteries surrounded by tall glass buildings that lined the streets. When the flow of traffic came to a complete halt, anxious moped and motorcycle riders made their own paths, sneaking in between cars in the middle of traffic and onto concrete paths as they wove through pedestrians along the walkway.

Minutes after the traffic had given way, our bus moved ahead, and then we came to another stop, this time by what seemed to be a brick fortress with a black wrought iron entrance gate. The swinging double gates were attached to stone walls higher than E-Paw's head. But the bus didn't enter the entrance; instead we were allowed to exit the bus then enter the main gate. E-Paw and E-Mae retrieved our belongings and followed a group of people to another group of people waiting to verify our paperwork.

"How many children do you have?" A tall Thai man with fair skin and stiff hair stared slightly down at E-Paw.

"Three," E-Paw replied.

"You can stay in the *sala*, but remember to see the counselor for flight itinerary and travel instructions." The man pointed over to an open pavilion, where we could see a large crowd of people who had already huddled with one another and their belongings.

"*Kolp kun kup.*" E-Paw politely thanked the man in Thai.

"*Pai,*" E-Paw said as he heaved our belongings to an open space barely big enough to fit the five of us at what appeared to be the center of the oversized pavilion.

This confinement was not America either—there weren't a lot of Farang, what's more, the seas of Asian eyes stared back at us. What stuck indelibly with me all these years about Camp Lumphini was the water fountain in front of the pavilion that amused Thurng and I. Nok didn't care for it, but the smooth carved bowl filled with water up to the knees of little children our age tempted us to jump in. So, on that afternoon, we not only cooled our feet in the water but also made several attempts to submerge ourselves in it.

That evening we returned to the gathering of people, some of whom were quite friendly with E-Paw and E-Mae. Food was brought out to us in huge silver vats and pots that were still steaming. It reminded me of what was given to us back in Camp Phanat Nikhom. By now, we'd grown used to staring at those familiar hot vats of food brought out before us day after day. Normally, it was the sort of soups that had been stretched out with water so bland that they were missing the authentic spices of a Lao or Thai dish like lemongrass, kaffir, and red chili. We could have used E-Mae's homemade anchovy sauce. But no one really complained about how the food was being served—the only thing I ever heard was the growling in my stomach of it not being enough.

Before the sunset that evening, a large group of people gathered under the pavilion. Like us, each family held close together in their own huddle, separated by belongings or just a few feet of space. We leaned on each other, resting on bags, and comforting one another in our own dialect. Some had already dozed off snoring, mothers tucked their babies close to their bosom, and just outside the main gate the sounds of ongoers could be heard shouting with the speeding lorries. Every now and then cars would beep their horns and tut their sounds. But from the inside of the thick concrete walls, I got only a glimpse of the ongoers.

The following day, I woke up to the heat already making me uncomfortable around the ring of my neck.

"E-Paw, can we go play in the water fountain with the other kids?" Thurng asked.

"Okay, but you have to wear your clean shorts and wash yourself really good before you go in and after you get out," E-Paw said. "And you have to make sure you look out for each other, okay?"

"*Err . . .* " I gave E-Paw a smile.

That day, Thurng and I played in the well of water until its flowing fountain was shut off. And then it was dinnertime again. After dinner, we returned to our area under the crowded pavilion.

"Alright, we're leaving tonight," E-Paw said after he received word that we were ready to board our plane.

It was frightfully exciting to hear those words coming out of his mouth.

19

ON OUR WAY TO AMERICA

On that hot and crowded evening at Camp Lumphini, E-Paw's dream of coming to America became his reality. With the sun slowly sinking over the tall buildings towering over the main entrance, our charter bus came humming and hissing in again. The gate opened and a crowd of people moved toward it. We eased our way out through the gates and stood by our designated bus. Along the streets, the city lights glowed bright, adding to the yellow and orange glow in E-Paw's nicotine-hungry eyes.

Minutes later, the bus hissed and moved off again with streetlights, headlights, neon lights, and billboards blinding me in every opening I peeked through.

"We're heading to the airport," E-Paw said.

He looked exhausted, but then he returned to a stiff figure, half-awake and half-sleeping as he stared at the front of the bus. Still, in my little head, I was waiting for "America" to pop up on the next corner. As Nok and E-Mae sat silently in their seat with their eyes sunken and exhausted, Thurng's eyes gleamed at Bangkok's busy highway, rising and bending bridges, glittering temples, and advancements that were too far from a fresh mind to fathom.

Almost an hour later, a larger airplane than I had ever seen was floating with its blinking lights above the bus. Nok and Thurng stared at it with overwhelming amazement of their own.

"Woah! *Yun!*" I said, pointing at the airplane that just whirled over us.

Without any warning, the bus came to a sudden halt and another hiss came out from underneath it. In the sky pulsing lights flickered from the wings of the airplane, adding their sparkling glow to the constellations. Some of the planes appeared linear in flight, while others circled the field brightly like fireflies floating gently through the air in the night. Along the runways more lights lined the tarmac.

"*Pai!*" I heard E-Paw's voice from behind urging us to move up with the other passengers as they exited the bus.

Outside the bus, I was overwhelmed by the darkness now brightened by the overhead fluorescents and headlights of standing cars and buses. In the distance, a plane slowly lowered itself like a graceful bird gliding on its wings to the ground. Its wingspan widened and the roaring of its engine sent a vibrating chill to every bone in my body, as it headed in our direction on the runway. I turned to look over at Nok, and her eyes were affixed to it with curiosity like mine.

It was 6:00 p.m. when we crossed the parking lot with other refugees waiting to board the plane like us. Their sullen faces under the fluorescent lights made them appear like sleepwalkers meandering the streets at night. Heaving most of our heavy carry-ons, E-Paw guided us to a waiting lounge inside a glass building with more bright fluorescent lights. We crashed in a wide lounge with restrooms, a food counter, and words written in English that were too advanced for me to translate, even with my little red English-Laos pocket pal.

Inside the lounge another commotion was taking place. There were passengers who looked like merchants with crates of birds and small animals stacked next to their feet. From their dark skin and round eyes, and their spoken language, the Lao people in our group said that they were from countries called Africa and India. Curious looks were tossed amongst the groups of people, but no more warm smiles were exchanged. It was here that for the very first time I saw the whitest and darkest of men.

E-Mae, Nok, Thurng, and I took our seats and set our bags on the floor inside the lounge. In the meantime, E-Paw took off to ask a Thai woman at the check-in counter a question. As I sat on the cold seat, I could feel the chill through my shorts and naked thighs. Then I was hit with a foul odor that brought me back to the chicken coop, and I wiggled my nose as I built up my tolerance for it like I'd done in the past.

E-Paw returned with the envelope of documents the camp counselor told him to hang on tight to. He took a seat to the right of me and told us, "We're going to have to wait for the airplane."

I looked around the lounge again and saw the other passengers huddling in their own little groups. The cool air was becoming relentless; for the first time in the summer months, I felt the air change. Cold air blowing out from the vents around us gave me goose bumps along my arms and legs. *It's cold in America. There's hail and a time of frost.* I recalled a conversation about a wintry picture that the elders had back in Camp Ubon sent from America.

I wasn't the only one who complained about the chilly air. Nok was also feeling the cold.

"E-Mae, can I get my sweater, too," Nok asked, rubbing then folding her petite limbs inward over her seat.

E-Mae, who had been planning along with E-Paw, bought some food with the money they found deep in their pockets. E-Paw exchanged his palmful of *bahts* for no more than a few dollars. But they were planning for the worst—if it was up to them, Nok said that they would have brought a bundle of wood, the machete, blankets, and our banged-up utensils. Now E-Mae was happy to hand us our wooly sweatshirts, which no longer made me itch like the first time I wore it. Since E-Paw and E-Mae got wind of the condition and weather in America, they had been doing everything to plan for a world half the globe away. E-Mae helped us slip on our shirts and we quickly walked over to a large glass window that gave us a glimpse of the half-lit world.

"Look at that airplane!" Nok exclaimed.

"And look at the one landing with its lights!" Thurng said, pushing the glass with the palms of his little hands.

"You kids don't go too far from your mom; I'm going to step outside the sliding door for a bit," E-Paw said.

"Err, Err . . ." We reassured E-Paw.

I couldn't tell E-Paw, but I wouldn't have gone too far, because I was scared. All of my life these airplanes had marked the sky with white lines in a roaring thunder, and now we could read the insignia on the span of their wings.

"Nok, is this America?" I asked.

"No, we still have to get on the plane. E-Paw said it's far from here," Nok replied.

"Oh, look over here!" Thurng said excitedly, staring at another plane lowering itself on the runway.

"Err . . ." Nok and I nodded with Thurng as we both stared at the dark plane with its lights getting brighter and brighter.

Nok, Thurng, and I took E-Paw's advice and didn't venture too far past the fluorescent lights above our heads. But five hours waiting in an airport lounge for two little rascals was just too much time. Our mischievous little hands began examining everything that glowed and glittered, from machines stacked with candies behind the glass windows to sliding doors. Then we'd chase each other in and out, forcing the automatic doors to slide back and forth. Our little legs couldn't stay idle, and we teased each other to kill time by pulling and tugging on one another.

"Will you guys stop?! You're going to hurt each other, and you'll break something that E-Paw can't pay for!" Nok yelled with gritted teeth.

We halted then leaned against E-Mae's shoulders. E-Paw returned shortly with a quick smile as he joined our little group. His eyes slightly red, his face tan and yellow like he recently recuperated from jaundice. I knew exactly what E-Paw wanted: his cigarettes. He hadn't gone this long ever without his nicotine fix. Then E-Paw gave me another warm smile and mussed my hair once again as my eyes grew heavy, and I fell asleep to the bright blinking world with Thurng leaning against my shoulders.

It was midnight when Nok shook Thurng and I vigorously out of our sleep, waking us up to the hazy surroundings.

"*Pai*, we have to go now." She shook us again.

I got up and dragged my feet with E-Paw and the group of passengers waiting to board the plane. We met our tall and stout escort; he was a true blonde-haired blue-eyed Farang man who spoke fluent Thai and was also well-versed in Laotian. We were so impressed by his clear instructions in our very own tongue that E-Paw told us never to call anyone a Farang from this point on.

"Call them 'American,' after all, we're going to America," he said.

So that night we followed our American usher out through the sliding doors and didn't look back at the lounge we'd been camping out in for the entire evening. The group came to a complete stop in front of a luggage cart. The cart had a long flatbed, which looked like a mid-sized bus without the protection of its windows. Along the rails, a row of seats stretched across the metal rig, under its dark roof. The driver, with ushers hanging onto the metal rails, approached us, and without any questions, they loaded our baggage into the cargo carriage by the side of the cart.

The chilly night got even cooler, filling the air with all sorts of strange new sounds that commingled with the soft mumbles: chickens flopping their wings and scrambling inside cages, babies crying, sandals clapping hard floors, and our American escort telling us to hasten our pace and board the bus. We were in the middle of the crowd as we inched our way up to our seats behind E-Paw. I turned around, and behind me, E-Mae was still clinching a cotton pouch that she made for the few articles she had left from her inheritance from Grandpa La, and in her other hand, she made sure that Thurng was still attached to her.

The bus full of long and exhausted faces took off again, this time bringing us toward the plane sitting out on the edge of the dock facing the runway. With its life-size wings and engines just above our heads, the Pan Am airline logo stood out like a billboard sign stretching across the great hub of the plane. It was the same dark blue logo on the tickets that E-Paw had been safeguarding in the brown plastic notebook case since Camp Lumphini. I was still looking for the word "Boeing" that E-Paw and our Camp Ubon neighbors had often mentioned. Standing there breathless under its wings, scanning its belly with my eyes left to right—like a child in awe of seeing something so small in my sky, now enlarged, to something bigger than life itself. It was a grandiose moment for me, meeting my own *Pa Lur See* wizard, then standing before him speechless.

"Watch out for the steps and hang on to each other," E-Paw said with his eyes vigilant like that night we escaped from the village.

I quickly followed E-Paw and our American usher up the metal stairs to the entrance of the oversized airplane. Each step brought me closer to the stars, but since I had a great fear of heights, my heart was in my throat. Then the levity overwhelmed me, when I dared myself to look down as I grabbed the rail.

By the entrance stood a tall perky American woman with blonde hair tucked into a bun resting on her shoulders under her dark cap. The woman was dressed in a neatly pressed grayish-blue elegant dress suit with a blue handkerchief tucked in her blouse pocket. Her face was smoother and lighter than Narng's, and she had a soft smile with warm shiny red lips. We exchanged smiles with her, then made our way down the cabin's aisle where passengers were being seated by other flight attendants, who were almost a replica of the woman at the entrance of the plane.

Moving along the aisle that stretched to the back of the air-plane, one of the women in front of E-Paw took the Pan Am book-let in his hand and pointed him to our seats. Unsure of what to do, we hunkered down inside the large cabin and watched the rows of seats being filled with various groups of passengers, some carrying cases with small mammals. Inside the stench of chickens, ducks, and other small animals in cages quickly got our attention. I tilted my nose to blow air out my nostrils. But before long, we acclimated to the odor as other passengers settled down in their seats. Then their conversations grew louder with familiar and new dialects reverber-ating throughout the cabin. The assortment of spoken languages reminded me of being in a chattering bird's nest. The only foreign sounds I could make out were "R" and "S," which I associated with the conversation between the flight attendant and our American guide, who had been helping other refugees with their seats.

Seated in the row before us was a young Lao couple with their infant child staring over the headrest with dark marble eyes. In the commotion, he started crying, then the new mother cradled him softly to her chest. The shy woman tugged the little infant in the cradle of her arms, but he didn't stop crying, so she handed him to her husband, a man with long hair parted in the middle, who gently quieted the baby with his swaying elbows. He turned around to E-Paw and let out a smile big enough to catch E-Paw's attention.

"Where are you going?" E-Paw asked the man.

"We got sponsored to California," replied the man with his fine black hair brushing his collar bones. "What about you?"

"We're going to New Haven, Connecticut." E-Paw stressed the words in this fashion: New Hee-ven, Con-Nick-Tick-Cut.

With several raucous passengers anxious to be settled in their seats, the flight attendant quickly tucked away personal belongings, some of which were bulky and awkward for handling. But the upbeat women moved along the middle aisle with their hips moving with feminine grace. When the luggage and animals' crates were nestled into their appropriate slots, some of the friendly flight attendants made their way toward the cockpit. Then the voice of the pilot came over the cabin's speaker—this time it wasn't in Chinese, Vietnamese, or Khmer; it was in English.

Standing next to my seat, the flight attendant proceeded to show us how to work our seatbelts. After she was done, she went back to sit in her own seat by the entrance and buckled her own seatbelt.

Thurng, who was sitting next to E-Mae, was already occupied with little travel booklets and headphone sets.

"Don't break anything," Nok said from the seat behind him.

Another hour later, the plane began to taxi down the runway, leaving buildings and glowing tower lights behind. I stared out the window, and watched the images shrink, but it was stimuli overload as images were filling my little mind with new wonders of the world before me.

"Wow! Look at that . . ." Thurng said, with his eyes still wide open. His words quickly disappeared with the white lines drawn along the landing strip. Then there was a levity in my body and a knot in my stomach as the plane lifted skyward. I stared out the window to see the stars, my back still pressed against my seat.

"Don't get up out of your seat," I heard E-Paw's voice from behind me.

In my silence, I found a glittering star. It was a bright star but not as bright as the light from the wing of the plane. The delightful horizon was almost heavenly as it appeared as soft as sudsy foam floating in water.

"Look, it's so bright," Nok pointed excitedly at the stars.

"Err, Err . . ." I nodded, sitting there speechless, as I stared out the window next to me.

"We're close to the heaven," Nok said excitedly as we searched for more stars.

I soon dozed off with Nok and Thurng. Five hours later, I woke up and saw a city illuminated with bright lights outside the window.

"I think we're in India and the plane is refueling, and they're letting some passengers off the plane," E-Paw said while peeping through the window next to him.

"They say that America is a half a day's ride from here," said the traveler sitting behind E-Paw, whose destination happened to be Florida.

"They say that it's warm in Florida all year," E-Paw said, studying magazines he found in front of him.

When I nodded, my eyes still open, E-Paw and the nearby Laotian passengers continued their humming conversation; they sounded like a fan buzzing me to sleep. Thurng was still out like a light in E-Mae's lap, and Nok, who sat next to me, looked dazed and sedated. The few words that we expressed to each other were about how strange and cold the modern world appeared, when the plane would come to a complete stop, and where exactly America was.

"E-Paw, when are we getting to *Ar-May-Lee-Gar*?" Nok got air-sick and was wishing for the plane to land.

"Soon." E-Paw said, placating us each time we asked.

E-Paw's dark tan face was now tinged with slight yellow from the overhead light. But E-Mae said that he'd turn yellow if he went without his tobacco.

After a day of being stuck to our seats, America was still nowhere on our horizon. Instead of the golden street of glamorous light, the morning sun came piercing through our windows. Outside our windows, puffs of clouds floated effortlessly like giant balls of cotton. We were surrounded by them, over, under, and beside us. Nok and Thurng also gazed at them. While there was amazement in Thurng's expression, Nok was still fighting the chills and wishing for the feel of dirt and sand beneath her feet.

We stared out the window and soaked in the heavens, but our attention soon turned to the wide projection screen with an American movie already playing. We all watched the movie, and we enjoyed the action, but the dialogue was still quite foreign to us. Nok went back to the covering of her little blanket, and Thurng and I stayed occupied with our own curiosity. Thurng ransacked the compartment and pulled out more magazines written in English. When he couldn't hold himself together, he would shove the headphone jacks in and out of the connector.

Shortly after our first movie ended, breakfast arrived. We tasted our first glass of orange juice, which left us licking our lips and sucking our teeth for the sweet citric tangy taste. Next came the breakfast rolls with small packets of grape and strawberry jam and butter. We ate them like they were candies as they melted in our mouths. We licked the packets clean and when we ran out, we would just look at the flight attendants, as they would return with more for us. We even avoided being sinful by not wasting the leftovers; if we had any, we did what E-Paw and E-Mae told us to do and saved them for when our hunger struck again.

Throughout the day we slept, played with the toys that the flight attendant handed us, and ate more delicious food that came out from under the silver cart. The elegant and fine-pressed women were also nice enough to give us kids the blue Pan Am pins. They even helped us clip them on our shirts.

"Thank you!" We said and nodded to their glowing faces.

Then they brought out sweeter crunchy and soft snacks that kept Thurng and I enticed with their surprises. Nok ate her food, but from the looks of her gloomy expression, she was still uncomfortable from being airsick.

"Make sure you two don't do anything bad," she would tell us from the front seat, as she was now sitting next to E-Mae, and Thurng and I were together with E-Paw snoring behind us.

E-Paw slept during the day like he used to do back in the Sirindhorn Reservoir. Sometimes when his snores got louder and he would start to talk in his sleep, we would give him a little nudge to shake him out of his dreams. We knew that E-Paw was appreciative; even he would agree with us that his nighttime habits kept us up some nights.

Although there were people who looked at E-Paw strangely, no one really complained about his snoring in the plane. Besides, there were plenty more unsettling things happening on board, like the baby crying throughout the night, a lady vomiting from being airsick, and people nonstop chattering.

But before lunch E-Paw woke up to the plane breaking through the puffs of clouds. We came to an opening, and I could see a peninsula of land and little islands not too far from it surrounded by a large body of water. The sound of the captain came through the loudspeaker, but his words were not clear. The flight attendant stood in front of our aisle and pointed to a blinking light, indicating that we needed to put on our seatbelts.

There was slight turbulence, and the plane slowly descended toward the land mass. Since we boarded the plane, it seemed like this plane ride would never end. I looked down again, and there was a plateau that looked like our *nah* with dikes surrounding the green fields. As the plane approached the landing strip, dotted white lines appeared over the blacktop. Then a flood of thoughts filled my head again: *This must be America, but this America looks empty and vacant like our uncultivated fields. Can this be the America that our predecessors have been talking about, and where is the snow that was in the pictures that we received from America?*

I turned to E-Paw, "E-Paw, is this America?" I wanted a confirmation of the land of heaven, since we had already been as high as a cloud and far above an expanse of plateaus.

"I'm not sure where we are, but they say that they are refueling the plane," E-Paw told us. I watched E-Paw; his eyes were bloodshot; he was drifting in and out from what appeared to be insomnia.

Then different dialects filled the cabin, as other passengers stood up from their seats, stretched their achy limbs, and needed to use the bathroom. In sync with the crowd, Nok, Thurng, and I got up and shrugged our bodies and extended our arms and legs. Then we waited for the other passengers to use the bathroom before taking our turns.

"You can't stand and squat down on the toilet seat like we did back at the camp, the seat is too high, and you'll slip off. You're supposed to sit directly on the toilet seat," E-Paw said after his observation from making his bathroom trip.

"Pai num gun (we'll go together)," E-Mae said. "Besides, there are switches, buttons, and moveable things that Thurng is likely to get his little hands on."

We'd never seen anything like the modern toilet. It was another marvel and we stood before it, at first staring at it, and then studying it like we were trying to buy a new car. We had graduated from using leaves and sticks to bowls of water, and now bath tissues. It was wild. It was beyond our imagination that after we were done all we had to do was say goodbye to what we had left behind by simply pushing a button. No more bringing along our own water or even a shovel to dig a hole and bury it from sight.

Before flushing our waste, we asked E-Mae, "Where will it go? And will this fall and hit someone down on the ground?"

"*Bor* (no)," E-Mae said. "Americans are modern people, they are very clean, and they don't just toss away their waste like us."

We returned to our seats after feeling relieved, and together with E-Mae we learned how to use the toilet somewhere in the sky that day. E-Paw estimated that we had another hour to wait. Then we were told to remain seated as the plane started to edge itself along the runway again, picking up speed. Swoosh! Like a bird we were up and gliding through the clear sky and soaring toward the clouds again. The ground slowly shrank in size and became one with the blueish green Earth below. As the plane floated along the cottonlike clouds, the flight attendants wheeled their carts along the aisle. It was lunchtime. Thurng and I waited anxiously for our meal. Our eyes automatically widened as the aroma of chicken soup filled the cabin, our stomachs growled, and our mouths watered, waiting to satisfy every bit of our hunger.

We received our bowl of soup and gobbled it up like we'd done in the past. The food lacked the spicy hotness, but soon, I learned to love the creamy savory taste of cheese on bread and the tomato sauce in chicken soups. The taste of butter spread on rolls and warm soup was delicious, but without any sticky rice to go with it, my stomach was left feeling empty. E-Paw, E-Mae, and Nok received their food as well. Unlike Thurng and I, the sweet and creamy taste of the foreign food left them in state of bewilderment. But what they hesitated to finish, Thurng and I gladly devoured.

"You know if you finish your food and leave the bowl empty, you can get some more." Thurng devised a plan to feed our ever-so-insatiable hunger.

"Err." I nodded to Thurng.

Thurng was right. Soon after we finished our food, the flight attendant came back and stared at us like we were two poster children starving in some developing country. Then our polished plates would be taken away from us, and a few minutes later, more rolls and jams were put on our plates. Again, we filled our insatiable hunger and stuffed the leftovers in our little snack bag. I smiled at Thurng, giving him an indication that his clever plan had worked again. With our stomach filled, Thurng and I went back to joining Nok. Nok ate her food, but after a few bites, she gave a hard swallow, then handed us the rest of her leftovers.

Shortly after we overstuffed our bellies, the bread and butter felt like it was rushing through my veins. I felt my heart beating and body drained from all energy. Thurng seemed to be going through the same ordeal, as he curled up in his seat and slowly closed his eyes.

Then suddenly, in the middle of my sleep, I woke up to a light trembling under my feet and thunder-like sounds that I felt in my bones. I brushed my eyes with the back of my hand and saw that everyone, including Nok and Thurng, were up and alert. I looked outside the windows over Thurng's left shoulder; I saw a huge landmass that came together with a great body of water like two large pieces of a puzzle.

I took a great sigh and let the air seep into my chest and out through my nose. Then the pilot's voice came through the speaker over the cabin above our head.

"We are landing for gas again. And we can't get off the plane yet—it's still taking us to America," E-Paw said. We still didn't know where we were.

"This may be the real *Farang*," said the young Lao man who was now fighting air sickness.

We were thrilled to see it from the sky—it was filled with lights and tall buildings.

"You see kids, we got to go to *Farang* after all," E-Paw said with a smile that stretched the wrinkles on his cheeks and forehead.

Another hour later, the plane was taxiing off the runway again. By this time, this routine was getting to Nok, who looked nauseated and pale. Thurng cradled in with his stuffed animals, and I slept like the time we had escaped through the jungle and mountain. E-Paw said that we kids missed some of the grandest views of the bluest blue water and the brightest of clouds with the sunlight literally piercing through.

On what E-Paw estimated to be our third day on the plane, we circled over what appeared as a massive city with far more buildings, boats, bridges, and cars than either Thurng or I could have ever counted. Not only were we surrounded by these amazing modern inventions down below, but also in the sky, other planes circled the airport like turkey vultures gliding through the air over a piece of animal carcass.

"It's New York. See all the tall buildings and intertwining roadways?" E-Paw said after gazing out through the window. I'd heard of New York before from E-Paw, who'd always insisted on knowing the exact location of New York and Connecticut. "We're almost there, just a few more hours and we'll see Paw Seel and his family."

That morning, we landed at Newark Airport. We stood up with our escort's instructions to gather our belongings out of the plane. Before he dispersed the small group of Laotians, he led us to a revolving stair they called an escalator—something that I thought would pull me inside of it if I wasn't quick enough to step off when I was out of rungs. In the waiting lounge, he gave everyone their instructions and what gates to proceed to. For us, he pointed to an airplane that had been waiting outside next to the runway. Then we heard the people in the group yell out to each other, "Thank you, and *soak dee, soak dee!*" The Lao bachelor waved to us and let out a huge smile as he grabbed his bags and made his way toward a gate on the far end of the main corridor.

"*Err, err, soak dee.*" E-Paw and E-Mae returned their farewell. "*Kolp Jai!*" E-Paw repeated, then shook our long blonde-haired escort's hand heartily, appreciating him for who he was: a true American.

"Nothing happen, nothing happen, *soak dee.*" The man smiled and made his way to another gate of his own, and we never saw the man who had helped in guiding us to our new home again.

We had finally arrived in America, and E-Paw wasted no time. He hauled a large suitcase and heavy bags. We followed him toward a smaller plane, hanging on to our belongings and keeping up with his pace. I wondered what E-Paw had planned, who would pick us up, and where Paw Seel and his family were, since we were going to live with them. I saw faces, but only the Americans. They glanced quickly at us as they hauled their luggage and bags. I didn't dare to stare directly into their eyes, which I realized now could be blue, hazel, brown, or green. But their skin was still white, sometimes pink, and I wondered what they saw when they looked at us. *Did they see fear, or pity for our aimless souls wandering in their lounge?*

When we reached the plane, the pilot smiled at us and grabbed the piece of paper from E-Paw. Then he helped us to board his plane. Our plane this time was a Learjet, with two large propellors hanging on each side of its wings before its engine and one more propellor on its nose. We noticed that there were a handful of people already seated, and it appeared to be at full capacity.

Once the American pilot with a big smile, wavy dark hair, and mustache made his final checks, and all the passengers were strapped in, the lighter plane sped off along the dotted lines on the landing pad. My tense body started to get light again, as the plane rose to a daunting height above the ground. Compared to the Pan

Am Boeing that flew us to America, this plane looked like it might crack and fold in a good gust of wind. Even more horrifying, I could see through the panes of its flimsy windows the flappy rudder and the naked steel bars bolting its wings to its body, and in front of us, we could see almost every move the pilot made.

But I was quickly drawn to the clear view of the modern world from above. I stared down toward the massive city with a child's glee. Then I gazed in awe at the buildings and every immaculate object I could study while the plane flew over them. With my heart still beating underneath my brown sweater, I was captivated by the hundreds of cars crossing the great bridge strung with huge gray cables across the water. On the busy highway, cars and trucks now resembled little crabs marching in a single file. My heart was beating faster and faster in my chest with each observation, but I did not dare say anything to E-Paw or Nok who sat next to me.

The world of steel, concrete, and glass was still freshly beyond my little imagination. Nok was still airplane sick, but Thurng and I were in our glory as we pulled ourselves closer to the windows at the sight of cars and buildings with smokestacks that bellowed puffy white clouds like the ones floating next to us.

"Look!" Thurng said, pointing to winding bridges and sparkling skyscrapers.

A half an hour later, our flight across the great city and blue ocean ended, and we arrived in Connecticut. The plane landed in a smaller airport with more planes just like the one we were on. The trembling plane came circling over the landing pad, surrounded by jetties and marshes not too far from tall grass, an inlet, and a large city with skyscrapers nestled along the coast. As the plane began to dive downward toward the runway, I felt the jitters from the plane as if someone grabbed me by the shoulders, picked me up in the air, and shook me with both hands.

Our nonstop flight finally came to an end that day, as the flimsy aircraft landed gently on the runway of Tweed Airport in New Haven. Sizing up the airport through the cockpit, I noticed that this time the runway appeared to be smaller with fewer planes. When the plane came completely to a halt, my knees were still shaking, and no one said a word to each other, not even Thurng.

20

ARRIVING IN AMERICA

June 1981

Numb from jetlag, I was happy to stand on solid ground. On the tarmac, the pilot passed E-Paw our luggage and bags and the two strangers exchanged smiles. E-Mae grabbed our little carry-on bags; she had an exhausted pale look on her face. Moving along with E-Mae, Thurng held onto his plastic bag of bread rolls and jam packets, as he readied himself for what seemed to be another flight. Following the other passengers, I stepped off the plane onto the tarmac with my legs stiff as a log. I grabbed my little plastic bag of food that Thurng and I were saving and a white cotton bag I had been carrying for E-Paw with his thick *Thai Sisavad Fables* book, pictures, and notebook. I looked at Nok behind me, and she had an "I don't care" look on her face. *Several years later, Nok would tell me that she was afraid that they would put us on another flight.*

Behind the small crowd of passengers, we exited the runway through the opening of the metal fence. In the parking lot a group of people watched us with curiosity. In the crowd among the American, I noticed Asians who strongly resembled us. It was Paw Seel, the sponsors from the Jewish Family Service, and with them, a Lao man, our translator. Their faces brought smiles to ours. For the first time in the past months, a jolly look appeared on our pale sunken yellow faces. I didn't know where Paw Seel and our sponsors were taking us, but I could feel the rush of excitement flowing through me.

Then there was an outburst of words in English and Laotian being tossed together from all directions: *"Sa bai dee!* Hello! Welcome to America! Thank you! Hi, how are you?"

"You didn't die, and you're here already," Paw Seel said, putting his hands on E-Paw's shoulders.

"I'm here," E-Paw replied in Lao with a huge smile to Paw Seel and our welcoming group.

One by one, the joyful Jewish sponsors came over and shook E-Paw and E-Mae's hands; some even then threw their arms around them. The greeting was unusual for me; I was afraid that they would touch me on my head. I remembered E-Paw telling me to avoid any hand contact above our shoulders with anyone outside the family. He said it would be disrespectful and insulting, leading us to break our own discipline in Buddha's teaching. Then they approached Nok, Thurng, and I. At first, I cringed at the sight of their towering height and their green and blue marble-like eyes and white skin.

"Hello, how are you? I'm John and this is Barb and Ruth. What's your name?" John said, bending down to meet our eyes.

"Hi, how are you?" E-Paw said, smiling with his pale eyes now glowing with gratitude.

The rest of us smiled, then nodded our heads along with E-Paw like a handful of people with limited English proficiency. I stood there staring shyly at the circle of smiles. The months of preparation at the Ubon Camp's English school left me without a single word. Like Nok, I gave my best face to the friendly people and moved closer to Thurng, who kept his silence as he leaned against E-Mae and hung on to her hand.

I didn't realize it at that moment, but in those friendly smiles and humble faces were the people who gave light to our new hope. There before us were our miracle hands—the evidence that amongst all evil there was still a beacon of kindness and caring in human beings. Once I realized the gift they had given us of another chance in America, I sought to return it.

"Well, let's go home," said John.

"Okay," Paw Seel added.

All our belongings went into the trunk of the sponsor's two-toned beige-cream Oldsmobile wagon, and E-Paw, Thurng, and I squeezed into the backseat of the car. Paw Seel took the front seat with John at the wheel and our Laotian translator pressed in the middle. E-Mae and Nok got into a blue station wagon with our cheerful brown-haired, blue-eyed sponsor, Barb, her two kids, and Mae Seel. Out through the windshield of the car, we watched our sponsor John speeding off through a street lined with multi-family houses along our left and right.

With Judith's brown Dodge van (with Peter, Jenny, and Lou—the other sponsors) trailing behind Barb's blue Ford, the cars followed each other down the long stretch of road with two- and three-story house covered with glass windows, siding, and shingles to top off their roofs. Farther down the road we came to an intersection with lights changing from red to green. John merged onto the highway with a huge gray bridge arching over the mouth of a river, which I had seen while sitting on the plane.

"How long was the plane ride?" asked Paw Seel.

"I took note of when it landed and I asked the people around me, and I jotted down at least two and a half days. It took us eastward toward India, over a lot of mountains and blue oceans, and Farang, and then we finally landed in Newark Airport. At one point I fell asleep during a landing. But I was afraid that the planes would never land." E-Paw chuckled.

"Are you tired?"

"Yes, it was cold, but the urge to smoke got the best of me." E-Paw smiled while he stared through the windshield of the car.

E-Paw's words blew with the wind from the windows that had been slightly open with the cranked handles. The wind was cool, but not as chilly as the air in the plane's cabin the night when we had to throw on our sweaters and request a blanket.

"This is what they call the Q-bridge," the Lao translator informed us as we rode over the bridge.

From the backseat, I could see more buildings jutting up toward the blue sky. There were houses of different sizes and colors and many brick buildings along the banks of the river. Beyond the inlet of the river toward my right, a monumental statue that reminded me of the Statue of Liberty stood above a tall sheer cliff on a mountain. Below the bridge large white cylinder-like oil tankers were scattered. By the harbor, there were dark oil tankers and smaller white boats throughout the New Haven harbor along with dark piers and stone barriers out by the larger bay under a gleaming sun and blue sky.

"These roads are called I-91 and I-95. There are many speeding cars that go through here," added the translator.

"Hmm . . ." E-Paw replied as he stared through the windshield, looking at different structures suddenly appearing before him.

The winding highways came together in loops and bends that caused me to lean against the car each time John followed its path. The curvy stretch of highway finally straightened itself when we approached the entrance to the city.

"This is the city of New Haven," John pointed out to us.

As John drove, we got a glimpse of the towering building they called the "Knights of the Columbus" and the New Haven Coliseum with its parking garage visible from the highway. The ride also took us through the heart of New Haven and Yale University, where we gazed at cobblestone paths and marble buildings with its gothic roofs.

Our journey "around the world" came to a complete stop in front of a three-story house. We got another surprise when we saw Paw Seel and Mae Seel's children: E-Laa, their youngest daughter, who was no bigger than Thurng, with round shoulder-length black hair; Tien with long black hair down to her lower back; and Ai Mai, a teenager with a bright white smile. Then there was the eldest son, Ai Mee, who was more reserved and expressed his happiness to see us in soft and friendly words. They all came out from the house with wide smiles and excited hands that reached out to greet us. When we finally stood before one another, we exchanged smiles, and our friendship quickly rekindled as it had always been there like two intersecting roads.

Led by Barb and John, we climbed the stairs, passing double glass doors with clear crystal knobs to the second floor, where Paw Seel and Mae Seel and their family lived. When we finally got up to the entrance of the third floor, John, who was taller than all of us, had to lean away from the slanting ceiling by his head.

"Welcome, this is your new home," John said, touching E-Paw on the shoulders.

E-Paw returned the biggest smile and said thank you, as he laid our bags in the living room with three windows that overlooked Whalley Avenue. Our sponsor and Paw Seel gave us a tour of our new home. To our surprise, it was fully furnished with a set of golden beige velvety sofas, a refrigerator filled with food, a gas stove, a toilet and running water, and the best part of it all, a television set sitting there waiting to entertain us in our own living room.

We followed E-Paw and collapsed our legs on the golden beige sofa, which became the best seat in our new home. For the first time since we had left the Sirindhorn Reservoir, the comforting feeling of the warm smiles made me feel like I was home for good.

EPILOGUE

Almost forty years later, after assimilating to a new life in America, I returned to Laos. I was going to visit Vung and Narng in Thailand with E-Mae, Nok, and her husband, Harry. I planned on going all the way to Laos and had tossed the idea back and forth with Nok and Harry, but they gave me an absolute "No." Each time I had mentioned it, the dark bitterness showed itself in Nok's heart-shaped face.

She gave me a warning through clenched teeth: "Why would you want to go to Banh Dong? It's still under communist influence, and they took everything from us."

I couldn't tell Nok that I'd made a promise to Uncle Wan that I would visit him when we spoke over the phone one day, just a few years before he passed away. Inside my head, I could still hear his voice: *Buc Laa, they'd put a gun to my head, forced me to tell them which way you went. I didn't tell them, so they fired a bullet over my head.* His words had haunted me ever since. I knew then that the ultimate sacrifice during our escape from Laos wasn't my family's struggle to make it to America—it was my uncle and his family who protected us when we were most vulnerable.

Before crossing into the border of Laos, I had also visited Narng in Bangkok. She and her son picked us up at Suvarnabhumi Airport. When I first saw her, I thought, *there she is, my long-forgotten sister, in the flesh.* I smiled at her and gave her a hug. She didn't return my affection; culturally, it was an improper gesture. Still, I gave her a hug. My sister was there again with me, but this time, like a kind loving stranger.

While staying with Narng I learned that her four children gave her a total of ten grandchildren. I embraced them as my nephews and nieces. We drank and danced to Thai pop Luk Thung music, and even a Bon Jovi song ("It's My Life"), on the roof of the house they'd rented.

One hazy night I was on Narng's balcony, staring down at a vacant lot with a pack of hungry dogs meandering its empty ground. I saw that I was no better than them. I had been drinking and thinking about how I would face my own demons in Laos. It appeared that the world before me had moved on, but I was still stuck in my own time capsule. I was running from my own demons of words, invented fears, and pangs lodged deep in my soul.

The running and moving around like nomads was over, but the suffering remained. I wanted to let it go, but I didn't know how, and I certainly wasn't going to commit suicide—I didn't have the audacity to do so. I stood there alone, soaking up the city lights, while tossing pieces of chicken to those wandering canines. I washed my tears down with the warm bitter Thai Chang beer. I drank and I spit postnasal drip and rubbed away the tears swelling in my eyes. I ended up giving all the chicken in my hands to the dogs. They deserved better. I was thinking about my own pup at home in America.

I wished I could've given the hungry dogs more than a handful of grilled chicken. I told myself that I had to go—I needed to face my own demons. I needed closure. I'd be stronger if I could return to the place where we almost died. Or should I follow Nok's voice of reason? I took another gulp of beer, it hit the back of my throat, and I felt the alcohol streaming into my body, blood, and numbing veins. From the kitchen window, Narng saw me crying on her balcony; she didn't know what to do for me. She turned to Nok next to her, who gave her a gesture to let me be. Leave me alone.

After four nights in Bangkok, all of us packed ourselves tightly into Narng's son's pickup truck to visit my brother. My nephew made several stops for food and for us to loosen our stiff limbs.

The ten-hour ride came to a halt at Vung's Village, and I saw his family for the very first time. Staring at me were Vung's wife, two sons, and three little grandchildren. His wife received me with her smile and hands right away, while his two boys and I sized one another up comfortably from five feet away. We'd known of one another's existence as family members, but to see each other in the flesh was a grandiose moment that got us psychoanalyzing each other the entire afternoon.

Vung didn't have much, but he had a *nah* surrounded by tropical fruit trees and quacking ducks and gawking chickens. On his farm, his family collected sap from hundreds of rubber trees for a nearby rubber factory. They also grew yucca and raised tilapia in the pond near their house. And they were heavily involved with ushering monks at their village Buddha temple.

Cousin Vee was also Vung's neighbor. They stayed together through the years as cousins and good friends. Cousin Vee also married a Thai woman and had two beautiful kids of his own. In the village, his family owned a little package store and had a *nah* and raised livestock like Vung. He was still tall and slender. When he saw us, he let out a soft smile that stretched wide on his friendly face.

During the time we stayed with Vung, Aunt Dee and five of her twelve children crossed the border from Laos to see us. We spent the entire day and night recounting the before and after of our escape. There I learned how Grandpa Oosu and Uncle Wan passed away, each in their own bed. When my cousins were returning home to Laos, I saw that as an opportunity to complete my own circle. It was another chance for closure.

The following day I returned to Laos with Narng and my aunt and cousins. This time, my nephew drove us through Ubon, an hour north toward Chong Mek and the Laos border. Before we reached our destination, we stopped to have lunch on a sandy beach of Little Pattaya, a string of bamboo and grass huts sitting on empty barrels stretching out into the Sirindhorn Reservoir, where I searched the stretch of water for the dark spares of protruding tree limbs. I found none that day; they too were long gone.

After we'd washed up from our meal, my nephew took us through Chong Mek, or our Banh Nong Mek. There along the main road I had hoped to connect my childhood memory to my reality. Narng herself couldn't show me to my point of interest. The roads leading to Thai and Laos customs' entry were freshly paved, and bright green signs flashed in my view. I had to accept that the village of Banh Nong Mek that once became our home now existed only in my mind.

When we reached Banh Dong, I stood in the verdant rice field with Narng, staring at Uncle Wan's dilapidated hut and his tombstone next to Grandpa Oosu. Aunt Dee and her grown children were there, and they were eager to help me piece together the lingering memory of those days running along with them on the *nah*. I searched for any clues to add to a vivid childhood memory. I found little—the world had already moved on, and Grandpa Oosu and Uncle Wan were long gone.

That day, Aunt Dee said something so profound to me that I'd kept it as my own secret. She recounted, "Years after you'd left for America, your brother Vung came to visit me. He stood there before those tombstones, shivering and then bursting out into tears like a lost child. I didn't know what to do for him. I think he was looking for you and your parents."

I had never mentioned that to anyone except Nok several

years later; I didn't want to add shame and guilt to Vung's painful memory.

After we left Ubon Camp, Vung and Narng both became Thai citizens through marriage. But on that day while we were standing there together under the hot sun before the green fields, Narng pointed at the very spot where she had held her vigilant eyes for E-Paw during those day he'd been hiding and crawling amongst those stalks of rice that were tall as her shoulders. It was there that I finally had closure; I had come full circle.

Before making my way back to the Thai border that day, there was a feast at Aunt Dee's house. My Cousin Buc Dur and his eldest sister, Cousin Yai, joined us. While we ate grilled mud fish and snails pulled from the rice field with hot spicy papaya salad and sticky rice, drank warm Lao Beer, watched homemade fireworks, and danced to Lao Mor Lum music played on the portable cd player, I learned that Grandpa La remained religious, active, and disciplined with his natural remedies until the age of 105. And soft-spoken Grandma Dao passed away peacefully at the age of 82.

When I returned to America, I told myself that I had to move on . . . with all of my family as the village in my heart, and my grandparents and uncle as the spirits in my soul.

ACKNOWLEDGMENTS

This book is written in honor of my father. Without his unwavering love for us, America would just be the mere thought of a golden and glittering place that existed only in our imaginations.

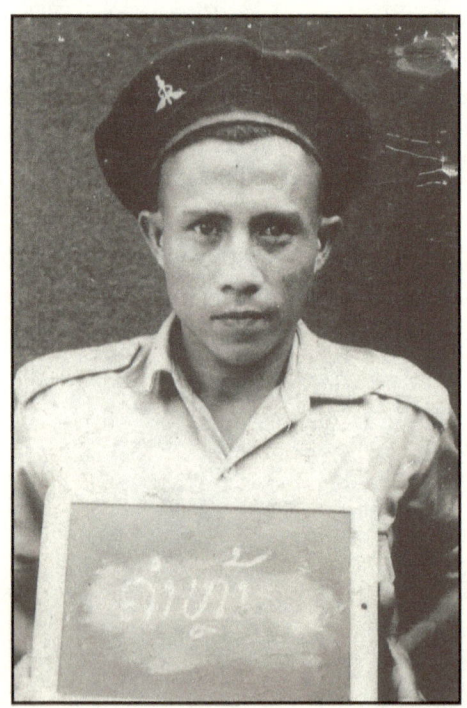

264

Ubon Refugee Camp March 1981

A SPECIAL THANK YOU

The village echoes a lifetime in my heart while I was growing up as a Laotian living in America. The humbling sincere kindness of family and friends, and the support system that made it special for me. All of which became the ethical principle foundation that kept me grounded. The timeless value of respect and honor for one another, the nurtured ideas of collaboration and self-sacrifice, and a sense of gratitude that came out of deep appreciation for the simplicity in happiness that made me Lao. Most of it came out during the mingling and laughter of villagers working diligently together while preparing meals, lending a hand in cleaning up, sharing salt and spices with the neighbors and loved ones. They were all memories of the village in heart and mind.

So, to you, my villagers, I wanted to say, thank you for all of your support from my heart. Your support, kind words, inspiration, and profound insights have helped carry me to the end of my book.

To Mother Nature, Buddha, Kubar Somfdee, Paw Yai, Mae Yai, E-Paw, E-Mae, Paw Seel, Mae Seel, Uncle Wan, Vung, Narng, Nok, and Thurng.

To our Jewish Family Service sponsors, our light of hope during a time of need.

Katy, who seeded the idea that I should write a book.

Lara, my editor, whose profound editorial insight gave me the confidence to complete this book.

Libby, my designer, for the kind words of encouragement and dedication to bring my vision to life.

ABOUT THE AUTHOR

Bounthavy Soukthideth resides in Connecticut with his family and two dogs. He seeks peace through acts of kindness while accepting life's circumstances. He aspires to return the kindness he has received by sharing his experiences of resettling in America.